I WILL IN ME POLITICS

THE MAURICE HICKEY DIARIES

PAT SHORTT

PAT SHORTT started in comedy when he left art college. With Jon Kenny he created D'Unbelievables, Ireland's most popular comedy duo. Together they performed their unique and critically-acclaimed brand of comedy in theatres all over Ireland, the UK and the United States as well as various countries across Europe. As a solo artist Pat's one-man shows, including 'Pat Shortt Live' and 'You Won't Get Away With That Here', were very popular and his work hailed as 'comic genius' by *The Irish Times*. An actor of note, Pat has appeared in many plays and films, most recently in the lead role of Josie in the movie *Garage*, which was awarded the CICAE Art and Essai Cinema Prize at the Cannes Film Festival.

An accomplished musician also, Pat has recorded with many bands and toured extensively in the US with The Saw Doctors. In 2006 he scored the big hit in Ireland with the song 'The Jumbo Breakfast Roll' under the guise of showband singer Dicksie Walsh. Pat's television credits include Tom in 'Father Ted' (Channel 4), and Bobby in 'The Fitz' (BBC). Pat can currently be seen in the popular television show 'Killinascully'. This successful series features Pat in a variety of roles and was created by him for RTÉ.

JIM O'BRIEN

JIM O'BRIEN is a freelance writer based in Rosenallis, County Laois, and he has worked with Pat Shortt on the Maurice Hickey diaries. Jim was formerly a journalist with the *Irish Farmer's Journal*. He and Pat have known each other since college days and have collaborated on a number of ventures including the first series of 'Killinascully' and scripts for Pat's stage shows.

I WILL IN ME

POLITICS

THE MAURICE HICKEY DIARIES

PAT SHORTT

ILLUSTRATIONS BY ALAN CLARKE

THE O'BRIEN PRESS
DUBLIN

First published in this form in 2007 by The O'Brien Press Ltd,
12 Terenure Road East, Rathgar, Dublin 6, Ireland.
Tel: +353 1 4923333; Fax: +353 1 4922777
E-mail: books@obrien.ie
Website: www.obrien.ie

I Will in Me Politics is based on columns which have appeared
weekly in the *Irish Farmer's Journal* under the authorship of
Councillor Maurice Hickey.

ISBN: 978-1-84717-084-2

Text written in consultation with Jim O'Brien

British Library Cataloguing-in-Publication Data
Shortt, Pat
I will in me politics : the Maurice Hickey diaries
1. City council members - Fiction 2. Diary fiction
3. Humorous stories
I. Title
823.9'2[F]

Front cover photograph and internal photographs © Great Graphics, Cork.
Illustrations by Alan Clarke, © copyright.

1 2 3 4 5 6 7 8 9 10
07 08 09 10 11 12

Printed and bound in the UK by CPI Group.

CONTENTS

A COBBLED HISTORY

You're welcome to my book. Little did I dream when I was asleep at the back of Master Canty's class in Killdicken that I'd ever be an author. I doubt it ever crossed auld Canty's mind either; he used to tell me that if I was ever hung for intelligence 'twould be a travesty of justice. Anyway, he's gone to the great classroom in the clouds and here I am with a book of my own under my oxter. Wherever Canty is, I hope he's as sick as a parrot – for all his auld lip, *he* never wrote a book.

Like most things in the Hickey history, this book is an accident. My grandfather became a councillor by accident and my father inherited the seat because he was the only member of the family who hadn't emigrated. I inherited the seat when my father died simply because the Mother thought 'twould get me out of the house and might even get me a wife. It has succeeded in doin' neither: I'm a bachelor councillor still livin' at home with her.

The idea for the book came to me on New Year's Eve a few years ago. The Mother and myself generally stay at home for that particular celebration. It's not that I'm allergic to goin' out, far from it, but both of us have a severe allergic reaction to Auld Lang Syne and the shlobberawlin' that goes with it. We sit in to watch the telly and talk.

We talk about the relatives that sent us Christmas cards and, more importantly, those that sent none. We discuss the youngsters in the extended family and how the ones who were in nappies only yesterday now have sour faces and earrings in their noses. When our conversation turns to the dead, we inevitably begin talkin' about my grandfather, Auld Maurice, the giant of the family, the first Hickey politician.

While my father was a quiet, practical kind of man, his father, Auld

Maurice was a legend. His political career began in the 1930s when, in a fit of stubbornness he stood for election to the county council. A cobbler by trade, he was well known for his craft, his straight talkin' and his determination to collect debts. It was this latter quality that drove him to put his name on the ballot paper.

The story goes that a local businessman and farmer who was runnin' for the council – and was tipped as a certainty – owed Auld Maurice for three pairs of shoes. There was no sign of him payin' up. Out of spite the grandfather ran against him as an independent, won the seat and held it for forty years.

Auld Maurice remained independent because no party would be able for him. He was a most cantankerous man. How he sustained a marriage that produced twelve children is a mystery. Its survival probably owes a lot to his wife's firm belief that this life is meant to be purgatory and the next heavenly bliss.

While Auld Maurice had a reputation for makin' fine shoes, he wasn't great in the customer-relations department. He was brutally honest about people's footwear needs, and the motto that the customer is always right wasn't one he paid any heed to. As far as he was concerned 'twas the customer's job to pay up and shut up; he was the cobbler and the people should be said by his expertise.

The Mother told the famous story of Auld Maurice and Mrs Collopy. It seems that the Collopys of Glenabuddybugga got a bit of money from an aunt who died in the States. Accordin' to the locals, the money gave them great notions of themselves. Anyway, Mrs Collopy arrived in to Auld Maurice with an order for a new pair of shoes. To show him what she wanted she produced a page from an American magazine picturin' a slender pair of women's shoes. 'Mr Hickey, my good man,' says she in an accent that must have come with the magazine, 'you'll make a pair of these for me and I'll pick them up at ten o'clock on Monday. You know my size. Thank you, Mr Hickey, and you have a good day.'

As she turned to leave, he asked, 'Who told you you could wear narrow shoes?' 'Excuse me, Mr Hickey, I'll wear whatever shoes I like.' 'Fine, so,' says he, 'I'll make you a narrow pair of shoes like the ones in the picture. There's only one problem. I'll have to stitch in satchels at either side of them to carry your bunions. Your feet will look like a pair of asses bringin' turf from the bog. I suppose that isn't altogether a bad thing, Mrs Collopy, as they'll be a constant reminder to you of where you came from.'

This straight talkin' lost him a certain amount of custom but also earned him huge respect. He held the council seat until his death in 1968 at the age of eighty. 'I don't know how Granny put up with him,' says the Mother. 'He was as cantankerous at home as he was in the shop or the council, but she was well able for him. 'Twas a constant battle of wits between the two of them.'

The Mother then told a great story I hadn't heard before. Auld Maurice insisted on eatin' his dinner alone while he read the newspaper. The grandmother hated this and it took very little to annoy her at meal times. One day, all the children had been fed and coralled into a corner of the kitchen. Himself was perched at the table with his paper, waitin' to be served. 'What's for eatin', woman?' he barked from behind the outstretched pages. Bein' Friday, the dinner consisted of spuds and eggs. The grandmother was about to lay his plate on the table when she stopped suddenly. Now, like every household of the time, they fattened a pig in the backyard and at that very moment, the family pig trotted into the kitchen. The grandmother spotted him and, bendin' down, placed the dinner of eggs and spuds on the floor. The animal duly tucked in. The slobberin' sound of the dinin' swine caused Auld Maurice to drop his paper. 'What's goin' on here?' he demanded as he glared at the sight of the animal with his snout in the china plate. 'Oh dear,' said the grandmother in feigned surprise, 'what's come over me at all? Amn't I after feedin' the wrong pig.'

With stories like this, myself and the Mother passed a most pleasant New Year's Eve. A year or two ago she told me if I was any good I'd write a book about all this stuff. There and then I started takin' notes in a copybook I keep under the bed, and here's the finished product.

IN THE NAME OF
THE FATHER

I suppose I'm luckier than most politicians. I have a simple recipe for protectin' my seat: I turn up at everythin' but only get involved in the few things that suit me. I learned this from my father, God be good to him. He held the seat before me and while he was sparse with his advice in my younger days, as he drew closer to the back door of Tinky Ryan's hearse he became more forthcomin' with his words of wisdom.

Whenever he wanted to give me the benefit of his experience he'd get a fit of throat-clearin' that sounded like Pa Cantillon's tractor startin' up after a frosty night spent outside Walshe's pub. In the months before he died he did an awful lot of throat clearin' and advice givin', once it seemed as if I might take on the council seat.

In one of his last shots of advice he warned me against givin' up my independent status. 'You'll get nothin' but abuse in a political party,' he warned. 'The fellas at the top in those organisations got there because they climbed over more corpses than anyone else. As a local politician they'll treat you like a gentleman when they're on the election trail, but you're only the servant boy once they put their snouts inside the gates of Leinster House.'

After he died, he wasn't cold when everythin' he said was borne out. The local TDs who wouldn't walk the same side of the street as him were huggin' and kissin' myself and the Mother. You'd see them comin' for miles with their Crombie coats and their funeral faces and each of 'em thinkin' their seat was safer now that there was no danger auld Mickie Hickey would be runnin' again.

What I couldn't get over was the plague of Senators that descended on us. Hoors I never even heard of arrived to the funeral from all sides of the country. Those who couldn't come sent Mass cards and wreaths. I couldn't figure out how the father was so well got in the Senate. When the funeral was over and things settled down, the Mother enlightened me as to the reason for the outpourin' of senatorial grief. 'Most of those fellas are elected by the county councillors,' she explained, 'and although you'll be an independent, your vote could mean life or political death for one of them shleveens. They have no shame. Imagine, havin' to tail-sniff your way into the chamber of the also-rans.'

It didn't stop there. A week after I took over the father's seat in the council I got a call from a Senator from the other end of the country who missed the funeral. He travelled down and took me for a big feed in a country restaurant. In the course of the meal he spoke about the loss of his father many years before. When he went on to describe his auld fella as a wonderful, devoted family man I nearly choked on my duck in plum sauce. The world and its first cousin knew that the man he was talkin' about died in the company of a woman who wasn't his wife. To say he died in her arms would be a most charitable description of the position he found himself in when he got the call to cross the great divide. *Sic transit gloria mundi.*

I'm a lucky man that my parents put me wise to all these hoors. Even if they didn't, the locals are sure to keep me on the straight and narrow. An incident in the pub a few nights ago made me realise that I wouldn't want to get notions above my station.

Tom Cantwell and myself were sittin' at the counter lookin' at 'Questions and Answers' on the telly. A well-known national politician was talkin' completely through his hat and after a while Cantwell looked over at me. 'You know somethin', Hickey?' says he. 'You have it about right where you are now. Don't ever find yourself in that fella's shoes. 'Tis one thing bein' a local gobshite but to be a national gobshite takes some neck.'

AN INDEPENDENT REPUBLIC

I'm an independent politician and I like it. A lot of people ask me why I don't join a political party, but 'tis great to be a lone ranger. The FFers would love to have me. They don't give a sugar what my political philosophy is, they just like a vote-getter. To be honest, my reserves of political philosophy are as plentiful as the supply of food in Mother Hubbard's cupboard.

Be that as it may, as an independent I have a lot goin' for me. For a start, I have to answer to no-one. I can make up my own mind on every issue that comes my way and vote whatever way I like. I don't have to waste time at party functions and meetin's listenin' to the same gobdaws sayin' the same thing they have been sayin' for the last forty years.

My party is a party of one. If I have a difficult issue to face, I retire to the jacks and do my thinkin' there. If a constituent calls to the house when I am answerin' nature's call, the Mother will tell them that I'm tied up at a meetin' of the 'full parliamentary party'.

Another thing about bein' independent is that I'm friendly with everyone at all sides of the political divide. In fact, I'm a listenin' ear when party men and women want to give out about colleagues that drive them mad and after a few drinks they all tell me they'd love to have the guts to go independent. But I let that kind of auld guff in one ear and out the same ear again because when the chips are down they are all party faithful. When you're useful they'll court you, but when you are of no use to them if you were on fire they wouldn't relieve themselves on you to put it out.

A marvellous thing about bein' independent is that you can blame everyone else for the disastrous state of the country and no matter who is in power you can regularly call for their resignation. You have to defend no-one except yourself.

The most important lack in the life of an independent is someone to keep you informed about what's happenin' on the national front. Any eejit will tell you what funerals to go to and where the local matches are happenin', but havin' no information or poor information on national issues can ruin a political life.

An independent I know once took a foray into national politics and his campaign died a death because of bad information. This all happened in the early seventies when elections were fought over issues such as contraception and divorce. This fella called into a pub after a day's canvassin' and wasn't there a crowd from RTE havin' a few pints in the same pub. They were delighted to meet an independent candidate and asked him if he'd do an interview. The man hadn't the luxury of a party machine or a PR guru to consult and went straight into it. Everythin' was goin' fine until they asked him what should be done about the contraceptive bill. 'Sure, like every other bill 'twill have to be paid. If we don't pay our bills how can we expect to run a country?' The story went all over the place and the poor man only got the votes of his immediate family.

But for all that, the life of the independent councillor is not a bad one, provided, like a horse, you stick to the course you were bred for.

THE SOMETIMES LONELY INDEPENDENT

I'm havin' nightmares about the up-comin' election. When you're an independent like me, you have no party organisation to back you up. I wake at night with lists of things goin' round in my head. There are posters to be ordered, leaflets to be printed. Then there's the few outstandin' favours for long-tailed families with a bundle of votes. Of course, there are a few policies and promises to be invented as well.

The most frustratin' part of bein' an independent is the fact that you can trust no-one to do the job right. You are totally dependent on voluntary help. If you as much as grunt at some supporters they are quite likely to tell you to stick your campaign up your nose, or up any other orifice they choose to mention.

As an independent, your so-called supporters can often be your greatest opponents. Take, for example, the Mother. The Mother always hated politics. At a wake one night, she had a sherry or two too many and someone asked her what bein' part of a political family was like. She stood up and declared: 'Politics is the last refuge of the looderamawn and the scoundrel. I should know. I married one, and I'm rearin' another.' Luckily, my friend Pa Quirke was sittin' near her. He finished his drink and in a swift damage-limitation exercise he offered her a lift home.

Well-meanin' friends can be a fierce liability at election time. The non-commissioned canvasser is the most dangerous ally a politician can have. I never tire of tellin' my supporters that no matter what kind of abuse or contrariness they get at the doorsteps the voter is always right. Nevertheless, at every election, some non-commissioned canvasser will lose the temper in a house that can produce a wheelbarrow load of votes. In the last election when I needed every vote I could get two incidents in particular brought me within a hair's breadth of political oblivion. Even now, recallin' these events brings a chill to my political spine.

Dixie Ryan, a non-commissioned canvasser purportin' to act on my behalf, paid a campaign visit to the home of Bockedy Grimes. Bockedy is a particularly cross man with bad feet and a huge family. There are ten votes for the takin' in that residence. When Dixie arrived, Grimes was bathin' his long-sufferin' feet in a bucket of hot water laced with poteen and mustard. He decided he'd entertain himself at Dixie's expense by launchin' into a diatribe on the uselessness of politicians in general and the uselessness of my good self in particular. Dixie tried in vain to get a word in, but he was told to keep his trap shut. When Bockedy finished, he folded his arms triumphantly, wrigglin' his feet around the bucket, satisfied that he had put me and all who supported me in our place. Dixie took one long, hard look at him and said: 'Do you know what's wrong with you, Bockedy? The wrong end of you is in the bloody bucket.' Dixie turned on his heel and left ten fine votes behind him.

The second incident involved a poorly-made poster. On the day of the election count, I couldn't understand how I got so few votes in the Honetyne end of the electoral area. A friend of mine in Honetyne had kindly made up, and put up, a few posters for me. It later emerged that the root cause of my low vote lay in the poster nearest the pollin' station. This particular one had been pasted on to a piece of cardboard that was originally part of a box containin' tins of anti-scour powder. The night before pollin', it rained in torrents and the lower end of the poster became detached from the cardboard. What resulted was a most unfortunate amalgamation of my election slogan and the slogan on the original box. As people approached the pollin' station, they were greeted by the sight of my smilin' face on a poster declarin': 'Maurice Hickey – for all kinds of calf's scour.' With friends like that ...!

PADDY'S PANDEMONIUM

Now, I'm no fan of the St Patrick's Day parade. However, in an election year, an independent local councillor would be committin' an act of political self-mutilation if he didn't participate in the local festivities.

I became involved in preparations from an early stage this year. I attended all the meetin's and made sure I wasn't landed with any job aside from reviewin' the parade. However, with two days to go, disaster struck. Mick Slattery and the boys on the FÁS scheme were busy puttin' up the scaffoldin' when Tom Walshe, our local publican and chairman of the community council, got a letter from County Hall tellin' him we had no plannin' permission for the reviewin' stand.

There was pandemonium. An emergency meetin' of the community council was called and we racked our brains to find a way round our dilemma. A brilliant solution came from the bould Breda Quinn, or 'Superquinn'. She suggested that we have a mobile reviewin' stand. 'If we put it on a trailer and have it towed up one side of the street while the parade is comin' down the other, they can't say a word to us,' declared a triumphant Breda. Everyone was delighted with the suggestion. Pa Cantillon said that the FÁS lads could build the stand on his silage trailer and he would tow it with his tractor.

On the day, everythin' started wonderfully. The parade was gatherin' at the Bally end of the village while the dignitaries mounted the trailer at the Honetyne end. At the first screech from Paddy McDonnell's auld bagpipes the parade and the reviewin' stand were to start movin'. It was from that moment things started to go wrong.

Cantillon had been on the beer all night and was asleep at the wheel of the tractor. Moll Gleeson, the local FG councillor, shouted at Pa to wake up and drive on. When she hit the roll-over bar a belt of her umbrella, Pa woke up of a sudden and started to move off at a snail's pace, as instructed. Unfortunately, he was goin' so slow he fell asleep again, and crossed over to the wrong side of the street. Meanwhile the parade, comin' down against him, had no option but cross to the other side.

What a disaster. There we were, on the reviewin' stand, lookin' in Mag Ryan's upstairs bedroom window while the Patrick's Day parade passed behind us. That wouldn't be too bad but Mag was actually in the bedroom, cuttin' her toenails. Little did she know that she had the 'great and the good' of Killdicken reviewin' her progress. When she looked up and saw the line of faces starin' in her top window, she screamed and fainted. The scream woke Pa and the tractor jerked forward, comin' to a complete stop outside Moss Kelly's upper floor. Poor auld Moss had been unwell of late and was perched on the throne in the upstairs loo when the reviewin' stand parked itself outside. Far from bein' perturbed by this very public invasion of his privacy, Moss, not havin' been out for a while, was delighted to see so many neighbours. 'How are ye all? 'Tis a great day for it,' says he, without flinchin'. 'At least 'tis dry,' says Moll Gleeson. 'Which is more than I can say for myself,' says Moss, roarin' with laughter. While we waited for Pa to get the tractor goin', Moss caught up with the news of three parishes. When we eventually got started he wished us all a happy St Patrick's Day and told us how delighted he was to see so many neighbours at one sittin'. At least there was one happy man in Killdicken at the end of Patrick's Day. Never again.

THE NANNY STATE

Well, my heart is broken with laws, bye-laws and regulations. The council, the government and the health board are gone mad. You can't burn a few bushes nowadays without the Thought Police from the council arrivin' with a fire extinguisher in one hand and the makin's of a summons in the other. I'm withered from it.

I'm told that this wholesale interference by the state is what they call the 'nanny state', hell bent on regulatin' your every move. There is now legislation coverin' what you may and may not do in every room in your own private house. They're tryin' to tell you what you can and can't eat, what you can have in the bathroom, how long you should sit in the sittin' room without exercise and the amount of telly you can watch. I don't know where 'twill stop.

Someone was tellin' me the other day that the state is bringin' in these regulations to prevent it from bein' sued for makin' people too fat, too thin, too wheezy or whatever. Did you ever hear the bate of it? As you probably know, I carry a bit of condition in front. To put it more plainly, I haven't been able to see my feet from a standin' position for the past ten years. Some people tell me I'm a bit strong, some people tell me I'm a bit on the heavy side and the more informed now tell me I'm obese. I think that means fierce fat. I was wonderin' aloud to Pa Quirke if I had a case against the state for my condition. I explained that in allowin' me to engage in habits that resulted in my current size, the state was an accessory to my so-called obesity.

Quirke thought for a minute and told me that if I took a case he'd support me all the way. 'Would you?' says I. 'Begod I would,' says Quirke, 'with a heart and a half. I'd go into any court and tell them that from a very young age, the state conspired to transform you from the handy little molehill you were into the mountain you have become today. I'd tell them how the local teacher, an agent of the state, used to frogmarch you down to the shop on your way home from school. I'd tell them how he would make you eat four bags of crisps, two bars of chocolate and three ice-creams every day. I'd tell them that after you finished the massive dinner your mother had for you each evenin', the postman, another agent of the state, would take you forcibly down to the Widow McMahon's, a first cousin of your mother. This good woman was convinced you needed feedin' and would land you up another dinner. I would tell the court that the postman used to sit across from you like a jailer till you ate every morsel.

Then I would recount for the court the horrific story of how the state used to force-feed porter into you as you grew older. I would tell them that every night, fifteen minutes before closin' time, the local sergeant would arrive in the pub and make you drink five more pints before the doors closed. He didn't seem to care that you already had ten drank. The court would surely be shocked when I'd tell them that once the pub closed, the guards would force you to queue at the mobile chipper. There they would make you order two quarter pounders with cheese, one large curry chip, one large chip with mayonnaise and a litre of coke. I would have the court in tears as I'd tell them how the guards, with truncheons drawn, would stand over you till you had licked the salt out of the chip bags. Then I would conclude with the chillin' warnin' that those same guards gave you every night, "Go home, Hickey, and don't even think of gettin' into bed till you have eaten half a block of ice-cream." You have a case against the state all right, Maurice. It's about as tight as your trousers.'

THE SMOKIN' BAN

The smokin' ban came upon us finally. It hit Killdicken like a ton of bricks on a Monday evenin'. At 8.00pm Tom Walshe's pub was a morgue. There were three people at the bar eatin' their nails while Tom was spendin' his time walkin' up and down behind the

counter mutterin' somethin' about the dubious parentage of Minister Micheál Martin. At about nine pm a few more had come in, but the silence remained and the tension grew. 'Twas like a scene from an old western film with them all sittin' around waitin' for the shoot-out to start. Some played nervously with beermats, Dixie Ryan kept rattlin' a box of matches in his pocket while Raymie Gleeson stared longingly at a packet of fags in front of him. Everyone was waitin' for the first one to light up, but no-one wanted to make things awkward for poor Tom, the proprietor.

The door burst open and in walked Madge McNamara. She was seventy if she was a day and a chain smoker since she was in fourth class. Everyone thought to themselves, if anyone will break this ban 'twill be Madge. She ordered a small one and a glass of water. She drank two sips out of the small one, took one sip out of the glass of water and slowly put her hand into the pocket of her cardigan. This was it. Madge was about to start the shoot-out with the lightin' of a Woodbine. She pulled her hand out of the cardigan pocket but there was no woodbine. She took a toothpick out of a small box and proceeded to chew it like Clint Eastwood. It was all too much for Dixie Ryan. He walked straight over to Madge and starin' straight into her face he shouted, 'Why aren't you smokin'? Is the ban too much for you too?' 'I'm afraid of no feckin' ban,' says she. 'I was at the doctor last week and he told me that if I didn't give up the fags he'd open me up and put my gallstones back in. I was so frightened I started to cut down and I had my last fag just before midnight last night. It is my pure intention to outlive Minister Martin.'

Dixie was deflated. He was waitin' for someone else to lead the assault on the ban and he would willingly follow. His options were runnin' out when in walked Pa Cantillon. Pa ordered a pint and looked around, confused that the whole place was in silence. He had a whispered conversation with the proprietor, finished his pint and left. After about twenty minutes the silence was interrupted by the sound of a tractor and the hollow thumpin' of an empty trailer. The tractor came to a stop outside the pub window. Pa came in and grabbed a few small stools. He took them out the door and returned for a few more. After five minutes he threw open the pub doors and announced to all and sundry that the official smokin' area was open. We all followed him on to the street and there was his silage trailer, with the back door open and about ten stools from the bar laid out inside. 'Ladies and gentlemen,' says Pa, 'for your comfort and convenience, the proprietor, Mr Walshe, invites you to avail of his all-weather smokin' facility.' Well, they trooped out to the trailer with their drinks and in two minutes a fog of smoke rose over the trailer the likes of which must have been visible from outer space.

It was then the *craic* started. Tommy Waldron arrived with the fiddle and Mrs Quirke turned up with the concertina. The spoons were produced. Songs that weren't sung in years were aired and the session of all sessions resounded from the trailer. At five past two in the mornin' Tom Walshe eventually cleared the place by startin' the tractor and engagin' the tipper. Every night since then, the trailer is the place to be. Not only that, there has been a massive call on silage trailers all over the county. They have an advantage over cattle trucks in that there is no residual odour. There are fears that there won't be a trailer to be got for the first cut of silage in May. There's a fella in Milltown Malbay who has found a double-wheeler, able to accommodate a Siege of Ennis and a Caledonian set. The ingenuity of the Irish in circumventin' authority is alive and well. Beneath every law lurks a lovely loophole.

A NEAR THING

I got the fright of my life durin' the week. I thought my political career was over and, to tell you the truth, I never realised how attached to it I had become. I inherited my late father's seat on the council. I took it on to keep the neighbours and the Mother happy. They all said that Killdicken needed a Hickey in the council. Since then a local organisation has grown up around me and they like nothin' better than fightin' elections.

Last week, the first meetin' of my supporters committee was convened. Here's a list of the members: Pa Quirke the postman, Pa Cantillon of the silage trailer, Tom Cantwell, who hangs around for any sup of loose porter that might become available, and Dixie Ryan, who is what one might call a single-issue canvasser – he was on board last time to fight the smokin' ban, who knows what it'll be next time. Then there is the Mother, the power behind the throne. She says nothin' at the meetin's but has to give everythin' the royal nod.

Breda Quinn, or Superquinn, joined the campaign team after Christmas. I was excited by her decision to join until I overheard her tellin' Moll Gleeson why she was puttin' her not inconsiderable weight behind my campaign: 'I do one mad thing every ten years, and campaignin' for Hickey is it for this decade.'

I arrived at the parochial hall for the meetin' this week to find it in full swing with the bould Superquinn in the chair. 'Sorry I'm late,' says I as I made my way to the top table. 'Sit down there with the rest of them,' says Superquinn, 'you won't have things all your own way this time.' I was absolutely stunned and fell back into a chair in the front row. 'So, Mr Cantillon,' says the bould Breda, 'you think we should have an open nomination procedure for the candidate or candidates that might wish to contest this seat?' 'Indeed I do, Madame Chairperson,' responds Cantillon. 'I am of the opinion that Councillor Hickey has not delivered as much as a filled-in pothole for Killdicken or Glengooley since he assumed the mantle of councillor five long uneventful years ago. I believe he is nothin' but a carbuncle on the hindquarters of the local political scene and we all know what should be done with carbuncles.' I was so gob-smacked I thought my false teeth were welded together. I couldn't open my mouth.

'Thank you, Mr Cantillon,' intoned Superquinn. You'd imagine she was runnin' a tribunal in Dublin Castle with the airs and graces she was developin'. 'And, Mr Ryan, I believe you have something to say?' says she, callin' on Dixie. Up he stood, obviously sufferin' from nicotine withdrawal. By the time he cleared his throat and began to speak I was beginnin' to return to myself, only to be knocked flat again.

Dixie, soundin' like he had swallowed a gravel pit, began with the sweet stuff but it wasn't long until he began to spew out the vinegar. 'We all know that Councillor Hickey is a grand fella. He is likeable and doesn't get on the wrong side of anyone. However, his likeable nature can't hide his uselessness. Since he came to power, we've had the devastatin' outbreak of foot and mouth, the points system has made nervous wrecks of us, the Americans have invaded Iraq and the smokin' ban has threatened everythin' we hold dear. It is plain to see that we need a change of independent councillor in Killdicken and I propose that we select Tom Cantwell, a man with a huge capacity for—' At that stage Superquinn interrupted him in case he slandered Cantwell who was snorin' through his own nomination. 'Could I have someone to second the nomination of Thomas Cantwell?' she shouts. I wasn't feelin' too well, but when I saw who seconded the proposal my whole body froze. The hand that was highest in the air to second Cantwell's nomination was the hand of none other than my own Mother. A betrayal that went back to the womb. I never knew the meanin' of gutted until that moment.

Before I could do or say a thing, Superquinn was closin' the meetin' while Dixie was tryin' to wake Cantwell to tell him he was runnin' for election. At that stage I waved my hands frantically and said I wanted to speak. Superquinn had a silly grin on her face when she called for order. I closed my eyes and with a shake in my voice I told them that this was the most devastatin' moment of my life and that this date, the first of April would ... I stopped dead in my tracks when I realised the day and date that was in it. I looked around to see my Mother shakin', Superquinn holdin' her sides, and tears of laughter pourin' down Pa Cantillon's cheeks. I felt weak. The room went round and round and I woke in the back of an ambulance on the way to the hospital in Cashel. To paraphrase Mr Shakespeare, 'Nothing became my seat like the losing of it.'

CITIZENSHIP

All this hullabaloo about citizenship is worryin'. Why we have to have a referendum on whether children actually born in the country have a right to it beats me. As far as I'm concerned, any child born in Hollow Street or the Coombe has more of a right to put on an Irish jersey than some who have worn it in the not too distant past. The powers that be tell us they're amendin' the constitution in order to close a loophole in the law. I am of the belief that legal loopholes or loose interpretations of the law are very useful things. You'll never know the day nor the hour that you might need them.

A loose understandin' about who you are and where you're from is especially important in rural Ireland. For instance, when I introduce myself to people tellin' them I'm Councillor Maurice Hickey from Killdicken, I'll be asked immediately, 'But who are you?' I will often reply, 'I just told you who I am.' A certain impatience afflicts the questioner who then asks, 'But what Hickeys are you?' It is customary at this stage to completely ignore your paternal antecedents and talk about who your mother was. This seems to satisfy all curiosity. In fact, people will often interrupt you and tell you things about your relations you'd prefer not to know.

'Well, my mother is ...' 'Sure, don't I know who she is now, she's Higgins from Honetyne. Her mother's people were sheep shearers from Ballyullan. I hope you're better than them. They were no addition to any place.' When people start tracin' you through your mother's people, they seem to think they can say whatever they want.

To get back to the closin' of loopholes and loose identity, tightenin' this sort of thing could have serious implications for some rural GAA clubs. It is a well-known fact that cousins from Dublin, New York and London have found themselves togged out in the colours of the parish they were visitin' for a few weeks durin' the summer. They'd be given a new name, a new identity and told to keep their mouth shut for the duration of the match in case their accent gave them away.

Two years ago, Glengooley was playin' Balltrasna in the semi-final of the county junior football championship. One family, the Geoghegans, between first cousins and brothers had five family members on the panel. They all got stuck in Holyhead on their way back from a family weddin' in England. The Glen boys couldn't get the match postponed and after they had fielded all their subs, they were still short one player for a team.

There was a tall, lanky scoorloon of an Australian cousin visitin' the Casey's in Portmore for the summer. He had a reputation as a bit of a windbag, boastin' about everythin' Australian, especially the 'Footie'. He was asked to tog out and play as 'Uinseann Geoghegan'. Even the locals had trouble with that particular name. The Aussie readily agreed, even though he knew nothin' about the game and less about the player he was impersonatin'.

Glengooley manager, PJ Muldowney put the Aussie in full-back with clear instructions to 'jump like a so-and-so kangaroo and bury at least two of the forwards in the first ten minutes.' The Aussie played a blinder. He caught everythin' that came near the square and fisted it to safety. He frightened the daylights out of two members of the full-forward line. At the beginnin' of the second half the Glen was ahead by a goal and five points. Everythin' was goin' well until a small, knacky corner-forward continued to get the better of the Australian and started to tantalise him. When he called him 'Skippy', that was the last straw. At the arrival of the next ball, the Aussie wrapped the corner-forward around the goalpost. The ref came boundin' over, whistle blowin' and book out. There ensued an animated conversation with the Australian. Then the Aussie cupped his hands around his mouth and shouted to the manager on the sideline, 'Wot's moy bleedin' nime, Pee Jai?' Needless to say, the Glen didn't even contest the objection.

'I'LL CONFIRM NOTHIN''

The Mother reminded me durin' the week that my cousin's son, my godson, is about to make his confirmation. She told me to be sure to get some nice new euro notes out of the post office for him. Between gettin' the lawnmower fixed, payin' the Easter dues and now this, I won't have a bob left for the election campaign.

Anyway, I called over to see the cousin and give him the few euros while they were still fresh in my wallet. I asked him if he was ready for examination by the bishop and if he knew his catechism. He looked at me as if I had two heads and asked what 'catechism' meant. His mother came to the rescue and told him to show his religion books to Uncle Maurice. Well, compared to my time, his religion book was like an adventure story in a comic book. Gone are the days of the fierce examination and waitin' in trepidation in case you got a question about the Blessed Trinity or explainin' one of the seven deadly sins.

I remember one year, Canon Carey, the parish priest, was in the school for one of his sessions preparin' the confirmation class for examination by His Lordship. He asked young Tom Walshe, now our local publican, to recite the ten commandments. Tom was flyin' it till he got past the fifth. Then he ran into a few linguistic snags that nearly sank his prospects of becomin' a 'true and perfect soldier' of the faith. 'Fifth, thou shalt not kill,' declared Walshe with his hands behind his back and his chest out. 'Sixth, thou shalt not milk a donkey,' he continued confidently, before finishin' with a warnin' that 'Thou shalt not cover your neighbour's goods.' He then warned that one should not 'cover' one's neighbour's wife either! The whole class was chewin' the desks to stop themselves laughin'. Canon Carey couldn't see us; he spent most of his life goin' around with his eyes closed. However, we were terrified that the Master would catch us laughin' and the priest in the room. God only knows what he would do to us.

I have one other clear memory of a preparation session conducted by the said Canon Carey. While he went around with his eyes closed, everyone said he missed nothin'. He got news everywhere he went, not by askin' questions but by makin' statements that people corrected. So he'd say to someone like me, 'Ah, young Hickey, ye have seventeen cows now.' Of course I'd respond by correctin' him and tellin' him the right number of cows. This is how he calculated how much we should be payin' in dues. He knew everythin' about everyone's business.

He was examinin' us for confirmation but a quiet youngfella, Tommy Maguire from Honetyne Upper, refused to answer even one question. The priest asked him who made the world, who died on Good Friday, who divided the waters of the Nile, but Tommy just kept his arms folded and stared straight ahead. Finally, Canon Carey went up and remarked to the master that young Maguire didn't appear to hear very well. 'Oh his hearin' is all right, Canon,' says the Master, 'there must be somethin' else wrong with him.'

The canon went back down to Tommy's desk and tried to draw him out, 'Ah, Young Maguire, you must be the quietest little man in the four parishes! You haven't answered one question for me.' Without lookin' at the priest, Tommy answered like a marine under interrogation: 'Me Father told me tell you nothin'. He says you're a hoor for news.'

A CANTANKEROUS ELECTORATE

The canvassin' for the local election started in earnest this week. I'm worn out already and my bad hip is actin' up. I've been on a waitin' list for seven months and I was sure the job would be done in time for the election. Anyway, by the time the canvassin' is over my rear end will be in a sling. I find myself goin' down on one side all the time, a bit like an auld Cortina with a broken spring. I come at everythin' sideways. But it's an ill wind that doesn't bring some good fortune. The state of my pelvic attachments is a great talkin' point on the doorsteps and testament to the fact that my position as a local councillor hasn't improved my place on the waitin' list. All jokin' aside, I meet people every day in sheer agony, waitin' for the simplest operation. Not all of them deserve too much sympathy.

At the Bally end of the village there lives the most cantankerous hoor that God ever put into shoe leather. He'd fight with his own toenails. He lives alone since the wife and himself had a so-called amicable separation at a time when any kind of separation was taboo. They've been apart now for the best part of twenty-five years. The same man can't live with himself, not to mind anyone else. He had occasion to go to hospital last year to have an in-growin' toenail removed. The neighbours said it was the toenail that had applied to be removed from him.

He was no sooner in hospital than he was broadcastin' his story. Anyone that was misfortunate enough to be within three yards of him was told that he had been waitin' six months for a bed to have the toenail removed and his health was deterioratin' rapidly every day while he waited. When he was told that his operation was to be delayed by two days he was fit to be tied. The next mornin' when the matron was doin' her rounds he called her over to his bed. 'Who are you?' says he, 'Oh, I'm the Matron,' she replied pleasantly. 'Well, let me tell you one thing, Mrs Matron,' says he with the air of a man about to deliver a killer punch, 'you wouldn't run a feckin' henhouse.' There was pandemonium. He was told if he didn't apologise he would be discharged immediately. In a situation not too different from the one in which Frank Dunlop found himself in the Flood Tribunal, he was given two hours to 'reflect on his position'.

After two hours he declared that he was ready to apologise to the Matron. She came to his bedside with an entourage of medical and clerical officials who were paid to be somewhere else. He cleared his throat and said, 'Matron, I wish to withdraw my remarks of this mornin'. I was wrong, I have to tell you that in all likelihood you probably could run a feckin' henhouse.' Within minutes he found himself on the steps of the hospital with his in-growin' toenail fully intact. He's in the process of suin' everybody in sight and there are no offers to remove the toenail.

I have been avoidin' his house like the plague. He has wasted enough state resources without wastin' mine as well. While I'm no fan of the government, patients like this fella add a lot more strain to the system.

The state of my hip continues to be a talkin' point on the doorsteps. I was just beginnin' to glory in the fact that I was a walkin' wounded symbol of the poor state of the health services when I was cut down to size. I was hobblin' down through the village last Friday with my bunch of canvass cards, gettin' loads of support and sympathy. Then I heard the voice of Superquinn bellowin' from the other side of the street: 'If it isn't Hopalong Chastity and his sundance tailend. Hickey, 'twould take some health service to straighten you out.' My back, my legs, my ego and my political future need a massage.

WATCHIN' YOUR BACK

It's great weather. You couldn't ask for better conditions for canvassin'. Everyone is in good humour and they're all promisin' me the auld number 1. I'm too long in the tooth to believe everythin' I hear, but a positive white lie is easier to take than a blatant refusal. However, not all is well with elections in this little country of ours. There is a cuttin' edge after findin' its way in to the rivalry between candidates that can often backfire on all of us. Years ago local elections were more like a hurlin' tournament than a political contest. There was determined but friendly rivalry. The same can't be said of the present time. Candidates would cut one another's throats for a few votes or even a few transfers. The internal rivalry between candidates standin' for the same party is ten times worse than the inter-party stuff. And in modern electioneerin', spin and PR have added to this rivalry and one-upmanship. We are all tryin' to get the photo opportunity or the bit of good news that is better than the next one.

Up to recently, this ill will in the bigger parties was workin' to my advantage. My relationships with all the candidates from the main parties was great, I was talkin' to everyone and everyone was talkin' to me. None of them were talkin' to one another. However, I became a victim of my own spinnin' and the whole thing spun out of control.

An incident happened that at first worked beautifully to my advantage. Two candidates from one of the bigger parties ran into one another while canvassin' the one house. There are ten votes in the same house so it was a juicy little preference producer. Well, the mother and father of a row blew up between the two candidates when they met in the kitchen with one claimin' that he had always canvassed this house and always got the votes. The other fella told him to get lost, it was a free country and he'd canvass whoever and wherever he liked. The woman of the house was disgusted at what was happenin' and told the two of them to get lost. 'A plague on all yer houses!' says she. 'From now on the votes in this house are goin' to Hickey.' She cleared the two looderamawns and their respective entourages and I put a sign on the gate: 'Hickey Canvassers Only. All Others, Hop It.'

Needless to say, I was delighted with this and decided to do an Alistair Campbell on it. I contacted the local press and had my photo taken beside the sign at the gate. Unfortunately the woman wasn't at home at the time and the first she knew about this was when she opened the paper on Wednesday. I got a phone call from her that singed the hair around my left ear. She left me in no doubt that I had overstepped the mark and she'd see me in hell before she or anyone in her house voted for me.

While I was flattened by my own stupidity I consoled myself by sayin' that the ten votes I lost were ones I hadn't expected to come my way. The incident didn't stop there, though. When I opened the paper this Wednesday, there was a full-page interview with the woman in question. She gave a detailed account of the row between the candidates in her house, how she hunted them and what happened when I had the photo taken and published without her permission. That wasn't bad enough, but the article was centred around a huge photo of the woman hangin' a poster of mine upside-down on her clothesline under the banner headline, 'Hamfisted Hickey Hung Out To Dry.' There was also a photo of the new sign on the woman's gate, featurin' a picture of an Alsatian accompanied by a warnin', 'All Canvassers Are Legitimate Targets'.

IDEOLOGY & FECKOLOGY

I have a crowd of Yanks visitin' at the moment. What a mess to be in at the height of an election campaign. Bill Ryan, a cousin of the Mother arrived with his new wife Berle, along with her three daughters, Leanne, Beth and Charlene. In fairness, the three daughters are in their twenties and gorgeous-lookin'. However, Bill and Berle have been tryin' to run my campaign.

I thought I had gotten rid of the whole lot of them when I suggested they take a bus tour of Connemara, west Mayo and north-west Donegal. They were all ready to go when Bill announced that he was stayin'. He reckoned that 'Cousin Mossie' could do with some help. But the women went off on the bus.

Bill's participation on the canvass was nothin' short of disastrous. After two days I was sure I hadn't a hope of retainin' my seat. By the time the canvass is over I'll *need* feckin' help – from the fellas in white coats. You see, a lot of my voters are drawn from the crowd I meet in the pub, the post office or in the queue for bargains in the Co-op shop. They like a smoke, they like a drink and a small number of them have a sort of an allergy to a day's work. Now, when it emerged that, politically, Bill is to the right of Genghis Khan, we ran into ideological difficulties on the campaign trail that could yet leave me without a council seat.

On my canvass, the woes and problems of humanity are heaped at my feet. I listen and nod, and then give out about the government, concludin' with an assurance that 'I'll see what I can do'. This formula works for me – and for every other independent that ever wore out shoe leather lookin' for votes. It didn't wash with Bill.

We arrived at Hauly Donnellan's on the Bally road. Hauly worked for years in the local quarry. His lungs and chest carry a ton of quarry dust which isn't helped by the cartons of fags he goes through. When he isn't coughin' he's smokin'. The wife died two years ago and the children are all over the world. All the poor auld devil has left are the fags and the few pints. I knocked at the door and out he came, coughin' and splutterin' like a TVO Ferguson on a cold mornin'. He complained about the smokin' ban, the price of drink, the price of his chest medicine and the fact that his roof was leakin' for six months and the council sent no-one to fix it. Before I had time to sympathise with his predicament, Bill tore in to him. He told him if he'd just 'quit the goddam cigarettes' he'd have no need to buy the 'goddam drugs'. Forgettin' what country he was in, Bill continued his rant, tellin' a visibly shocked Hauly that if he got off his 'butt' and got a job he wouldn't be waitin' for 'Uncle Sam' to fix his 'goddam roof'.

As we left the house, I hadn't the gall to ask Hauly for the vote. He was so taken aback by Bill that he couldn't even cough. We went to four more houses where Bill continued to peddle his neo-conservative wares with gusto. He told Mary Glennon that her house was a health hazard after he slid on a cold rasher left out for the dog. When Maggie Moloney appeared in all her finery to give out about there bein' no playground for the children, he advised her to save the money she spent on make-up and take the youngsters to Disney once a year. Maggie has never been past Clonmel.

I called off the canvass before we were physically attacked. Bill was buryin' my election hopes with every word out of his mouth. I shook him off and went for a pint. While I was in the pub, it was announced on the nine o' clock news that former US President Ronnie Reagan had passed away. No sooner was the news over than Bill came in and stated that he was goin' straight back to the States for the funeral. I told him he was right to go, that I always found it's the funerals you don't go to are the very ones people remember. When Berle and the girls came back from their bus tour the followin' day, Bill had all the bags packed. They all hugged and kissed one another when Bill told them the sad news. They shed a tear for Ronnie, put on their funeral faces and we all hit for Shannon. Havin' sympathised on their loss for the umpteenth time, I saw them off at the departure gate. With great relief, I stopped on the way home and drank a fulsome toast to the memory of Ronnie Reagan who, in dyin', resurrected my council seat.

A NEW SYNDROME

I have discovered a new condition. It is experienced by people who have nearly lost their political lives on one or more occasion. The condition is known as NPDS, Near Political Death Syndrome.

I got a severe dose of it durin' the last local election count. I arrived at the count centre at about eleven o'clock, thinkin' that I'd be well on the way to victory. I went up and greeted Teresa Stapleton, the returnin' officer. Teresa has held this position since my father's time. At every count she sits in the one place and doesn't move from it until the last candidate is elected. They say that since she put on the bit of condition, the chair has nearly to be amputated from her at the end of the last declaration. Before I arrived that mornin', there had been a bit of high drama when the chair in which Teresa had ensconced herself proved not to be up to the task and disintegrated. She tumbled backwards off her podium and ended up in an unceremonious heap in the middle of a collection of ballot boxes. They got a cushion and repositioned her on a temporary seatin' arrangement.

As I arrived at the count centre, I was a bit nervous that my American cousin, Bill, who had been on the canvass in the early stages might have done a bit of damage. When he went back to the States, I returned to visit the houses he had canvassed with me but the reception I got was about as warm as a polar bear's snout.

Back to the count. Early tallies showed that I'd need to buck up on number ones and number twos if I was to have any hope of retainin' my seat. My electoral area is a four-seater and I always took the third one. I was surprised, but in no panic, when Fine Gael took the first seat ahead of Fianna Fáil. After the second seat was taken by the FFers I went down town for a pint before my own elevation. On my return, I nearly dropped dead when I discovered that Percy Pipplemoth Davis of the Friends of the Sunflower party was about to take my seat, the third one. I was sick to the pit of my stomach. This blow-in, this woolly-jumpered tree-hugger was about to displace *me* from the family seat at the council. The insincere auld bag of bones had the nerve to come over and hug me sayin', 'Maurice, it will be such a shame if you aren't with me in the chamber.' I told him he had no idea what a shame it would be. I wanted to tell him that the proper chamber for him had the word 'pot' attached to it.

I couldn't figure out what was happenin'. I was in a state of collapse when it emerged that Pipplemoth Davis and the last candidate would be elected without reachin' the quota. The count went on and on and on. Timmy Ryan, a Pee Dee convert was closin' in on me and I was movin' at a snail's pace. In fairness to the FFers and the Fine Gaelers, they were gathered around me tryin' to figure out what was wrong. They said that the Honetyne boxes were very poor for me and I normally got a big vote there. In fact, they said that the turnout in Honetyne appeared to be very low.

I was sittin' in a corner, very dejected when Pa Cantillon and Breda Quinn (Superquinn) arrived to console me. Cantillon was full to the throat. He had been on the porter all mornin'. He was no sooner sittin' beside me than he looked up at the returnin' officer and whispered to me, 'Isn't that Teresa Stapleton from Borrisnangoul?' ''Tis,' says I. 'She has been the returnin' officer here since my father's time.' With that he stood up and staggered his way through the countin' area to the podium and climbed up to shake hands with her. She wasn't at all pleased with this invasion of her realm but decided that prudence was the better part of valour and stretched out to take the hand of the very unstable Cantillon. He fell forward, knocked over her table, knocked her off her seatin' contraption and landed on top of her in the middle of a pile of empty ballot boxes.

Sergeant Miller woke up of a shot and while he was tryin' to get Cantillon to his feet, Superquinn was helpin' Teresa to re-establish herself. As she straightened the ballot box on which the returnin' officer had been perched, Superquinn let out a shout. 'Hey, hey, hey!' says she. 'This box is full.' Well, there was consternation all round. Since her first seatin' accident of the day, the returnin' officer had been sittin' on one of the Honetyne boxes and it full of votes. A total recount had to take place, the quota had to be rejigged and to my great relief I took the third seat. Pipplemoth Davis took the last seat from the Pee Dees after a marathon count.

Where the returnin' officer had put her backside nearly deprived me of a place to put my backside for the next five years. Pa Cantillon is tellin' the world and its mother that he single-handedly rescued my political life. My recovery from Near Political Death Syndrome will cost me dearly in porter for Cantillon.

PITCH INVASIONS

After our recent democratic exertions, life is returnin' to normal in Glengooley, Killdicken and environs. Normality in this world is characterised by funerals, football matches, auctions, marts, fights, fallin' outs and makin' ups, with an acceptable level of skulduggery underpinnin' everythin'.

Summer is a time when all these ingredients are most headily mixed. You can often experience the whole lot in one few hours. We had that experience ourselves just two days after the election. The extended spell of fine weather has seen more good hay saved than was saved in total since the famine. Come next spring, the animal population of the country will be in the finest of fettle. The shine off their coats will dazzle the sight in vets, dealers and tanglers. Anyway, the downside of this bumper fodder harvest is that there is hardly a young fella available for football and hurlin' before nine o'clock in the evenin'.

Last Saturday evenin' our lads were playin' the Bally boys in the first round of the championship. The match didn't start till half-nine. 'Twas a fine long evenin' but a half-nine start was stretchin' it. At twenty-five past, cars were flyin' up to the dressin' room and fellas covered in hayseeds, smellin' of lubrication oil and soaked in diesel jumped out. They all followed the same pattern. They'd open the boot of their souped-up motors and pull out jerseys, togs and socks from under tool boxes, bits of drive shafts and half-finished bottles of orange, lemonade and other dubious concoctions.

At half-nine the ref threw in the ball while fellas were runnin' on to the field, pullin' up togs, hoppin' on one leg while tyin' the laces on the other boot. Mick Kelly, the goalie from Bally, was pullin' on his jersey as he ran to take up his position in goals. He ran straight into the nettin' and only that

Mag Slattery had a scissors in her handbag, he'd still be enmeshed in the back of the net.

The game started in good spirits and half-time came without a row. It also arrived without a score. People at this end of the country are not made for the big ball. The second half told a somewhat different story. Tim Cantillon, a son of my friend Pa of silage-trailer fame, came on as full-forward for our crowd. Tim, like the father, is in the contractin' business. He has a mower, baler and wrapper on the road. He was put markin' Tom Cregan, a young farmer playin' in the full-back position on the Bally side. Unknown to some people, there was a lot of tension between the two. Cregan had been waitin' for two weeks for Cantillon to bale his hay. Cantillon's man had knocked it two weeks ago but now the weather was about to break and there was no sign of the baler and wrapper. Tensions were high. When the first ball came in, Cantillon went up for it but as he stretched into the air he got the full power of Cregan's left elbow into the gut. He doubled over while Mick Kelly, the goalie, cleared the ball.

The ref followed play but the row went on between Cregan and Cantillon. It had more to do with hay than football. As Cantillon rolled around the ground after the dig in the guts, Cregan stood over him shoutin': 'Get up, you liar. You left my hay on the flat for the last two weeks and there you are, above at Lady Buttenshaw's savin' her few miserable auld sops. You're just like all the Cantillons, full of snobbery. Ye were always in the back pocket of the gentry, ye crowd of sleeveens.' Cantillon wasn't long gettin' over his injury and before anyone could shout 'Ref!' he had Cregan buried in the back of his own net. At this stage Kelly, the goalie, became involved and the ref halted play. He ran down to the goalmouth furiously blowin' his whistle. As he reached the melee he tripped over a stray football boot and found himself entangled with the combatants. Mag Slattery and her scissors came to the rescue again.

Just as they disentangled themselves, an umpire came over and whispered somethin' to the ref. This particular referee is full of his own importance and is known to one and all as 'Captain Peacock'. He blew his whistle and called the two teams together: 'Gentlemen, while you were dishonourin' this game with your despicable behaviour, one of the great exponents of our national games was called home to his eternal reward.

Gentlemen, the great Mitch Hogan has passed away. May the Lord have mercy on him.' All heads were bowed. Captain Peacock continued: 'In honour of this man and in the name of all that is good and decent about our association and its games I propose that we now abandon this particular fixture. Havin' played fifty-eight minutes, each team has managed to score one point. Need I say more?'

He blew his whistle. Someone shouted: 'Mitch Hogan would've loved a game like this. He'd have been in the middle of the row.' Someone else shouted: 'We'd have beaten ye anyway.' The row took off again. The ref had to be escorted off the pitch. Both teams have been suspended from this year's championship and every second mourner at Mitch Hogan's funeral had a black eye, a bandage or a limp. What a wonderful little country.

GREATNESS, GRABBERS AND GOMBEENS

I was within a hair's breadth of greatness this week. I had the chain of office in my hands, ready to put it over my shoulders when it was snatched from me by the most low-down piece of skulduggery that I ever experienced. I spent the rest of the week distressed, disappointed and distorted. The Mother tells me I'll wake three parishes with the roarin' of me in my sleep. It even pains me to think about it.

What happened? I'll tell you what happened. I was knobbled, shafted and hung out to dry. Early in the week the new council met to elect the mayor, and appoint the chairs of the council committees and people to various bodies and sub-groups. There was a fair number of independents elected this time round. However, they're not all like myself. To be honest, there is a rare collection of cranks and looderamawns sittin' in the chamber on independent tickets.

First among them is Mindy Morrissey from Glenabuddybugga. She campaigned on a promise to have a bye-law passed preventin' young wans from wearin' the low-cut jeans and the high-cut *geansies* and blouses that show off their belly buttons. Seemingly it upsets her, no end. She'll not let Tomeen, her husband, out to town without the darkest pair of sunglasses you ever saw. She says that the sight of these belly buttons drives his blood pressure sky high. (If Mindy herself took to wearin' the garments in question, her navel would be hangin' somewhere near her knees.)

Then we have Terence Bullockfield, who arrived here from God-knows-where about two years ago. He teaches yoga and transcendental meditation to a big enough number of people. Since the church fell on lean times, all kinds of star-gazin' is growin' in popularity. Mr Bullockfield got the whole lot of his 'students' to vote for him and got in.

Another of the independents is the sunflower saver, Percy Pipplemoth Davis. Now, he is two ends of a treacherous hoor. And here lies the cause of my devastation.

On the mornin' of the first council meetin' the above-mentioned trio, myself and the three ODI's (ordinary decent independents) met. It was agreed to put me forward for Chair of the Council and mayor of the county. Lo and behold, didn't the Fine Gaelers and Labour approach us. Together we had a majority of one over the combined forces of the FFers, the Pee Dees and the Shinners. In record time a deal was struck. It was agreed we'd have a rotatin' mayorship. I would get the chain for the first year and after that the others would take their turns. I was nearly speechless with excitement. I went home and told the Mother. There were tears of pride in her eyes as she fussed around pretendin' 'twas a great inconvenience. We went straight to Treacy's in Clonmel where I bought a new suit and a new pair of shoes. The Mother dug out my old copy of *Buntús Cainte* so that I could brush up on the *cúpla focail* and she cleaned out a cupboard in the parlour to hold the chain of office. All my years of public service were about to be rewarded.

The new councillors gathered in County Hall on Monday evenin'. I was like a seven-year-old at the Feis. I had my speech learned off and I couldn't stop clearin' my throat. As proceedin's commenced I noticed that Pipplemoth Davis and Mindy Morrissey were missin'. A Fine Gaeler requested an adjournment to give the missin' members time to turn up. The outgoin' mayor, who was chairin' the meetin', said he had apologies from both and, before we could do a thing, the FFers had Mick the Snipe Brosnan elected and there he stood, the smug auld looderamawn with *my* chain around his thick neck. I was stunned. You might as well have planted a mallet between my two eyes. My astonishment soon turned to disbelief and anger when I realised that my missin' independent colleagues weren't missin' by accident.

The evidence of their dirty deeds soon came to light. In his openin' address to the Council, the new mayor announced that a key plank of his programme for local government was public decency. He declared that he would institute bye-laws compellin' anyone availin' of public buildin's or facilities to be covered from the neck to the knee in garments that reflected 'acceptable standards of public decency'. That auld prude, Mindy Morrissey, had sold me out for the sake of her husband's blood pressure and her own hang-ups.

However bad that was, the treachery of that eel, Percy Pipplemoth Davis, would have made Judas blush. When it came to the election of the Chair of the Environment and Housing Strategic Policy Committee, wasn't Pipplemoth, in his absence, proposed by a Pee Dee, seconded by a Shinner and elected. That he may get fourteen kinds of the itch.

I left the County Hall in a daze. I took a taxi home, returned the new suit to Treacy's and spent the rest of the day on my own in Walshe's snug. The only relief I am gettin' from my anguish comes from the pleasure of plottin' my revenge.

CHANGIN' TIMES

I love the summer. Everythin' is quiet, only the farmers are workin' flat out. But it has been so dry recently that even they are laid back, now that all the fodder is saved early. Most people are in what they call 'holiday mode'. Anyway, the pressure of the election is over, the weather has been grand and Killdicken was like an open-air holiday camp for the past few weeks.

The thing about peace and quiet is that they have a habit of bein' shattered. I'm reminded of the warnin' we'd get goin' to dances: Beware of the quiet ones. The same could be said about quiet times; they're the lull before the hurricane.

The shatterin' of our mid-summer magic began in the most unlikely of places – the church. On Saturday evenin' we all trooped into Mass and everythin' seemed normal enough, until it came to the time for the sermon. We had no sooner sat down and prepared ourselves for forty winks than Fr McGrath declared that there would be no sermon. We fairly perked up when he asked us to stay back after Mass for an Important Message. Everyone was stunned. We didn't know what to expect.

Well, the whisperin' took off as soon as the baskets started to go around. By the time we got to the 'Our Father' I had heard four different rumours. The most charitable of these had poor Fr McGrath dyin' of cancer. One story had him in trouble with the bank – seemingly he was in a bank in Clonmel durin' the week and was called out of the queue into the manager's office. Accordin' to another tale he was runnin' off to Scotland to the landlady who owns the B&B where he stays every year on his fishin' holiday. It appears that her husband died durin' the year and Father has been over twice already. It didn't strike people that he went over once for the funeral and the second time for his usual holiday. I gave up listenin' when I was told as gospel truth that himself and Tom Nolan, the Credit Union Chairman, were bein' investigated by the guards after losin' most of the credit union funds in Cheltenham last March.

By the time it came to communion, our parish priest was a roarin' alcoholic, a ravin' sex maniac, a swindler and a gambler. At the end of Mass, when Father went into the sacristy to change out of the vestments, people were breathless at the prospect of what was goin' to emerge on his return to the altar. One delicate-minded little man gathered his wife and teenage children and frog-marched them out of the church. He was heard to say, 'I will not have my family exposed to this sort of thing.' Obviously, by the time the rumours got to him they deserved to be X-rated.

When the misfortunate priest reappeared you could hear a pin drop. He stepped up to the pulpit, cleared his throat thoroughly and began: 'My dear people, as you know the Church has been going through some rough and lean times. In this little parish of ours we cannot expect to escape the cruel winds which buffet the Church in these dark days. Here in this little haven, we too have to accept our share of bad news.' At this stage every jaw had dropped wide open. Upper sets of false teeth were collapsin' onto lower jaws as people waited expectantly for every word.

'I myself have had my difficulties,' continued Fr McGrath. 'I have found it a very, very lonely time to be a priest.' Pa Cantillon leaned over to me and whispered loudly: 'I'd put a thousand euros on the Scottish lady. I'd say she has him. Ha, haa, the Flower of Scotland herself.' 'Shh,' says I, 'give the man a chance.' Fr McGrath continued: 'It will get even lonelier as fewer and fewer priests are available for work in parishes up and down the country. Allied to that, the Church is not the wealthy organisation people perceive it to be. The value of Church savings and investments has collapsed as interest rates plummet. We have had to resort to sometimes unorthodox methods to supplement Church resources.' Tom Cantwell gave me a dig from behind: ''Tis all gone on the horses, I'm tellin' you. The whole feckin' lot is still runnin' around Cheltenham.' I ignored him, as the man at the pulpit seemed to be comin' to a conclusion, 'This brings me to the nub of the issue. Less priests and less resources mean less service. This will inevitably result in fewer masses. From now on there will be no Saturday evening Mass in Honetyne; there will be one Mass there at ten am on Sundays. Saturday evening Mass will continue here in Killdicken, but there will be only one Mass here on Sundays and that will be celebrated at twelve noon.'

There was uproar. Most people were ragin' that no-one had been asked their opinion. Some were ragin' that none of the more raunchy rumours proved to be true. I was speechless with relief. I had visions of the place bein' infested by the feckin' media. By the time I recovered my equilibrium, Superquinn was on her feet givin' a rousin' speech about Mass rocks and Redcoats and priests bein' hung and the faithful bein' hunted and shot. Before I knew it, a sit-in was organised and they're not leavin' till the bishop himself appears. I'm afraid 'tis only beginnin'.

THE GLARE OF PUBLICITY

The parish is in a serious state of crisis since Fr McGrath announced a change in Mass times and a reduction in the number of Masses. There was outrage when the news broke and a spontaneous sit-in in the church went on for the most of last week. About twenty parishioners refused to leave the church when Fr McGrath made the announcement. They vowed to sit tight until the bishop came and explained himself.

The people on the sit-in were not the people you'd normally associate with this kind of action. Ten of them were daily Mass goers with an average age of about seventy-three. These were the most militant of the lot. They didn't care what happened, but they weren't movin' till the bishop arrived. When some of the locals suggested to Moll Tierney, who is ninety-one, that she should leave the protest to the 'young ones', she said: 'I'll see the bishop in this church, be it in this life or the next. And if he wants to see me in this life he'd better hurry up.'

We've had the media crawlin' all over the place like a rash. Superquinn took over operations and appointed herself spokesperson for the 'Killdicken Twenty', as they became known. She got all kinds of headlines like, 'Killdicken Queen Defies Church Princes'. She was on Joe Duffy for half an hour on Friday and the next thing she'll be on the Late Late. She has become somethin' of a celebrity. It's a good job this didn't happen before the elections or she'd have been persuaded to run and my seat would have gone west.

Poor auld Fr McGrath was in an impossible position. He'd have preferred to leave things as they were, but he couldn't. In fairness to the crowd on the sit-in, a small bit of consultation beforehand would have gone a long way. Now, to keep the lines of communication open, he put the heatin' on at night for them and left the sacristy open so they could use the toilet and boil a kettle. A bit late.

As the days went on the whole thing turned into a kind of carnival. Mornin', noon and night people were bringin' sandwiches and tea to the church. The churchyard was a hive of activity as crowds travelled from far and wide to support the 'Killdicken Twenty'. However, Fr McGrath had to draw the line when our local publican, Tom Walshe, arrived with a barrel of porter and a crate of spirits, wine and sherry for the protestors.

On the fifth night of the sit-in I decided to intervene. I went to Fr McGrath to see what I could do. He was in very bad form. 'Look, Maurice,' says he, 'I've been landed with this. A bunch of know-alls in high places in the diocese have put together a programme of what they call rationalisation. Mark my words, the bishop will not come to Killdicken because he won't be let. That crowd of sharks he has around him would make Alastair Campbell and Peter Mandelson look like the feckin' Teletubbies.' He pulled out a bottle of whiskey and by the time I stood up to go home I had difficulty negotiatin' my way to the front door, not to mind negotiatin' an end to stand-off at the church.

I woke the followin' mornin' with a head like a bucket and the Mother roarin': 'Get up, get up, you looderamawn, and come down to the telly. They're talkin' about the sit-in.' When I went down she had Sky News blarin'. 'Last week the Vatican indicated that Pope John Paul II is considering a return visit to Ireland. However, he will find a very different country to the one he visited in 1979. The people are in open revolt against the authority of the church. Nowhere is this more evident than in the little village of Killdicken in southern Ireland where parishioners have occupied their church to protest against changes in the times and locations of services. We go over live to Killdicken where Lauren Simpson is talking to Breda Quinn, the leader of this revolt.'

Well, the bould Superquinn appeared in all her glory, wearin' a bandana around her head and a T-shirt with the slogan 'The Bishop or Bust' emblazoned across her ample frontage. She rattled off her speech about the Penal Laws, Mass rocks, Redcoats and persecutions. She declared there would be no surrender until the bishop came to Killdicken to explain himself. Unfortunately, she didn't stop there, she went on to demand the abolition of celibacy, the democratic election of Church leaders and the ordination of women. 'Oh Jesus, Mary and Joseph,' gasped the Mother.

'They'll be sendin' a feckin' aircraft carrier from the Vatican. We'll be blown off the face of the earth.'

Whatever about sendin' an aircraft carrier, someone must have put a blow-lamp to the bishop's tail-end. I rang Dixie Ryan to give me a lift to the church and by the time I got there, the bishop, Fr McGrath and Breda Quinn were givin' a press conference announcin' the end of the sit-in and the reinstatement of all Masses. As I elbowed my way towards the cameras and the microphones, Superquinn shouted: 'Here he comes, our esteemed public representative, Councillor Maurice Hickey, late as usual. Hickey, even the Church got here before you.' There goes my career in international politics.

DRIVIN' LESSONS

It's as plain as the nose on my face that I need to do somethin' about the fact that I can't drive. For years I've been late for council meetin's, conferences and all kinds of official functions. Over the last few months the Mother has been pilin' on the pressure about the drivin'. She tries to sweeten it sayin' that the few euros in travellin' expenses would come in handy. To crank up the pressure, she took to goin' to Clonmel twice a week for the shoppin'. 'Twas highly embarrassin' to see her out on the main road hitchin' lifts. She'd come home in the evenin' moanin' about how handy it would be if I could drive.

Havin' made discreet enquiries about drivin' lessons and tutors, I found a retired English cop in Borrisnangoul who was cheap. I was told he provided a car for the lessons and he would keep his mouth shut. If it got out I was takin' these lessons, I'd be the laughin' stock of the county. I met the tutor, Peter Sanders, in a pub in Clonmel and he took me to the quietest road in Ireland, the bog road between Borrisnangoul and Honetyne. Anyone travellin' that particular route is either transportin' poteen or lost.

Peter was described to me as a quiet, patient man. I'm afraid I broke both his silence and his patience. We only managed one lesson and it was an absolute disaster. I sat in behind the wheel at half-past ten and it was quarter to twelve before I managed to get movin'. Every time I tried to start, the car would buck-leap around the place like a bad-tempered stallion. After fifty-four attempts, things eventually came together and I took off.

Miraculously, Peter was able to talk me through gettin' from first gear into second and, sure, at that stage I thought I was flyin'. As I belted along the bog road I relaxed and chatted to him about where he was from and how he liked Ireland. I completely forgot that I was doin' the drivin' until I noticed a look of horror come over Peter's face. I turned to the windscreen and to my own horror I was on the grass margin at the wrong side of the road with the car beginnin' to slide sideways into a drain. 'The brake, the brake, press the brake pedal, the middle one!' screamed Peter. My foot frantically searched for the brake and landed on the accelerator. With a thud, I wedged the car in between the two banks of the drain. We couldn't open either of the two front doors. Peter was able to squeeze into the back seat, open the back window and climb on to the boot.

Luckily a local was passin' on a tractor and he pulled us out. The only damage to the car was the caked mud from the drain on the front wings. Of course, once the car emerged from the drain our rescuer recognised me. 'Councillor Maurice Hickey, what has you stuck in a boghole in Borrisnangoul?' 'Oh, I was only passin',' says I, 'when I saw this clown of an Englishman stuck in the ditch. Sure I couldn't leave him stranded. I had to stay here till help came. There's no doubt about it, when you take these fellas off those big motorways, they can't drive at all.' The man on the tractor made a comment about takin' the man out of the bog and drove off. Peter stood there and stared at me as if I had just hit him across the face with a shovel. 'I don't believe what you've just said to that man,' says he, his eyes poppin' out of his head. 'Now, now, Peter,' says I, 'I'll pay you handsomely for the privilege of makin' a driver out of me. Just remember, the customer is always right, especially the one that pays well. Now we'll try again.'

This time Peter opted to take me into a meadow where his brother-in-law had just saved hay into round bales. I was doin' all right until I clipped one of the bales on my way up a hilly part of the field. As I came down the hill the dislodged bale began to follow me. I looked in the mirror and nearly died when I saw this monstrosity bearin' down on the back window at speed. I panicked, hit the brakes and the runaway bale bounced up over the car and for some reason stopped dead in front of us. I lost control and crashed straight into it. Peter had blood drippin' from his forehead and through tears of frustration he begged me to get out of the vehicle. He told me to expect a bill for damage to his car. He said that if he ever saw me behind the wheel of a car again he'd call the guards. In his opinion I should be banned from drivin' for life.

I got home later that evenin' to find a strange car parked outside the house. When I asked the Mother who owned it I nearly died when she said that she did. 'I applied for my drivin' test at Christmas,' says she. 'When I got the call I took lessons in Clonmel twice a week for the last six weeks and I passed my test yesterday. I was between two minds about buyin' the car, but when I heard today that you crashed into the same bale twice in the one meadow, that was enough. I decided I'd take my life into my own hands rather than put it into yours. So I bought my own car there and then. Now, Maurice, give me a list of the conferences you have lined up and a few blank expense forms.'

KILLDICKEN GETS ITS OWN SUMMER SCHOOL ... WELL, SORT OF

God be with the days when every parish had its annual carnival with swingin' boats, chair-o-planes, bumpers and merry-go-rounds. I can still remember watchin' the big fellas from sixth class on the swingin' boats tryin' with all their might to get the boats to do a full round of the bar they were hung on. And you'd have to be fierce careful passin' the chair-o-planes because some misfortunate youngster was sure to get sick as he swung through the air.

These carnivals are a thing of the past. We've gone up-market. Nowadays a parish isn't worth its salt if it doesn't have a summer school. Local organisations and publicans dream up these events in an attempt to attract crowds and make money. They rake through the parish register lookin' for someone who is dead and famous, and they name a summer school after him.

This year I was so busy with the election I never realised that a summer school had been organised in Killdicken. Normally I'm dragged into every dog-fight in the place but I didn't know a thing until I read a notice in the parish newsletter about a Summer School Committee Meetin'. I was deeply offended at bein' kept in the dark. I went straight to Superquinn and asked her what she knew.

She took great pleasure in informin' me that she was chairperson of the Mick Coughlan International Jew's Harp Summer School. When I quizzed her about who was involved she told me that they had decided to keep away from the 'usual suspects' like the clergy, councillors, TDs and celebrities. 'This will be a people's summer school,' says she. 'Mick Coughlan was a man of the people. On Friday night I will welcome everyone and the openin' talk will be given by a nephew of Mick, Nigel Coughlan from London. If you really insist, maybe you can say a few words at the closin' ceremony.'

I was reelin' with shock. 'A few words at the closin' ceremony!' I shouted. 'I've been relegated to the back door of the championship without gettin' a ghost of a chance to play anywhere near the front door. You haven't heard the end of this.'

Not to make myself out to be too much of an auld sulk, I went to the openin'. There was a huge crowd in Tom Walshe's. The thung-a-twang of jew's harps would deafen you. Joe soaps who hadn't the price of anythin' bigger had turned up with these miserable instruments stuck in the hollow of their mouths and they pluckin' sideways as if they were tryin' to dislodge a piece of tough steak from their teeth.

At about ten o'clock, Superquinn called order and welcomed everybody to the first ever Mick Coughlan International Jew's Harp Summer School. She then called on Nigel Coughlan to officially open the school.

Nigel, a very well-dressed, dapper man in his sixties, took the mike and addressed the crowd in a posh BBC accent. 'Ladies and gentlemen, I am truly delighted to be here in Killdicken. It's a sort of homecoming for me. My father, Tom Coughlan, and his brother, Mick, were born here. This, of course, is the centenary of Mick's birth. His genius for music was first recognised by his mother. Family legend has it that at twelve months, when he wanted his bottle he would play the first few bars of 'The White Cow's Hind Tit' on the jew's harp. Before he was ten years old he was known throughout the length and breadth of the county for his talent. By his early twenties, along with an ever-growing musical reputation, he had developed quite a reputation for carousing, drinking and general loose living. In 1928 at the age of twenty-four he married Lizzy Flanagan from Clonmel. She had two sons and a miserable life, compliments of my uncle.'

You could hear a pin drop in the pub. People were gettin' fierce fidgety and uncomfortable. Tom Walshe wasn't sellin' as much as a drop of drink. Nephew Nigel went on to paint a picture of life endured by Mick's family that made *Angela's Ashes* look like *The Sound of Music*. Eventually Mick's wife left him and took the children to Boston where she married a doctor. The sons, in turn, joined the medical profession. Mick himself died at a *fleadh ceoil* in Clonmel in 1966 after swallowin' his jew's harp while playin' a few Kerry slides. Unfortunately the jew's harp didn't slide and it choked him.

'This brings me to the second purpose of my visit to Killdicken,' continued Nigel. 'Tonight I am delighted to launch my book, *Tom and Mick: A Study of Irish Male Dysfunction*. When Breda Quinn first contacted me I couldn't believe how lucky I was that the Mick Coughlan Summer School coincided with my book launch. Thank you so much, Breda, for your invitation. Everyone, do enjoy the rest of the summer school, do buy the book, I know you'll love it.'

There was dead silence when he finished. As the crowd shuffled out, Tom Walshe tried to revive things. Turnin' to Pa Cantillon, Tom Cantwell and Dixie Ryan he shouted, 'Well, lads, ye'll have the same again in honour of the great man.' Dixie lifted his head from his chest and whispered, 'No thanks, Tom. After that lecture 'tis the pledge we'll be takin'. The summer school was on its last legs before the first night was over.

As I left I whispered to Superquinn: 'Breda, the next time you have a brainwave like this, it might be a good idea to round up the usual suspects. They'd be better than a loose cannon like Nephew Nigel any day.'

THE PARISH NOTES

For the past forty years, Mary Moloney has written the Killdicken parish notes. Poor auld Mary has been in hospital with high blood pressure since the first week in August and since then there has been no regular news from Killdicken on the paper. The editor of the *Weekly Eyeopener* contacted Lilly Mac in the post office to know if anyone would compile the local notes until Mary is feelin' better. Lilly asked around but whoever she approached refused. She went to Fr McGrath and he called a meetin' in the presbytery. After goin' around in circles for an hour, Superquinn (who's at every meetin' in the place) suggested that 'since Councillor Hickey has little enough to be doin', maybe he should write them. They'll probably be as inoffensive and harmless as himself.' I got the job.

I was furious at Superquinn's snide remarks and made up my mind that what I would write would be neither harmless nor inoffensive. I rang the editor and she agreed that the notes should be 'sharp and newsy'. I put pen to paper.

KILLDICKEN/GLENGOOLEY/HONETYNE NOTES
Hickey Hammers Council

Councillor Maurice Hickey has once again proved himself a champion of the people. In a hard-hitting statement he slammed the poor state of the road between Killdicken and Honetyne, saying there isn't a tyre left on a bike or a spring on a car. According to an outraged Councillor Hickey, 'Tractor drivers have taken to standin' up while drivin' on this road. If they sit on their spring-loaded seats they risk being fired through the roof of the cab when they hit a pot hole.' The tireless councillor demanded immediate action by the roads department of the council.

Summer School Fiasco

The first ever Mick Coughlan International Jew's Harp Summer School was described by many locals as a damp squib. The school got off to a very shaky start when, at the launch, Nigel Coughlan, a nephew of Mick Coughlan, painted a most unsavoury picture of the late musician's personal life. The future of the summer school is very much in doubt. Poor attendances at both lectures and classes, along with the failure of the Budnanossal Céilí Band to turn up for the closing *céilí*, have left a sour taste. Talking about sour taste, the organiser of the event is gone to ground and unavailable for comment.

Fifty Years of Bedded Bliss

Surrounded by their seven children and thirty-eight grandchildren, Mary and Tom Cregan of Cossatrasna celebrated fifty years of wedded bliss on Sunday last. At a function in Tom Walshe's public house, Tom and Mary were presented with a brand new, king-size, double bed. A great night was in progress until Tom and Mary were encouraged by a local photographer to get into the bed and pose for him. At this point the local Gardaí raided the premises, impounded the bed and charged Tom Walshe with running a house of ill-repute. Locals were astounded to hear that the happy couple is to be charged with offences against public decency. The day in court is eagerly anticipated.

Glengooley Collapse

Glengooley Junior Footballers were taken apart by a rampant Bally on Saturday evening. By half time, Bally had built up a convincing lead of 2.11 to a single point. The second half was even more disastrous when Bally boys added a further 3.18 while the Glen failed to register a single score. According to sources in the Glengooley camp, fourteen of the Glen players had spent the day at Tim Clancy's wedding and had left the table to play the match. Asked to comment on the defeat, one team member remarked, 'Sure, we were stuffed after the feed at the Gooley Arms, we hadn't the energy to fight, not to mind play a match.'

Heat and Light

Parish Priest Fr McGrath is concerned at the number of people lighting candles and putting little or nothing in the money-box. 'They might be fooling me and fooling the parish finances,' says Fr McGrath, 'but they can't fool God. He knows who is and who isn't paying. I wouldn't be surprised if some of these prayers backfired.'

Huge Funeral

A huge crowd turned out to pay their last respects to Nan Griffin, late of Killdicken, who was buried after a long illness on Thursday. Nan, a well-known character in the area, worked for thirty years as milk in-take supervisor at the local Co-op. In his sermon, Fr McGrath told a crowded church that her experience with large volumes of traffic made Nan eminently suitable for her last job as lollipop woman for the local school. According to Sergeant Michael Miller, Nan put Killdicken on the map: 'During her time at the Co-op and at the school she could create a traffic jam out of nothin'. For the last thirty years this was the only village in the county to feature regularly in traffic news on national radio. I wouldn't like to be in the queue for the pearly gates if Nan has anythin' to do with it.' God be good to Nan.

IF YOU GO DOWN
TO THE WOODS TODAY

One of the few perks I got since my re-election to the council is the vice-chairmanship of the Tourism and Heritage Committee. It's a harmless enough job and the expenses aren't the worst. There's also the chance of the occasional junket.

I didn't expect this to be a burdensome office until a few weeks ago when the community council reconvened for the autumn. The last item on a fairly uninspirin' agenda was a post mortem on the summer. In an atmosphere of doom, gloom and recrimination, Superquinn went into full flight, bemoanin' our poor fortune as a destination for visitors and givin' out about local apathy. The jew's harp summer school was sabotaged by locals who either did nothin' or, worse, poured cold water on the whole event,' she thundered. 'I have to say the attitude of our local independent councillor, Councillor Hickey, along with his comments on the local paper were very damaging. His attitude is all the more galling given that he is vice-chairman of the council's Tourism and Heritage Committee. Our local tourism resources are ignored. Pa Cantillon has the finest walks through his forestry and around by the banks of the Dribble and he can't get a penny of support. I think Councillor Hickey should be called to account here tonight, in front of his own people.'

I broke out in a cold sweat and found my mouth dryin' up as I began to panic. I hadn't expected to face this kind of abuse. But Superquinn was on the warpath.

Luckily, Tom Walshe, the publican and chairman of the community council, came to my rescue. 'Now,' he said, 'Councillor Hickey can't be held accountable for the tourism season. You might as well blame him for the weather. Could we put this item on the agenda for the next meetin' and perhaps Councillor Hickey will have news on the council's tourism plans for the area? We'll meet as usual on the last Thursday of the month.'

I was shakin' like a leaf at the end of that. Thank God for Tom Walshe. He told me I'd better put on my thinkin' cap before the next meetin'. I went straight home and poured myself a stiff whiskey before hittin' the bed. The followin' day, salvation came from a most unusual quarter. In the village I met Percy Pipplemoth Davis, the councillor of the tree-huggin' variety. He looked unusually flustered. The hoor normally looks like someone on a permanent holiday. Anyway, he rushed up to me and said: 'Maurice, the very man! I'm in a most disastrous fix. My nature-walking group was to host an international walk in Wicklow next weekend but there has been a landslide on the route and we can't find an alternative. We have about two hundred people coming, some from as far away as Sweden.' I couldn't believe my luck. Another chance for Maurice to shine. 'Percy,' says I, 'I have the very solution for you.'

I went straight to Tom Walshe and he convened an emergency meetin' of the community council where, with the greatest of glee, I stared straight into Superquinn's face and announced I had secured a major international walkin' festival for the parish. Pa Cantillon was delighted to open up his walks free of charge provided we organised plenty of publicity. The whole committee went into overdrive and, within hours, beds, sandwiches, and entertainment were organised. When I told Percy that everythin' was ready he seemed a bit nervous about the publicity we had planned. I was fairly annoyed that the hoor wasn't far more grateful for all our efforts. I couldn't figure out what he was playin' at.

I contacted the local papers and went on the radio waxin' lyrical about this major international walkin' festival. We had a huge banner across the main street that read: 'Killdicken Welcomes International Nature Walkers.'

The mornin' of the walk we were in Pa's yard at cockcrow. We had the Burco boilers bubblin' in the old milkin' parlour and enough tea and sandwiches to feed an army. I had the local photographers and reporters on the spot. Just before the walk started, in a speech fit for the openin' of the Olympics I declared the International Nature Walk open.

What happened next put Killdicken and Glengooley on every newspaper and on every radio and television show in the country. The two photographers will never again see a poor day.

Just as I declared the event open, the walkers returned to their vehicles, removed all their clothes and off they went as naked as the day they were born. All I could see was a sea of wobblin' backsides wanderin' down the silage yard, through the gate and out across the field to the forest walk. Pipplemoth Davis walked past in his pelt, with a smirk on his face. He looks even more miserable in the nip than he does fully clothed.

After the last bottom went by, Superquinn glared at me. 'Hickey, if your bare backside wobbled past this minute I'd take great pleasure reddenin' it with an ash plant. You are some eejit.'

The followin' day the front page of every national paper carried photographs of the assembled nudes alongside pictures of the astonished faces of myself, Tom Walshe, Pa Cantillon and Superquinn. The headlines will be forever emblazoned on my memory: 'Killdicken Bares all', 'Oh My Glengooleys', 'Get 'em off ye, Killdicken'.

NIGHT CLASSES ON TAP

I don't know about you, but I find that September is like the beginnin' of a new year. In the name of self-improvement people take on all kinds of daft things for the winter. The Mother suggested that I should enrol for night classes, recallin' that when I was at school durin' the day the timin' didn't seem to suit me. 'Most of these classes don't start till eight o'clock at night and you're generally out of the bed by that time,' says she. 'Spendin' a few nights educatin' yourself would be better than wastin' your money and your time down in Tom Walshe's.' I promised her I'd get the night class booklet from the VEC and I'd find somethin' to study.

I didn't want to start a row with her, but I wasn't impressed with the way she dismissed the educational merits of Tom Walshe's licensed premises. A night in Tom Walshe's can be of huge educational value. I regard it as the Academy of Life. Sittin' at the bar on a quiet mid-week night is often far better than watchin' National Geographic or the Discovery channel.

A few weeks ago, I was in the bar at about half-eight on a Wednesday evenin'. There were about three other regulars in and we began talkin' about the bird life in our little area. 'Well,' says Pa Quirke, the postman, 'it's a little-known fact that a very rare species of crane visits the Dribble.' 'Is that so?' says I. 'By God, it is,' says he. 'This particular breed of crane lives on eels, but it doesn't always manage to kill the eel before it swallows it. Very often an eel will pass right through the crane from one end to the other.' 'You're not serious,' says the publican. 'I am,' says the postman. 'I spend a lot of time on the banks of the Dribble and one day last year I watched a certain crane eat the same eel at least ten times. I declare to God, at the finish he was so tired he had to put his poor backside up against the bridge to give it a rest.'

Wonders of the universe such as this feature frequently in the conversation at Walshe's counter. Dixie Ryan, a local smoker of note, gave us a lecture last week on the benefits of tobacco, the likes of which I had never heard. He told us that a neighbour of his, a woman in her eighties, went into hospital with internal bleedin' and only for she was a smoker she would have died on the operatin' table. 'She had been feelin' poorly and went to the local doctor,' says he. 'The doctor diagnosed internal bleedin' from a fall she had a few weeks previously comin' home from bingo. In he sent her to the hospital and straight up to the operatin' theatre with her. They opened her up and there was blood floodin' around everywhere. Her insides were like the engine room of the *Titanic* after she struck the iceberg. Now, they can say what they like about smokin', but let me tell you it saved May Geraghty's life. She smoked sixty fags a day since she was twelve, but hadn't all those years of smokin' sealed her lungs with layers of tar. There was no way the blood could have got in to them. Make no mistake about it, if the lungs had flooded she'd have gone down quicker than the *Titanic*. May is still alive five years later and smokin' like a chimney,' concluded a triumphant Dixie, before succumbin' to a severe bout of coughin'.

At Tom Walshe's counter, you'd hear of cures for warts, you'd hear about quare things fellas did as far back as the Whiteboys and the Tans, and you'd get the unauthorised biographies of the great and the good.

One of the favourite topics for discussion was strayin'. The country is full of stories of people who went astray near holy wells and never came back. One night we were talkin' about this when one of the older men began to name people who are reputed to have gone astray. As soon as he named the individuals and their families there was general agreement that those concerned had every reason to get lost. Be it bad debts or frosty marriage beds, it was plain to see that these strays had a lot to stray from.

I'm tellin' you, there's no need for night classes as long as the pub remains an institution in Ireland. Even in this era of the smokin' ban, the unofficial intellectual life of the country is found around the counter of the local. Only the other night I was privileged to get a lecture on a revolutionary way of givin' up the fags. A commercial traveller, who regularly stays in Killdicken, told us he got the cure from a Kerryman. The procedure involves takin' a hair from the tail of an in-foal mare as close to her backside as possible. You then thread the hair through a fag and light up. 'Does it work?' gasped Dixie Ryan, half-afraid that it might. 'Well,' said the commercial traveller, 'accordin' to my Kerryman friend, any man that has tried to get a hair from an in-foal mare that close to her backside never again had need of a smoke.' Ah, what an academy.

MEETIN' OF MOTHERS

Since the Mother learned to drive, she has lost the run of herself. Perched at the steerin' wheel, she's like a mother superior as she pontificates on every subject under the sun. She runs regular campaigns aimed solely at my good self. When she gets me in the car I'm a captive audience, strapped into the passenger seat with no alternative but to listen. This week, love and marriage were her chosen topics.

She had obviously been savin' this particular subject for a fine long journey in order to cover it comprehensively. She was drivin' me to Westport in County Mayo to a conference on inner-city decay. I was like a condemned man strapped to the chair, waitin' for the inevitable, which came in massive doses of high voltage. 'Maurice, you will have to settle down,' says she, approachin' her subject with her usual circumlocution. 'Really, aside from the demands of your public office you live the life of a teenager. You go from the bed to the pub, with the occasional meetin' thrown in. You need the discipline of a strong woman in your life.' I was stunned. Here was this woman, who had towered over my existence since as far back as I could remember, tellin' me that I needed another such woman. 'I'm afraid,' says I, 'that there is no vacancy in that department at the present time. The position is more than adequately filled by the woman in the drivin' seat.' 'Now, now, Maurice,' says she, 'save your sarcastic remarks for the council chamber. This is your mother you're

talkin' to.' She told me that she heard Dixie Ryan was goin' to Lisdoonvarna next weekend and she had organised for him to take me.

I flew into a rage. I called her an interferin' auld busybody and told her 'twas none of her business if I decided to spend the rest of my life in an intimate relationship with a jennet. Well, she turned on me, callin' me the most ungrateful wretch of a son that ever walked. The row was so severe that she took her eyes off the road and we came flyin' into a bad bend near the convent in Dunmaggit. I screamed when I saw the high wall comin' straight for us. As the Mother tried desperately to control the car it rounded the bend on two wheels and we went straight through the convent gate, careered across the front lawn and crash-landed into the grotto. Just when the car came to a halt, the statue of the Blessed Virgin came loose from its moorings high up on the grotto and landed upright on the bonnet of the car. There we were, the Mother and myself, starin' out the windscreen of the car and the Mother of God starin' back at us.

I slowly turned my head to see if the Mother was all right. Not only was she all right, she was sittin' there like the cat that licked the cream. 'Now,' says she, 'just look at what Our Blessed Mother had to do to make you listen to your own mother. She has to jump on to the bonnet of the car before you'll take notice. This is a sign. You're goin' to Lisdoonvarna with Dixie. Now, we'd better extricate ourselves from this mess. We'll pay up and shut up or these nuns will sue the backside off us.' The nuns came out, fussin', and the Mother waved my cheque-book at them. Miraculously, the car was driveable and we hobbled back to Killdicken. There was no point tryin' to get to Westport. The problems of inner-city decay would have to be solved without my valuable input.

Anyway, I did what I was told and took off with Dixie to Lisdoon. We hit the place on a Thursday evenin' and did all the hotels. Dixie was so busy dancin' he forgot to smoke. I spent two days traipsin' after him from ballroom to bar to ballroom. On Saturday afternoon we were out at Ballylacken Castle. I must have been lookin' particularly miserable because a man I never saw before came over to me and asked me if I was all right. We got talkin' and it turned out he was a matchmaker. He told me he had the very woman for me. I informed him I was well capable of gettin' my own woman if I wanted one. He was as persistent as a half-cut bullock and convinced me to meet him and the woman in question at the parish church after Saturday evenin' Mass.

I got away from Dixie and arrived at the church at quarter-past eight to be greeted by the matchmaker. He told me the woman was waitin' at the grotto. I nearly ran at the mention of the shrine, but held tough. I walked to the grotto and stood beside a woman starin' up at the statue of Mary. Slowly I turned to look at her and who do you think was starin' back at me from under a scarf? None other than Superquinn herself, the bould Breda Quinn. 'Mother of God!' screamed Superquinn. 'Begod,' I shouted, 'that's twice in the past week that woman has interfered in my life with disastrous results. I'm tellin' you now, I'm goin' straight home. I'm movin' out from the the Mother, and I'm declarin' to God, man and whoever else will listen that I'm a bachelor from now till the day Tinky Ryan measures me for the six-by-four.'

SICK, SORE AND SORRY

Followin' my bizarre encounter with Superquinn in Lisdoon I didn't even bother to look for Dixie Ryan. I took a lift home with a relief milker from Dromtrasna whose conversation skills were in mercifully short supply. The journey to Killdicken passed in blissful silence and I was dropped at my own door at about three in the mornin'. The Mother wasn't expectin' me and as I rooted around the flowerpots for the back-door key I woke her. Thinkin' I was a robber, she opened the bedroom window and gave the window box a nudge with the sweepin' brush. I roared in pain as it landed on my back. In a flash she was at the back door, clobberin' me. There I was, face down on the ground, covered in mosspeat, and the Mother goin' mad with a brush.

'You low-down guttersnipe,' she shouted. 'Attackin' a poor widow woman in her sleep when there isn't a man in the house to defend her.

You'll get your reward. I've rang my alarm and the guards will be here to deal with you.' With that Sergeant Miller's car appeared and he jumped out, half in uniform and half in his pyjamas. 'It's all right, Mrs Hickey! It's all right. I'll take it from here,' says he, grabbin' the brush off her. I still hadn't gotten my wind back to explain who I was when he turned on me: 'Get up, you pup, till we have a look at you. Get up!' With that he gave me a wallop across the back that I'll never forget.

I eventually found my voice and shouted: 'Tis me! 'Tis me! Ye feckin' eejits.' 'Who's me?' demanded the Sergeant. 'Maurice, Maurice Hickey, ya big looderamawn of a guard,' says I. 'You couldn't be Maurice,' says the Mother. 'Maurice is in Lisdoonvarna.' 'Maurice is feckin' home now, isn't he?' says I. 'I declare to God, it's an awful state of affairs when a fella can't even come home to his own house without bein' assaulted by his family and the forces of law and order.'

We all calmed down and the Mother took us in for tea. The sergeant apologised but added, 'Can you blame us for tacklin' you?' says he. 'You could have been anyone.' I was in agony. I was sure the blow from the window box had knocked bits off my backbone. The wallop from the sergeant must have left a mark from my shoulders to my rump. I could neither sit nor stand.

As the Mother made the tea I knew by the looks she was throwin' in my direction that there was no sympathy for me. She was burstin' to know what brought me home so soon and why I hadn't the trace of a drink on me at half-three on a Sunday mornin'.

'So you were in Lisdoon,' piped up the sergeant, hopin' to thaw the frost that had descended on proceedings. 'Any luck?' says he. Only for my back bein' so bad I would have flattened him with a belt of a fist. The Mother grunted as she strutted across the kitchen with the teapot. She was like the Queen of Sheba with her long dressin' gown and the hairnet stretched over a mound of curlers. 'Any luck? Any luck? That's what we're all wonderin',' says she.

'Sergeant,' I asked, 'is there a law against people not mindin' their own business? Would someone who is a serial interferer and busybody get a custodial sentence?' The sergeant coughed, spluttered and then muttered: 'Well, Maurice,' says he, 'I never came across such a law. That's not to say it doesn't exist.'

'Well, there should be a law protectin' people like me from people like herself, Breda Quinn and Dixie Ryan,' said I. 'Now, I'm goin' to bed and I hope I can sleep through the agony in my back. On Monday I'm goin' to the doctor and I might even go to the solicitor to see which of you two I'll sue first. Good night.'

I stayed in bed for two days. The Mother and I avoided one another like the plague, a difficult job in a small house. On Tuesday evenin' while she was at bingo the sergeant called in. He looked fierce worried. 'Maurice,' says he, 'Breda Quinn didn't turn up for work today or yesterday. That's totally unlike her. I believe you met her in Lisdoonvarna.' I was stunned. I told him everythin' about the few days and especially about the encounter at the grotto. By the time we adjourned to Tom Walshe's bar I was shiverin' with shock. I began to imagine that all kinds of awful things had happened.

When we got to the pub it was full. I felt everyone was lookin' at me. There was a touch of a wake about the place. People were even talkin' about Breda in the past tense. Just as things began to get seriously morbid, the door flew open and in she walked with Dixie Ryan. He was smilin' like a Cheshire cat and she was sportin' a diamond as big as the Rock of Gibraltar. She looked ten years younger since the night at the grotto. 'Well, congratulations,' says Tom Walshe, 'and how did all this come about?' 'I'll tell you,' says a triumphant Dixie. 'Myself and Councillor Hickey went to Lisdoon together. Breda appeared and hopped off the councillor's big belly but I caught her on the rebound. How about that?'

I have to face the Mother after all this.

DOWN BUT NOT OUT

Breda Quinn's return from Lisdoon with Dixie Ryan on one hand and a whopper of a diamond on the other flattened me. While everyone in the pub was congratulatin' the happy couple, I knew they were lookin' at me with a mixture of sympathy and mad curiosity. They were dyin' to know what had happened. I was in a most unenviable position. Would I stay in the pub or would I go? If I left too soon they'd say it was bad form, if I stayed too long they'd be askin' had I any respect for myself. People can be cruel. From my school days I remember learnin' about the Roman Coliseum where gladiators and poor auld slaves fought wild animals in the name of entertainment. It often struck me that if you built a coliseum in every town and village you'd fill it regularly with crowds comin' to stare at other people's misfortune. I'm in bad humour.

Anyway, after about a half an hour of excruciatin' merriment in Tom Walshe's I went up to the happy couple to pump hands and kiss the air. As I greeted the radiant Breda Quinn, I was thankful for the noise in the pub. It meant no-one could hear what passed between us. 'Oh Maurice,' she shouted as she took my hand and rammed the diamond into my palm, 'I'll never forget our meetin' at the grotto in Lisdoon. What happened since was the greatest miracle of all time.' 'Well,' says I, 'for me 'twas the greatest escape of all time!' I didn't wait for an answer, but turned to Dixie. 'Well, Maurice,' he thundered as he pulled my arm half-way out of its socket, 'it's true what they say, ha? Where one man sows another man reaps. Ha?' With that he gave me a slap on the back that was worse than the wallop I got from the Mother's window box. 'Dixie,' I spluttered, 'I wish you many, many, many years with her.' As I extricated my hand, I said to myself: Drink enough now, Dixie, and enjoy your last few fags because once the glow wears off she'll straighten you. I don't know whether that was prophecy or wishful thinkin'.

I slipped out the side door of Walshe's hostelry and made my way home. I felt like the Florida coastline after another big wind. As I made my way down the street I was gettin' very sorry for myself. Every step seemed to bring back memories of the disastrous parts of my life in Killdicken. At the parish hall I couldn't help but think of the set dancin' durin' a Scór competition many years ago. I was wheelin' with a girl of substance from Glenabuddybugga when I became detached from her, spun off the stage and landed on the adjudicators' table. Needless to say, the Killdicken/Glengooley team didn't progress to the next round.

As I passed the church I was reminded of my days as an altar boy. I'll never forget the funeral of a fella who wasn't particularly renowned for temperance or fidelity. Towards the end of the ceremony the thurible, with its smoulderin' incense, came apart, sendin' hot incense and charcoal in all directions. The sacristan had just bought a new fire extinguisher so I dashed into the sacristy, grabbed it, returned to the scene of the fire and covered priest, coffin, undertaker and the chief mourners in a mountain of foam. As the mess was bein' cleaned up the priest went down to apologise to the widow. She wasn't a bit put out. 'Father,' says she, noddin' in the direction of the husband's coffin, ''twill take more than foam to put out the fire that's burnin' under that fella's arse at the moment.'

Before I got home I stopped in front of the Brothers' school and thought of the many times I made an eejit of myself there. One day I was asleep in biology class and Miss Donoghue had just given the capacity of the bladder. She heard me snorin' and shouted, 'What is the capacity of the bladder, Mr Hickey?' I woke suddenly and heard Pa Quirke whisperin', 'Twenty-five gallons.' 'Twenty-five gallons, Miss,' says I confidently. 'Mr Hickey,' says she, 'You'll never be short of a job. The fire brigade will be delighted to take you.'

By the time I got home the memories had me in a pit of gloom. I was prayin' the Mother would be gone to bed. I found her in her dressin' gown at one end of the kitchen table starin' into a cup of Horlicks. I sat down at the other end, admirin' the tablecloth. 'Well,' says she, 'I heard.' 'Heard what?' says I. 'I heard about the happy couple that came back from Lisdoonvarna leapin' like feckin' gazelles.' She was drippin' with sarcasm. 'Mother,' says I, 'I don't want to fight with you, but–' She put up her hand and stopped me. 'There'll be no fightin' because I'm finished playin' Cupid. As you can see, my aim isn't too good.' 'Your aim is fine,' says I, 'except that I ducked and Dixie got my arrow right between the eyes. It will take him a long time to know what hit him.' 'He'll know soon enough,' says the Mother, and the two of us broke down laughin'. The followin' mornin' I woke to a new lease on life. The Mother had the finest fry you ever tasted sizzlin' on the range. After the breakfast I strolled down the main street of

Killdicken with a spring in my step and the sweet smell of freedom in my nostrils.

THERE IS NOTHIN' SACRED

Of late I've been so wrapped up in my private affairs it might appear I have neglected my public responsibilities. Nothin' could be further from the truth. The sun never sets on the work of the elected public servant. People don't even give you a chance to answer the call of nature. Once you're elected, the public think they own you and there is no recognition of privacy and no respect for what the modern shrink calls 'personal space'.

This was brought home to me a few weeks ago when I attended the funeral of the mother of a councillor friend of mine. The world and its first cousin turned up to the funeral. The councillor told me afterwards that at least thirty so-called mourners used the opportunity to approach him about council business. In one case a woman came up and after the most perfunctory expression of sympathy proceeded to introduce her daughter, just home from England with a husband and two children. She wanted to know what he could do about gettin' them a house. Another fella shuffled up to him, nodded towards the corpse and whispered, 'What age was she?' 'Ninety-five,' answered my friend. 'Erra, she had enough of it. Any news on the plannin' for my slatted shed?'

I've done more council business at funerals, weddin's and wakes than I ever did in the County Hall. It's no wonder that we councillors go to faraway places for the odd junket. You'd happily sit through a three-day conference on the matin' habits of earwigs just to get away from the pesterin'.

I've had representations made to me in the most unusual places. Two weeks ago I went to have a tooth filled. Now, the dentist is not a constituent of mine but no sooner had he frozen my jaw than he began. 'Councillor Hickey,' says he as he revved up the drill, 'I am appalled at the way county councils do their business. They are a law unto themselves. Do you not think so?' With that he drove the drill into the innards of the bad tooth. I attempted a grunt but he started again. 'Have you heard about the horrendous problems I'm having with extending my lodge on Lough Derg? Are you familiar with it? Are you?' Here I was, prostrate on a chair, with two eyes blazin' down at me from the masked face of a man wieldin' a drill. I'd have felt safer in Abu Ghraib. It seems the council concerned had turned down an application for retention on a five-bedroom extension to his 'lodge', an extension he had built without plannin' permission. 'This development is in total sympathy with the natural surroundings,' he intoned. 'For heaven's sake, it was designed by one of the most renowned architects in the country. I am a responsible citizen and I'm being treated like a hoodlum.'

If only my mouth wasn't frozen as solid as Shackleton's arse, I'd have been happy to tell him that the whole country knew his daughter had just got her degree in caterin' and hospitality and the five new bedrooms were Daddy's way of givin' her the start. While he drilled and poked and stuffed and packed, he continued his diatribe. There's a lot to be said for the general anaesthetic. Anyway, as he lodged a fistful of cotton into my jaw he told me that I was just like the rest of them, I couldn't answer one of his questions. I wanted to tell him that it isn't easy to get answers from someone with half the North Pole jammed into one side of his face and half the Mississippi cotton fields stuffed into the other. I also wanted to tell him that the Kilkenny football team has a better chance of winnin' the Sam Maguire than he has of gettin' retention for his palace. I held my fire, but on the way out I nearly shot the receptionist with a mouthful of cotton when she casually demanded €130 and told me come back in two weeks.

Believe it or not, that's not the worst that's happened me. While I was in Clonmel with the Mother on Saturday I went in to a hotel to answer the call of nature. I was no sooner enthroned than I heard someone shout, 'Maurice, Maurice Hickey, are you here?' Thinkin' somethin' had happened the Mother I answered positively from my cubicle. 'Ah, Maurice,' the voice came back, 'I thought I saw you comin' in. This is Mick Mitchell from Borrisnangoul. I was wonderin' did you do anythin' about a grant for thatchin' the mother's place?'

Now, maybe I'm a bit odd but I don't like answerin' the call of nature and constituents' queries simultaneously. In fact my body refuses to perform under those circumstances. I abandoned all operations, gave Mick a half-hearted reply and went back to the car to wait for the Mother. By the time she arrived I was in a serious state. Within two miles of home I had to ask her to stop in Scack Lane and let me into the bushes. I was no sooner positioned than I looked up to see Tim Stakelum lookin' down at me. 'A great day for it, Maurice,' says he. 'Oh my God, Tim,' says I, 'I was taken short.' 'Ah, it's probably somethin' you ate,' says he. 'But now that I have you here I might as well tell you that I'm blue in the face askin' the council to repair that lane there behind you. It's a disgrace.' I went blue with pain but managed to make myself respectable and dashed for the car. I threw myself onto the back seat and groaned, 'Mamma, take me home quick before I burst.'

MEMORIES FLOOD BACK

Killdicken wasn't spared the recent floodin'. Our local river, the Dribble, decided to turn itself into a torrent for Halloween, with near disastrous results. We were in Walshe's havin' a few pints when the first signs of the trouble emerged. As usual, we were deep in conversation about matters of great indifference. Our chosen topic this particular evenin' was a hardy perennial. We were discussin' the changes in the world since we were young, with particular emphasis on the changes in the matin' habits of the current generation. We inevitably began comparin' the puritanism of our youth to the permissive society of today. While great deference was paid to the values of respect and decency of bygone days, 'twas hard to disguise our thinly-veiled envy for the world in which today's hot-blooded youth are growin' up.

Tom Cantwell was hangin' on to the edge of the conversation, drooped over a half-finished pint. He is always great for a summary of proceedings when he finds a hole in the conversation. Durin' a lull in the discussions he remarked: 'D'ye know somethin'? When I had the desire and the equipment I had no opportunity. Now that the world is full of opportunity, the desire isn't great and the equipment is even worse.' This comment was followed by a big 'Yo ho' from everyone. Now, if you ever take notice of the pattern of conversation in pubs, at a stage such as this there is either a complete change of topic or people dive in deeper. In this particular case people dived in and turned to me. 'Maurice,' says Pa Cantillon, 'I hear that Dixie Ryan isn't havin' things all his own way with the bould Superquinn. It seems he wanted to move in but she said he'd wait for anythin' like that till the second ring was on the finger.' 'By God,' says Cantwell, 'he was here on his own the other night and we got talkin'. I got the impression that he's fairly frustrated. He told me he felt like a man after crossin' the Gobi desert and just when he thought he got to an oasis he was told he had to spend a few months in the Sahara.'

As they all roared with laughter, I smiled to myself when I remembered an incident with Dixie in Lisdoonvarna prior to his whirlwind romance with Ms Quinn. He needed underwear and we went shoppin'. He purchased a large pair of red silky boxer shorts emblazoned in bright yellow with the slogan, 'I got lucky in Lisdoon'. Pa Quirke brought me back from my reverie. 'Come on, Maurice,' says he, 'you're stayin' very quiet.' 'Oh far be it from me to comment on things that are none of my business,' says I, 'but let me say I have reason to believe that Dixie had high hopes of drivin' on the provisional licence.'

With that I got down off the high stool only to find I had jumped into what I thought was a puddle of water. 'Jaysus, Tom,' says I to the publican, 'you must have a burst pipe or somethin'. There's water everywhere.' We all looked down and the floor was covered in about a half-inch of water. As Tom went to check the plumbin', Sergeant Miller came through the door, soaked to the skin. 'Come on, quick,' he says, 'the Dribble has burst its banks. We better get people to move upstairs or go to neighbours before it gets any worse.' He sent us around the village helpin' people with small children and older folks to get to places that were warm and dry until the worst of the flood had passed. My own mother was in Kilkenny visitin' her cousin, so I didn't have to worry about her. By the time I got home, all I could do was move whatever was dry upstairs and leave the rest to the river.

There was nothin' for it but go back to Tom Walshe's and see if there was a drink to be had. The electricity was gone and there is nothin' more miserable than sittin' in a dark house with water lappin' around inside. I was tryin' to figure out how to get to the pub when I heard a tractor pull up outside. Pa Cantillon had the same thoughts as myself and figured I'd need a lift. When we arrived at the pub it was packed. There were candles everywhere and about eight inches of water on the floor with everyone in waders and wellies. I called for two bottles of beer and was just settlin' on a high stool when the door flew open and in walked Dixie Ryan, carryin' Breda Quinn on his back. There was a big shout as he landed her on the counter. Tom Cantwell, surveyin' the sight of Superquinn gettin' a piggy-back, was heard to remark, 'I suppose that's what you'd call "Virgin on the Ridiculous".'

The waters of the Dribble went back as quickly as they rose and the followin' mornin', the main street of Killdicken was like a war zone. There was all kinds of unmentionable material around the place, items of every sort had floated in and out of people's houses. Retrievin' one's dignity had become as important as countin' the cost.

But you know, it's amazin' what comes to the surface when floods subside. I was makin' my way down the street to meet a council official from the engineerin' office when my eye was taken by a most intriguin' sight. There, impaled on the railin's outside Breda Quinn's front window was a large pair of red silky boxer shorts declarin' to the world in bright yellow that the owner got lucky in Lisdoon.

THE MOTHER OF ALL MINEFIELDS

The Mother handed me a massive headache last week. Her birthday is comin' up and normally there's never any great fuss. I'm careful to give her a present that's practical and useful. Over the years these presents have equipped the house for her and as I look around I see the fruits of many birthdays. There's the hoover I ordered from the Co-op, that lovely food mixer I bought at the ploughin' championship a few years ago, the quick-squeezin' mop and bucket, the Jamie Oliver cookbook, the set of fire-irons, the ironin' board – the list is endless. I hadn't picked a present this year but I wasn't too bothered.

That was until last Friday. Just after the dinner she announced she had somethin' important to say. 'Now, Maurice, for as far back as I can remember my birthday has been a non-event. The only indication that the day was different came when you unveiled your annual lousy present. It was always somethin' that reminded me of the drudgery I have to endure as an Irish mother. You and your hoovers, ironin' boards and fire-irons. Every year I felt like a slave gettin' a new pair of shackles. When I think of it, I should have reddened those fire-irons and branded you.' I was totally winded by this outburst, but she wasn't finished.

'This year, Maurice, my dear son, I want a birthday party. I want it held here in this house, not in Tom Walshe's shebeen or in some auld weddin' hotel. You will organise the whole thing and I don't intend to raise a finger except to put on my glasses to give my go-ahead to the guest list.'

With that she put on her scarf and coat and headed to the post office for her pension. I was left there with my mouth open and three weeks to organise a party. I began to think of all the things I needed to do: clean the house, buy the drink, organise food. Oh my God, the food! However, all these problems paled into insignificance when I thought of the guest list. The Mother had no idea of the lethal nature of the minefield she had laid down for me. You know as well as I do, when it comes to guest lists the people you leave out are of far more important than the ones you leave in. In the case of a local politician like my good self, drawin' up a guest list is like playin' Russian roulette with a nuclear missile. One false move and your political landscape is in ruins. This party was goin' to be a nightmare.

I decided to go for a walk. Whenever I'm under pressure I hit for the most isolated place in the parish, the Borrisnangoul road. Out there in the middle of nowhere I can see things completely differently. I was strollin' along tryin' to figure out how I'd rid myself of this troublesome party when I was distracted by litter. Some useless yoke had dumped a bag of rubbish in the ditch and the contents were blowin' around the place. I got a stick and poked at the material to see if I could find a name and address to pass on to the litter warden. I found two envelopes identifyin' the culprit as a well-known man from the Clonmel side. In the course of my search I came across a brochure advertisin' short breaks to Paris. That's it, says I triumphantly to myself as I read through the brochure, in the darkest hour, a light shines. Even in the depths of illegally-disposed rubbish, a man can find his salvation.

The Mother would surely prefer a trip to Paris than a night in her own house lookin' at a crowd of yahoos gettin' drunk at her son's expense. It would get rid of the party and the minefield of the invitation list, *and* keep the Mother happy.

I went straight home and phoned a cousin who works in a travel agency in Kilkenny. I told her I was thinkin' of takin' the Mother to Paris for her birthday and read out the details from the brochure. Before I knew it she had the thing booked and paid for and said she'd post out the tickets immediately. She told me I could pay her the next time I was in Kilkenny, there was no rush.

When Pa Quirke, the postman, arrived on Monday mornin', sure enough, he had a fine, bulky envelope for me. 'Did Quirke bring anythin' besides bills?' asked the Mother as she put away the breakfast ware. 'Well,' says I, handin' her the envelope, 'there's a little surprise for you.' 'From who?' says she. 'From your beloved son,' says I. Well, a suspicious look came over her face after she opened the envelope and examined the contents. I thought she was gettin' cross until all of a sudden she broke into a broad smile. 'Maurice, it is lovely, a weekend in Paris. But wouldn't it be better to have this as a surprise at the party?' I tried to answer, but there was no stoppin' her. 'Now, Maurice, I know what we'll do. You keep the tickets and I'll pretend I know nothin'. When you present them to me on the night of the party, I'll look so surprised you won't believe it.'

With a mischievous glint in her eye, she handed me back the envelope, the party and the minefield.

MOTHER, I HARDLY KNEW YOU

Well, this birthday party continues to give me major political and financial headaches. I seem to spend most of my time writin' and re-writin' guest lists in between fightin' with the Mother.

The whole thing has opened my eyes to many things about her. I discovered that she doesn't think much of my friends. She has some regard for Pa Quirke, the postman, whom she describes as 'the only one of your gang who performs any kind of a useful function in the community.' As far as she is concerned Tom Cantwell is a roarin' alcoholic who should be forcibly dried out and sent out to work pullin' weeds. Pa Cantillon is an excuse for a farmer whose land should be taken from him and given to someone with a bit of sense.

I thought she might have some time for Tom Walshe, the publican, him bein' the local successful businessman. I couldn't be more wrong. 'That drug dealer is not comin' to my party,' she exclaimed when she saw his name on the list. I was dumbfounded. 'Mother, he's no drug dealer,' says I, in a state of high dudgeon. 'He runs one of the best public houses in the county.' She wasn't impressed. 'He sells alcohol to people who either don't need it or can't do without it,' she retorts. 'So what?' says I. 'What else do you expect a man with a liquor license to do?' 'Listen,' she says, 'alcohol is a drug. People buy it for the sole purpose of alterin' their mood. It has no other use. It makes fools out of wise men and gives fellas that are jennets notions that they're stallions. Anyone who makes a livin' out of tradin' in this stuff is a drug dealer. If I had my way, I'd jail every publican in the country.'

This was turnin' out to be a most enlightenin' experience. In one short conversation my mother had advocated forced labour, land confiscation and the establishment of prison camps for publicans. I never realised that I was livin' with Killdicken's answer to Pol Pot. When I asked her if she wanted any alcohol at the party she left me totally confused. 'Of course I want alcohol at the party. I love the sin, but I hate the feckin' sinners.'

I was about to adjourn the meetin' when I remembered two erstwhile friends of mine that hadn't come in for scrutiny. 'What about Breda Quinn and Dixie Ryan?' says I. The very mention of their names was like throwin' petrol on red embers. 'That Jezebel Quinn and her cuckoo, Tricksie Dixie Ryan!' roared the Mother. 'That pair will not darken this door for as long as I live. And even if they darken it after I die, I'll haunt them and anyone who extends an invitation to them. Those double-crossin', fork-tongued, low-down lizards.' 'Begod, Mother,' says I, 'I didn't think you took what happened between me and them so personally?' 'Of course I took it personally,' says she, back in full flight. In the heat of battle she revealed a lot more than she had intended. 'Sure didn't I set the whole thing up. I convinced Dixie Ryan to take you to Lisdoon and I convinced Breda Quinn to go there at the same time. I had considered her to be a woman of substance and I certainly didn't expect her to turn her back on my son and waltz into the arms of that chain-smokin' auld gasbag. So now, you have it all. That's the truth of it.' She stopped suddenly, and, starin' at the floor, declared: 'You know somethin'? I think I won't bother with this blasted party at all.' Before I could say a thing she grabbed the coat and scarf and was gone.

Sittin' there I didn't know whether to laugh or cry. I needed some male company so I hit for Pa Quirke's. He was just back from his rounds and deeply embedded in an armchair beside a huge fire. 'Sit down, Maurice,' says he, ''tis an evenin' for nothin' but the nest. You look like a man that could do with a drink.' With that he reached into the cabinet and produced a bottle of ten-year-old Midleton whiskey. As he poured the drink I poured out my troubles about the Mother, the party, Breda Quinn, Dixie Ryan and Lisdoonvarna. By the time I was finished, I felt great. 'Twas better than confession. Pa went for the cabinet again and produced another bottle of the same vintage. I protested but he told me he had so much drink in the house he could sell it. 'The wife threw a party for my fiftieth two years ago and people brought so much liquor we haven't had to go near the off-licence or the top shelf since.'

The mention of a party and the long-term prospect of a well-stocked drinks cabinet immediately concentrated my mind. I asked his advice on the Mother's loomin' function and he told me to invite everyone and anyone. 'Put on a few chips and sausages,' says he, 'and the event will not only lubricate itself but will lubricate the house for many days to come.' Pa said his daughter would make out a few posters. He sent me home a happy man.

The Mother was havin' the Horlicks when I got back. Before she could say anythin' I told her the party was goin' ahead. When she enquired as to where this new-found enthusiasm had come from 'twas my turn to confuse her. 'Let me just say that I'm willin' to put up with havin' the house full of sinners for the sake of a decent supply of sin.'

THE GREAT GATECRASH

The Mother's birthday party eventually happened on a Friday night. I had asked her to give me a list of the relations she wanted to invite and I promptly phoned them. As well as personally invitin' people, I put up two posters, one in the post office and the other in the porchway of the church. The latter I put up on Monday mornin'. If anybody tackles me about not gettin' an invitation, I'll draw their attention to the public notices.

When asked what people should bring to the party, I told them to bring themselves and a bottle.

I was in a bit of a panic about the food until I spotted Sticky Stakelum's chip van in Clonmel on Saturday night. 'A solution with class,' says I to myself. Sticky is the only chip-van operator in the world who wears a dicky bow and chef's hat. He addresses his female customers as 'Madam' and the men as 'Sir'. Even when people are drunk, dishevelled and abusive, Sticky never forsakes his old-fashioned courtesy. 'And would Madam like sauce on that?' can be heard at the height of a barrage of abuse about his 'manky salmonella wagon'.

He is a genius at decipherin' the various grunts that emanate from his late-night diners whose speech functions have been dissolved in gallons of alcohol. 'And do I take it that Sir would like a double curry chip to accompany his quarter pounder?'

He was his usual courteous self when I approached him. 'Ah, if it isn't my good friend Councillor Hickey. Good evening, Councillor, and what can I offer you from my midnight menu?' 'How's the goin', Sticky?' says I. 'I'll only have a snack. Give me a large chip, a battered sausage, a quarter pounder with cheese, fried egg and onions and a large bottle of coke.' 'My pleasure, Councillor,' says he as he turned to the hot-plate with a flourish. 'Sticky,' says I, 'where will you have this yoke parked late Friday night, early Saturday mornin'?' 'Well, Councillor, as it happens, I have a window in engagements for the mobile catering facility this Friday night.' I told him about the party and asked him to park the thing outside my place between one am and two am on Saturday. I said I'd pick up the bill. He agreed and gave me my snack 'compliments of the management'.

Friday night came. The more staid relations appeared at about half-past eight and settled in to watch the news. Nothin' much happened until about eleven o'clock when a steady deluge of guests started to arrive. The place was packed, and everyone was in great form. Tommy Waldron brought the fiddle and, with Mrs Quirke on the concertina and Timmy Griffin on the box, they were knockin' out powerful music. A gang from Borrisnangoul and Honetyne tore into a Kerry set and I thought the house would collapse with the leppin' and yelpin'.

Everyone brought a bottle and soon the parlour table held a collection of liquor that would warm the heart. At twelve o'clock the formalities took place. The cousin from Kilkenny produced a cake and candles. I stood up and was about to launch into a speech when the Mother told me she'd get the brush to me if I didn't shut up. I wished her a happy birthday and presented her with the tickets for Paris. Lookin' suitably surprised she thanked everyone for comin' and since there was no closin' time she encouraged them to eat and drink plenty. I glanced nervously at my table of bottles. To create a diversion I announced the arrival of Sticky's chip van and informed the gatherin' that the grub was on me.

Things were too good to last. When I went out to see how Sticky was gettin' on I nearly had a heart attack. The queue for food was half-way down the street. To my horror, I saw two buses parked beside the 'mobile catering facility' and Sticky busily servin' mountains of grub to people I had never seen before. The occupants of the buses, a rugby team and supporters on their way back to Limerick, couldn't believe their luck when they saw the chip van. They thought they'd won the feckin' grand slam when they got the grub for nothin'. I tried shoutin' at Sticky but he couldn't hear me over the noise of the generator.

By the time I burrowed my way through the collection of hairy hoors at the counter, he was servin' the last of them. He spotted me and shouted: 'Marvellous party, Councillor. Wonderful people. Amazing appetites.' 'They're not at the party at all, you feckin' eejit,' I screamed back. With that, one of the rugby crowd turned and roared: 'Who said party? Hey lads, there's a party on here.' The two busloads descended on the house and drank every drop in the place. The Mother loved them. When they found out she was the 'birthday girl' they lifted her on to the table in her armchair and sang to 'the queen' all night.

It was seven in the mornin' by the time everyone left. The drink was gone, the house was wrecked, and Sticky's bill came to €535. Between that and the trip to Paris, the Mother's birthday did to my budget what the Olympic games did to the national finances of Greece. I was sittin' at one end of the kitchen table feelin' sorry for myself. Tom Cantwell was at the other end driftin' in and out of consciousness. Durin' a lucid moment he picked up Sticky's bill and with a big smirk on his face he handed it to me sayin', 'And would Sir like some VAT on this?' I threw him out.

HOW GREEN IS MY FOLLY

I needed a break so at the last minute I signed up for a conference on smog control. I didn't want to be draggin' the Mother to Dundalk so I took a lift with Percy Pipplemoth Davis. Bein' eco-friendly, his car runs on vegetable oil. I think he gets his supply from Sticky Stakelum's chip van, judgin' by the smell.

The conference sounded like a great opportunity for a change of diet and a good sleep. Auld Pipplemoth was all fired up about it. He was like a young fella settin' out for his first day in school with his folder, his recycled notebook, his fountain pen and ink. All he was missin' was the short pants.

More ominous, from my point of view, was his lunch basket and it packed with GM-free food. I was lookin' forward to a few drinks and a bit of decent grub on the road. Well, let me tell you, we didn't stop in a single town. He'd pull into a lay-by or a gateway, open his wicker basket and produce food you wouldn't give a budgie. I had a change of diet all right. For the mornin' break there were rice cakes, sesame seeds and vegetarian cheese. This was washed down with his own apple juice that tasted like boiled bog-water.

I was sure we'd stop in a decent hostelry for the lunch, but no chance. He took me up the Hill of Tara where the December wind nearly did permanent damage to my prospects of fatherin' children. In the middle of a high-dudgeon lecture about the plans to build a motorway in the next parish I had to ask for a free class. 'Percy,' says I, 'get me off this God-forsaken mound before I get double pneumonia. I don't give two knobs of goats droppin's if they build a feckin' airport here.'

We went down the hill in silence. Percy commented that I might be in better form after a good lunch. The very mention of food had me feelin' better. My stomach nearly seceded from the rest of my body when he opened the wicker basket in the carpark and handed me a bowl of organic couscous. He informed me it was a North African dish, a speciality among the nomadic tribes of the Sahara. Well, I'll tell you, this stuff was like eatin' a bucket of the Sahara mixed with molasses. No wonder these tribes are nomadic. With grub like this you'd always have to be within strikin' distance of a palm tree or a sand dune.

By the time we hit Dundalk I was starvin' and totally greened out. When we got to the hotel I couldn't wait to get to my room for a bit of peace. I nearly had a stroke when the receptionist said she had no record of a bookin' for me. I ended up sharin' with Pipplemoth. I made a quick visit to the room, threw in my bag and hit for the bar.

The conference was due to start with registration at seven pm and the Minister's speech at eight pm. I had an hour to recover from my day on the green side of life. I ordered a pint and a steak sandwich with onions and chips. Three pints later I registered, sat near the back and fell asleep. A dribble of applause that told me proceedings were over woke me from my slumbers. Adjournin' to the bar, I found a collection of councillors of similar disposition and enjoyed a night of intense cultural exchanges. This involved singin' songs and tellin' yarns that you wouldn't tell in the council chamber.

At three in the mornin' I retired to the bedroom. When I opened the door, the place reminded me of a church ready for a funeral. Pipplemoth was stretched out on the bed like a corpse. On his locker, an incense burner had the place smellin' of hot curry. Without turnin' on a light I grunted my way out of my clothes and threw myself into the scratcher.

I was woken a few hours later by a low hummin' sound, like a cow startin' to calve. I opened my eyes and as I looked around the room for the source of the sound I spotted him. Sittin' crosslegged on the floor, surrounded by candles and plumes of incense, was a naked Pipplemoth and him hummin' like a hoor. I didn't know what to do and after a few minutes decided the safest place was the bathroom. I tiptoed around him and in I went for a shower.

I had just covered myself with soap when there was an unmerciful screamin' from the bedroom. Without as much as a facecloth for coverin' I ran out and found Pipplemoth in contortions and in agony. His left leg was across his shoulder and the heel of the left foot was stuck at the butt of his right ear. He seemed to have gone into some kind of spasm and begged me to lift the foot off his shoulder.

I stood in front of him and, puttin' one hand on his head, I began to slide the heel under his ear to get it down his shoulder. He was groanin' in pain and I was gruntin' with the effort when the door opened and there stood a chambermaid, frozen with horror at the sight of two naked men in a very strange position. That wouldn't be too bad except the three councillors I had been drinkin' with the night before were passin' on their way to the breakfast. One of them stuck his head in and, grinnin' like a Cheshire cat, he commented, 'Isn't it early in the mornin' ye're at it, lads?' and off with him to tell the world. I paid my bill, cut my losses and went home on the train.

BACK IN PRINT

Mary Moloney rang me in a panic last Saturday. Her sister-in-law in New York had died suddenly and she had to leave immediately to attend the funeral. She asked me to do the parish notes for the next edition of the *Weekly Eyeopener*. With a certain amount of reluctance I agreed. This job had got me into fierce trouble already. I fell out with half the parish. You see, any time I take the pen in my hand I lose the run of myself and end up sayin' what I think instead of thinkin' about what I say.

For good or ill, here is a sample of this week's parish notes as they appeared in the *Eyeopener*

KILLDICKEN/GLENGOOLEY/HONETYNE NOTES
Pray Local for Christmas

À la carte Massgoers were on the menu in Honetyne church on Saturday evening. In the course of a sermon encouraging people to attend their local church Fr Timothy McGrath PP launched a blistering attack on what he called 'Eucharistic tourists'. He had harsh words for those who 'shop around for Mass as if they're looking for cheap petrol.' 'In this part of the country,' he declared, 'if you go for a walk on a Saturday evening or a Sunday morning, you are liable to be run down by mobile congregations in search of a fast Mass. These are the very people who will shout and roar in protest if there is a cutback or a change in Mass times. They'll be there for the action and the cameras but they're nowhere to be found when there is a bit of praying to be done.' He said that if these people were around at the time of the first Christmas, they'd have driven Joseph, Mary and the ass off the road as they whizzed past in their search for a 'spiritual take-away'. He concluded with the hope that people would 'pray local for Christmas and stay local for the rest of the year.'

Senior Citizens Vote With Their Feet

The annual Glengooley Senior Citizens' Christmas party had to be cancelled at the last minute due to poor attendance. Aside from committee members, the only others to attend the function were two musicians from the 'Honetyne Trio'. One local senior citizen commented that they were tired of the 'same auld stuff every year: packet soup, strong turkey, mushy veg and Christmas cake that had to be sliced with a chainsaw.' The disgruntled senior citizen continued, 'The music at the event would be better suited to a funeral home and you'd need to put on glasses to see the small sup of drink they'd give you in the bottom of a plastic mug.' A breakaway senior citizens group claims to have two busloads signed up for an alternative Christmas Party at *Upsy Daisy's* lap-dancing club in Clonmel.

GAA Magazine Causes Consternation

Publication of the Killdicken/Glengooley/Honetyne GAA Annual has given rise to much embarrassment in the club. Chairman, Mixie Dunne, has tendered his resignation following the inclusion in the magazine of an advertisement for vasectomy services in a certain medical clinic. Reflecting developments in the peace process, the advertisement adopts a very novel approach. It reads: 'Has the power-sharing arrangement in your house collapsed? Get those weapons decommissioned and revive your institutions. No photographs, no witnesses, no loss of power.'

In his letter of resignation, Mixie Dunne described the advert as an insult to everything the GAA stands for. He had strong words for anyone thinking of availing of the services of the clinic. 'It was never intended that our national games would be played by bullocks,' declared an outraged Mr Dunne.

Christmas Lights

As the Christmas lights went on in Killdicken, Postmistress Elizabeth McNamara (Lilly Mac) threatened to turn them off. At the switch-on ceremony performed in the post office by popular local councillor Maurice Hickey, Lilly demanded that the ESB bill for last year's lights be paid to her before Friday or she'd pull the plug. In a gesture of remarkable generosity, Councillor Hickey instructed Lilly to take the amount required out of his personal post office account and pay the bill. That's public service for you.

Santa's Farm

Local farmer Pa Cantillon has again handed his farm over to Santa for the Christmas season. The bearded man arrived on Saturday with his reindeers, elves and a very ample Mrs Santa. They have set up shop in the old milking parlour and the reindeer have been given the run of the farm. Santa will be delighted to meet the children of the parish and surrounding areas between ten am and nine pm each day.

Some locals are less than enthusiastic about Santa's return. May Hogan is particularly concerned to see the reindeer back. 'Last year they left me without a stitch of clothes for Christmas,' recalls an apprehensive May. 'They regarded my clothes-line as a plaything, and every time they came into my haggard they left with some articles of clothing stuck to their antlers. Last Christmas Eve when I went to get a clean pair of unmentionables for midnight Mass I had to corner one of the feckers in the haybarn to get them off him.'

Point-to-Point

The St Stephen's Day point-to-point will take place as usual at Hinchy's Field, Borrisnangoul. Five races will be held, the first off at eleven am. Entries should be given to Tossy Hinchy before closing time on Tuesday the 21st of December. Tossy requests that entrants indicate clearly whether they intend their horse to win or lose the race entered.

A STICKY END TO
THE CHRISTMAS DO

I love Christmas. I'd like to think my fondness for the season of goodwill is a sign of the child in me. I'm afraid it has more to do with my dedication to indulgence. I'm a bit like Mae West – I believe that too much of a good thing is wonderful.

It amazes me why people bellyache about the office parties, the functions, the food and drink that are forced on them at this time of year. No-one has to force-feed me. I can't get enough of the auld parties, the holly, the Christmas trees and the lights.

I particularly enjoy the Christmas bash that the council throws. It's great fun to see the councillors and officials lettin' their hair down. Regrettably, the plague of political correctness has infected events such as this with devastatin' results.

This year we have a new county manager, a new council and a new chairman. The manager and the chairman decided to celebrate the festive season by takin' everyone to the recently renovated Lisnagreen Castle. As vice-chairman of the Heritage and Tourism Committee, I'm particularly proud of this latest jewel in our tourism crown.

On the evenin' of the party we were to be at County Hall at half-five. The Mother dropped me in town at four o'clock and I told her to expect me when she saw me.

As I crossed the square I spotted Sticky Stakelum in his 'mobile catering facility'. 'Oh, Councillor Hickey,' he chimed, 'could I tempt you with some festive fare from my humble kitchen?' I wanted to tell him that his humble kitchen would be more temptin' if he gave me back half what I paid him for the Mother's party, but I held my tongue. 'Sticky,' says I, 'I'm on my way to be wined and dined compliments of the County Council at a banquet at Lisnagreen Castle. I have no need of your fare tonight, but maybe another time.'

Three busloads left County Hall for Lisnagreen amid much merriment at the prospect of another mighty Christmas do. When we arrived at the castle we were met by a piper and a troupe of medieval maidens who led us across the drawbridge into a courtyard lit by flamin' torches. 'Twas very atmospheric and had the makin's of a great night. One of the Fianna Fáil councillors sidled up to me and whispered, 'Hickey, they'll have to lay siege to this feckin' place to get us out of here before mornin'.' I agreed and rubbed my hands with glee. The crisp December air had me longin' for a bowl of punch and a gallon of hot whiskey.

To make a long story short, far from bein' satisfied, my longin's only got worse in that god-forsaken Norman rookery. Proceedin's kicked off with a reception lubricated by 'medieval' herbal drinks. What I drank smelt of horse's urine and tasted like a mixture of cabbage-water and snuff. I thought they must have served up the samples that went astray durin' the Olympic show-jumpin'.

After that bit of misery there followed a tour of the castle conducted by the county manager. Now, at his best, this man is a walkin' sleepin' tablet. He has no problem gettin' things through at council meetin's because we are all asleep when it comes to a vote. Let him loose on historical buildin's and he turns into a feckin' general anaesthetic. For an hour and a half we had to follow him around as he droned on about moats, towers and flyin' buttresses. By the end of it most of us were ready for horizontal mattresses. My Fianna Fáil colleague was grey in the face as he muttered, ''Twould be an ease if God took us.'

The manager hadn't the last syllable out of his mouth when the chairman instructed us to adjourn to the Great Hall for refreshments. This is it, says I to meself, let the party begin. But there was no improvement. We sat down at a table that must have been half a mile long. After an eternity the medieval maidens arrived with a dire concoction of cold pigs ribs, green cabbage – and nothin' else. Obviously this place was abandoned before Walter Raleigh arrived with the spud. Not a drop of strong drink was served. When urgent enquiries were made to the chairman we were informed that the manager 'regards expenditure on alcohol to be an inappropriate use of public funds'.

We got back to town after midnight and there wasn't one hostelry open.

My Fianna Fáil colleague offered me a lift home and as we got into the car I remembered Sticky Stakelum. We pulled in beside his wagon. 'Have you come for dessert, Councillors?' he enquired. 'No, Sticky,' says I, 'we want the full monty.' 'Was the banquet not to your liking?' he asked. 'Sticky' says I, 'we have just experienced a medieval famine served up with seventeenth-century Puritanism. Not a dacent bite or sup has passed my lips since I saw you nearly twelve hours ago.'

'Well, gentlemen,' says Sticky, 'you have come to the right place.' He brought us into the van, pulled down the shutters and fried up the finest feed I've ever eaten. But the best was to come. Sticky lifted a panel off the floor and pulled out bottle of poteen that was as sweet as anythin' that flowed through the Garden of Eden. At about five in the mornin' he phoned Priscilla, his wife, who cycled over and drove us all home in the 'mobile catering facility'.

As Sticky's wagon made its way through the night we washed down the last of the battered sausages with the dregs of the mountain dew and concluded proceedings with a rousin' rendition of 'Adeste Fideles'. Now, that's what I call a Christmas do. Long live Mae West.

A METRIC MESS

The new speed limits are causin' havoc in Killdicken. They're drivin' everyone mad and there is no mercy from the forces of law and order. The Clonmel guards are cleanin' up around here, handin' out penalty points by the squad-car load.

The Mother was one of the first victims. On Friday mornin' as we rushed to a funeral in Honetyne she got her miles and kilometres mixed up. She was doin' 50 miles an hour in the 50 kilometre zone when out of the ditch appeared a luminous yellow Garda jacket and up went the big hand of the law. She stopped the car with a warnin' to me to keep my mouth shut and leave negotiations to her. What ensued wouldn't get her the Kofi Annan award for peace makin'.

A young guard approached the car and she rolled down the window. 'What do you want, young fella?' she snapped. 'I'm late for a funeral.' 'Well,' says the guard, 'you'll be even later, now. Now tell me, Missus, what speed do you think you were you doing?' 'Is this a quiz?' she shot back. 'I haven't time for quizzes, I'm goin' to pray for the dead.' The young guard wasn't impressed and asked to see her licence. 'By the time I'm finished with you, you'll need to be goin' to the post office for a few pound,' says he as he filled out a speedin' ticket. 'You may not have noticed,' said the Mother, 'but while you were in Templemore learnin' how to pester the public we changed to the euro.' 'Well, Missus,' replied the guard, 'you may not have noticed, but speed is now calculated in kilometres per hour. You were doing eighty kilometres an hour in a fifty-kilometre zone.'

As she handed him her licence she asked, 'Where are you based?' 'Clonmel,' replied the guard. 'I should have known,' says she. 'And what brings you around here annoyin' the people? Is there a shortage of law breakin' in the town or what?' 'This is part of our division,' sighed the guard as he continued to write the ticket. 'Part of the division of spoils is what you mean,' continued the Mother. She was on a roll. 'This parish is like a piggy-bank for that station in Clonmel. Whenever they're short a few fines they send a little boy like you out here to rob the people. You're like Dick Turpin in a yella jacket.'

'Now, Madam,' says the guard, gettin' serious, 'I'd advise you to refrain from the insults.' This drove her mad altogether. 'So I'm "Madam" now, am I? I was "Missus" until you discovered I had a brain.' The guard tore off the ticket and handed it in the window with her licence. 'If your brain is half as sharp as your tongue,' says he, 'there's no fear of you. This is a fine for eighty euro. The offence also incurs two penalty points. You have four weeks to pay the fine or you can pursue the matter through the courts. If you are successful there will be no fine and no points. If you lose, the fine will stand and the penalty points will increase to four. Drive safely, your ladyship.' She pulled the ticket from his hand and turned on him with a venom normally reserved for the fox that steals her hens. 'May your pelt turn as yella as your auld jacket,' she hissed as she revved up the engine and took off.

After a mile or two I cleared my throat and remarked: 'That was a marvellous performance, Mother. I thought for a minute we'd end up in a cell in Clonmel.' I soon realised I should have left well enough alone. 'You were a great help,' she snapped, 'Cowerin' on the seat like a pup after piddlin' on the sofa. You're as yella as the feckin' guard and his jacket.' I kept my trap shut after that.

Later on I adjourned to Tom Walshe's for a pint where the new speed limits were the topic of conversation. I said nothin' about the Mother's encounter with the young guard but took great delight in the predicament of Dixie Ryan and one Breda Quinn as told by Tom Cantwell.

On Saturday evenin' at about seven o'clock the pair were in Borrisnangoul feedin' Dixie's cattle. It suddenly dawned on them that the lotto hadn't been done. Superquinn pushed Dixie into the car and told him to drive like hell. On the way, much to Superquinn's annoyance, he stopped to pick up Tom Cantwell. Accordin' to Tom, the two were fightin' so much they were half-way down the village when Dixie realised he was flyin'. 'What's the speed limit here?' he asked. 'Accordin' to the sign out the road it's eighty kilometres an hour,' answered Superquinn. 'No,' said Cantwell, from the back seat, 'the last sign outside the village said fifty kilometres an hour.' 'Erra, what would you know about it?' asked Superquinn. 'Well, there are two things I know,' says Cantwell. 'Number one, I'm certain I saw the fifty kilometre sign and, number two, I've a feelin' the fellas in the white car with the blue flashin' lights behind us saw the same speed limit.' When Dixie eventually stopped, one of the guards came up and tore strips off him. There wasn't a geek out of the bould Superquinn.

Pa Cantillon, who was sittin' quietly at the end of the counter decided 'twas time to smoke me out. 'Maurice,' says he, 'didn't I see yourself and the Mother stopped by a guard on the Honetyne road?' 'I suppose you did,' says I. 'She was caught by the kilometres.' 'A sore thing if it festers,' says Cantwell.

THE ENEMY WITHIN

Our little parish got a big jolt this week. The Mother brought the news from Mass on Wednesday mornin'. I was still in the scratcher when the door flew open. 'Get up and arm yourself,' she shouted, 'we have a fight on our hands.' 'What fight?' says I, 'are the Tans back?' 'No, you clown, they're closin' down the post office. Poor Lilly Mac,' says the Mother. 'Now, straighten yourself and go down to Lilly.'

I had the top taken off the egg when the full import of what was happenin' dawned on me. 'You mean,' I says to the Mother, 'there won't be a place to buy a stamp, post a letter or hear a bit of reliable gossip this side of Clonmel?' 'Maurice, you're a genius. Your grasp of complicated issues never ceases to amaze me. You're definitely Taoiseach material,' says she, drippin' with sarcasm. 'Get down there to the post office this minute and find out from Lilly Mac what's goin' on.'

When I got to the post office it was packed with concerned parishioners. Breda Quinn was the only one missin'. An upset Mary Costigan, who had worked with Lilly for twenty years, was makin' tea for everyone. Lilly herself was workin' at the counter, managin' to do the business and keep about five conversations goin' at the one time. The minute I went in the door, she shouted: 'Tay for the councillor. He's our only hope.'

After about five minutes, Lilly took me in behind the counter and down to the kitchen. She put Madge McInerney, chairwoman of Community Alert, in charge of the tea and told Mary Costigan to dry her tears and get back to her post at the counter. As she closed the door behind her she looked at me and smirked. 'I don't know how wise it was to leave Madge McInerney in charge,' she said. 'If we have a robbery she'll probably make tay for the robbers. Sure, the community alert money was stolen when she fell asleep beside the collection box at the church gate.'

When we got to the kitchen, I mentioned that I'd heard the sad news about the closure. 'Well, Maurice,' says Lilly, 'it's not as simple as it looks. What I'm telling you is for your ears only. You'd better sit down. Did you know that Dixie Ryan owns this property?' 'I never knew that,' says I. 'Well, he does,' says Lilly. 'I only rent it and the lease is up at the end of May.' 'Can't you renew the lease?' says I.

'That might have been possible a few months ago,' continued Lilly. 'But when the Quinn lady fell in with him, she took an immediate interest in his assets. I'd say she found a lot of them dormant. That's another story. However, once she heard he owned this place she came on a tour of inspection. I presumed she had her eye on the business so I mentioned to An Post that I'd retire at the end of the lease. The last thing I want to do is deal with a harridan like her. Only for that I'd hold out for another few years. Anyway, I'm not short of a few bob. I own a house or two in Clonmel.'

'My God, Lilly,' says I, 'this is unbelievable.' 'Ah!' says Lilly, 'there's more. When the Quinn lady got wind of the fact that I might retire she made a move that is backfirin' on her and on the whole parish.' My jaw dropped in amazement at the next instalment. 'Now,' continued Lilly, 'it appears that the Killdicken depot of the Co-op is to be closed. What's more, I've a nephew working in the Co-op headquarters and he told me that the Quinn lady has put in a bid to buy it out. Not only that, she has gone to An Post and told them she'd run the post office provided everything moves to the Co-op depot. An Post aren't too happy and told me they're looking at closin' the whole thing down. I'm tellin' you all this in case the Quinn lady appears with placards pretendin' to be the voice of the people.'

I was more angry than stunned. 'Leave this with me,' says I to Lilly. I went straight to the Co-op where Superquinn was closin' up for lunch. 'Oh Maurice, have you heard the awful news about the post office?' says she, with her funeral face on her. 'I have,' says I, 'and I also heard about your little plans to build an empire for yourself from the carcasses of the post office and the Co-op.' She went pale. 'That's only auld hearsay and gossip,' she snapped. 'You're worse to listen to it.' 'Breda, I know everything. Here's the deal. Lilly gets a five-year extension to the lease on the current post office and I say nothin' to anyone. Otherwise, I'll expose all your plans in the *Eyeopener* this weekend. Your business won't last piddlin' time if you close Lilly Mac.' 'The property is not mine,' says she, 'it's Dixie's.' 'Breda, we all know that you have Dixie firmly by the assets. One squeeze from you and he'll do anything. Tell him give me a ring.'

That night Dixie called to Lilly and gave her a new lease. The followin' day An Post agreed to take no action for the immediate future. I phoned the editor of the *Eyeopener* and next week's headline is in the bag: 'Hickey Hailed as Post Office Hero.' The most ruthless and cunning of them all – now, that's Taoiseach material, Mother.

THE VIRUS OF VALENTINE

Early spring would be the best time of the year if it wasn't for that cursed Valentine's Day. Without fail, the 14th of February doesn't pass without I findin' myself at the receivin' end of some feck-actin' or foolishness. I've had Valentine's cards sent to me that were so big they had to be delivered by courier van. One year I was presented with a blow-up doll in the pub. On another occasion a monstrous wreath with 'Luv ya Mossie' emblazoned in red carnations was erected at the grotto on the Bally road. I decided this year to deliver a pre-emptive strike. I paid a private visit to the postmistress, Lilly Mac, and asked her to hold on to my letters until a week after Valentine's Day. I'd collect them discreetly when it suited me. But even while I spoke, Lilly Mac handed me my post. She had a glint in her eye as she passed it to me.

The feast of red hearts hadn't passed me by. It burst into my life courtesy of one Madge Quigley. Now, I regularly receive letters from Ms Quigley complainin' about floodin' and its effects on herself and her beloved sheep. In a postscript to her last epistle she had generously offered 'to take the bare look off me'. In my reply I acknowledged her generosity and, while I didn't indicate an acceptance of her proposal, I stopped short of an outright refusal. In the language of the peace process, I opted for a fudge. But Madge is a bit like the DUP: if it's not in black and white it doesn't register. I didn't say 'No', so she presumed I meant 'Yes'.

So, here it was. The dreaded card. The envelope stood out as suspect. The size of the thing and the handwritin' were dead giveaways. 'This has the Quigley lady written all over it,' says Lilly Mac. 'You'd be makin' no mistake, Maurice, if you agreed to say half of the rosary with Madge. You certainly wouldn't have to worry about a pension plan.' 'Is that so?' says I as I gathered my post and headed for home.

When I opened the suspect envelope it was a Valentine's card of the homemade variety. On the cover was pasted a photograph of a black sheep while inside, in very neat handwritin', the followin' rhyme bleated out at me:

> *Baa, baa, black sheep,*
> *Have you any wool?*
> *Yes sir, yes sir, three bags full.*
> *None for the Master,*
> *Less for the Dame,*
> *'Tis all for my little boy who lives down the lane.*

To Maurice, my little boy. Do I wait in vain for you to come down my lane?
Love,
Madge

The card was bad but what came with it was worse. Enclosed was an invitation to accompany Madge to the South County Sheepman's Ball on Valentine's night. How in the name of God am I goin' to get out of this? I wondered. Don't get me wrong. Madge is a fine-lookin' woman; she's about the same age as myself, and is well-proportioned and well-heeled. But there are three big problems. Number one, I'm happy to remain a bachelor. Number two, the local papers would be covered in photographs of the event. I can see the captions already: 'Councillor Maurice Hickey and Ms Madge Quigley enjoying Valentine's night at the Sheepman's Ball.' They'd have us hatched, matched and dispatched while you'd be latchin' a gate. My third problem with Madge is her attachment to them feckin' sheep. Let me tell you, I wouldn't handle sheep if it meant securin' the affections of

Meryl Streep.

There and then I phoned her to make my apologies. I told her that I never leave my mother alone on nights such as Valentine's when the loss of my poor father is rekindled. Madge was havin' none of it. 'Maurice, you're lettin' your mother's apron strings tie you up in knots while the world is passin' you by. Make a break for it. I'm not takin' no for an answer.' I stuck to my guns and said I wasn't leavin' my mother alone. Madge was equally adamant and the phone call finished in deadlock. However, I knew I hadn't heard the end of it.

How right I was. When I came home from my walk the followin' evenin', the Mother was like a two-year-old. 'Well, Maurice,' says she, 'we'll have a great night at the Sheepman's do.' 'Who's we?' I asked. 'Well, now, I had Madge Quigley on the phone today,' she chirruped. 'She told me you didn't want to go to the ball because I would be left at home on my own. Sure, hasn't she solved the whole thing. Her Uncle Dan, a widower, is visitin' from Chicago and he's dyin' for a night out. He's takin' me to the ball, you're takin' Madge, and I'm drivin'.' The Mother may as well have driven a council steamroller over me. I was like a zombie. All I could say was, 'That's great news altogether.' I turned on my heel and went for a pint.

Comin' down the street, who did I spot leavin' the pub but Madge's Uncle Dan. I knew in my water he had spilt the beans about the Sheepman's Ball. As soon as I opened the door Pa Quirke piped up, 'Behold, here comes our leader, our guide and our shepherd.' With that, a well-oiled Tom Cantwell straightened up on his bar stool, stretched out his arms and intoned, 'If you love me, feed my lambs, feed my sheep.' 'I wonder,' mused Tom Walsh, 'does Madge Quigley realise that risin' the passions of a celibate councillor might have its ram-ifications.'

I WENT TO THE BALL

I tried hard to get out of it but all efforts failed. On Valentine's night I went to the Sheepman's Ball on the arm of Madge Quigley. The Mother was as excited as a teenager in the run up to the event. She spent a small fortune in Clonmel on the frock, the shoes and the hair-do. I thought the only cost for me involved the hirin' of a monkey suit, but when I went to be fitted I felt the effects of inflation from two angles. I discovered I'm three sizes bigger than I was the last time I bought clothes and the hire of the suit cost me what used to be the price of a new one.

When I brought the suit home, the Mother made me put it on to see how it looked. This led to another problem. Every pair of shoes I had resembled the surface of the moon under the shiny, black dress-trousers. 'Maurice,' says she, 'it's about time you put a few euros under your feet instead of down your throat.' I nearly calved at the notion of shellin' out another wad of notes on this blasted ball. 'How much will a pair of shoes set me back?' I asked. 'Well, you won't get a decent pair for less than seventy euros,' says she. 'Forget it,' says I, 'I'll go barefoot before I'll pay that.'

I decided I'd borrow the shoes but who'd have a black pair my size? There's Sergeant Miller, but he's surely five sizes too big, and there's the postman, Pa Quirke, but he'd tell everyone. How about Fr McGrath? He'd have loads of black shoes and he's about my size. I went straight to the presbytery and, sure enough, the PP was delighted to help. He couldn't believe how much I'd spent on the monkey suit. 'Sure, haven't I more black suits than I'll ever need,' says he. 'Say no more, Father,' says I, 'I'll only get depressed.' To make me feel better, he insisted on lendin' me a Crombie overcoat along with the shoes. I must say, the Crombie looked grand on me. I felt like a TD.

On Valentine's evenin' the Mother and meself got ready and off we went to pick up Madge and Uncle Dan. I must admit it was great to get dickied up. In fairness, the Mother looked fantastic.

When we arrived at Madge's, the uncle invited us in for a drink. Madge was havin' trouble with her hair so the Mother went down to the bedroom to help. Meanwhile, Dan and myself helped ourselves to the bottle of Black Bush. Eventually the Mother came back and when Madge appeared, I was

struck dumb. My misgivin's about the Sheepman's Ball melted away. I'll tell you, any man would have been delighted to have Madge Quigley on his arm that night.

We finished our whiskey and hit for Clonmel. By the time we got to the hotel they were sittin' down to the dinner. Madge and myself were parked at a table full of ardent sheep farmers and it was then the romance began to fall out of the night. In the face of Madge's radiance I had forgotten about her attachment to the sheep.

Another thing, my auld stomach isn't the strongest and it doesn't take much to upset it. The fumes from Uncle Dan's Black Bush mixed with the sheep-farmin' conversation at the table ensured that I was on a one-way ticket to the jacks. We had hoggets, ewes, lambs and rams for starters and soup. That wasn't too bad, but for the main course we had liverfluke, tapeworms and sheep that pulled their arses around the field. I was just holdin' on when, for dessert, they turned their attention to scrapie and castration. I made a dash for the loo that was faster than the charge of the light brigade. I'm glad to say I got there in time to keep my dignity intact.

I thought the worst was over, but the dancin' proved to be even more disastrous. Fr McGrath's shoes were obviously designed to provide good grip around marble altars; they weren't made for trippin' the light fantastic. When we got up for a waltz I felt as if I had suction pads on my feet. Madge wanted to know if I had cramps. I nearly came to grief entirely durin' the Siege of Ennis. An encounter with a substantial Carlow woman for the swing was a classic case of irresistible force meetin' an immovable object. While I was stuck to the floor in Fr McGrath's shoes, all twenty stone of the Carlow woman remained attached to my arms and continued to swing mightily. She twisted me into a hay-rope before collapsin' in a heap on top of me.

When I hauled myself back to the table I discovered that the Mother and Uncle Dan had gone home. Madge had arranged a taxi for the two of us. I suddenly found that I was glad to have Madge all to myself. By the time we left the hotel I was pepperin' as to whether or not I'd suggest meetin' again. On the journey home she chatted away about the events of the night while my head was in a spin of 'Will I? Won't I? Will I? Won't I?' Before I knew it we were at her front door. As she got out of the taxi she put her hand on mine and said, 'Maurice, thanks a million. We'll do it again next year if the Lord spares us. Now, I've a few ewes to lamb. Good night.' That put an end to my confusion – for the moment.

After the Ball

There has been fallout on all fronts since my outin' to the Sheepman's Ball. In short, the Mother is in love, there's a local weddin' happenin' sooner than I expected and my friendship with Fr McGrath is as strained as the peace process at the time of the Colombia Three. A number of things happened at the ball that didn't seem important at the time, but as the week went on they mushroomed in significance.

Where do I start? The Mother and Uncle Dan are like a pair of feckin' pigeons since the ball. You don't see one without seein' the other. I can't get a lift anywhere because they're off tourin' the country with Uncle Dan perched like a lord in the front seat of the car. The breakfast has gone from the full Irish to a self-service continental. Just when everythin' seemed to be goin' right, a feckin' Yank invades my life and kidnaps my mother. I suppose I'm what you'd call collateral damage.

Now, to this surprise local weddin'. I came on the information quite by accident. After the meal at the ball I gave a speech addressin' issues like roads and potholes and floods. No sooner were the tables cleared than I had a stream of people comin' up to me with all kinds of problems that needed council attention. I used the backs of a few auld pages I found in Fr McGrath's Crombie for takin' names, phone numbers and other details. I put the pages into the pocket of the monkey suit and thought no more of it.

At the end of the night didn't Fr McGrath's Crombie go missin'. I nearly lost my life. I was in a panic in the lobby when, out of the jacks came a young fella from Glengooley wearin' the missin' garment. I challenged him and he immediately realised he had picked up the wrong coat. Himself and the girlfriend went back to the ballroom to search for his own one.

The followin' mornin' I took the Crombie and the shoes straight back to Fr McGrath. He was delighted I had a good night and remarked that the dancin' would have done the shoes no harm. I didn't tell him what harm the dancin' nearly did me. When I got home I decided to follow up on the issues brought to my attention durin' the impromptu clinic at the ball. Havin' read through my notes taken on the back of the pages that I found in Fr McGrath's Crombie I concluded that a full day in County Hall was called for.

I was just about to put the pages away when I turned them over to have a look in case they contained anythin' important. 'Twas a good job I was sittin' down. There in my hand I held the official marriage papers of one Bridget Mary Quinn and a certain Richard Ignatius Ryan. I couldn't believe my eyes. Breda Quinn and Dixie Ryan are tyin' the knot on the 8th of April. Coincidentally, that's the same weddin' date as Charles and Camilla. It must be a specific day for auld shoes gettin' hitched to auld stockin's. Once I recovered from the initial shock, my next problem was to get these marriage papers back to Fr McGrath. I couldn't pretend I didn't know what they contained, havin' scribbled all over the back of them. There was nothin' for it but to face the music and own up.

At the presbytery that day I was greeted by a very sombre Fr McGrath. 'Father,' says I, handin' over the papers, 'I'm terribly sorry but these were in the pocket of the overcoat you loaned me. Not realisin' what they were, I took notes about constituency matters on the back of them. It was only when I went to follow up on the notes I saw that they were official marriage documents. Of course, Father, you know that this particular weddin' is close to the bone for me, but I won't say a word to anyone.'

Fr McGrath nodded solemnly and took the papers. He then asked me to wait at the door while he went back into the house. He couldn't have been more frosty and I couldn't figure out what was up. He returned with a small dustbin and a pair of fire tongs. With the tongs he extracted two small packets from the bin and held them up to my face, sayin', 'These items were in my coat when you brought it back from your night out.' Oh merciful hour, there in front of my nose were two packets of condoms.

Where did they come out of? I suddenly remembered the young fella who took the coat by accident and how I met him comin' out of the jacks.

I was about to attempt an explanation but the priest put up his hand. 'Councillor Hickey, don't waste your breath. My housekeeper didn't know you had the coat and 'twas she found these items in the pocket. She left them on the hallstand with a letter of resignation. She's gone for a week's retreat in Knock and God only knows what she'll do. Nothing will excuse this, Councillor.' With that he closed the door in my face. I'll be ringin' Adams and McGuinness to see how I might get out of this one.

CATCH 22

I haven't gone near Fr McGrath since the disaster with his Crombie. I'm avoidin' goin' to Mass in the parish so I've the Mother drivin' me to Clonmel. Thankfully, her 'boyfriend', Dan, has returned to Chicago and I have my means of transport back. She drove him to Shannon herself for the flight to the Windy City and I went with them in case she'd be upset. In fairness, they really took to one another at the Sheepman's Ball and had a great time tourin' the country since. However, the carry-on of them was fierce embarrassin' at the airport, with them holdin' hands and she lookin' into his eyes like a teenager.

After Dan checked in we adjourned to the bar for a few farewell drops of comfort before he left. When it came time to go I said my goodbyes and left them to themselves at the security gate. I was nearly at the exit doors and there was still no sign of the Mother followin' on. I turned back to see herself and Dan in the throes of a passionate kiss the likes of which you wouldn't see outside the chipper on a Saturday night. The Mother even had one leg lifted like they do in the films. When she eventually caught up with me she informed me she was goin' to Chicago for Easter. More to be worryin' about.

On the way home, I decided I'd better tell her about the PP, and what his housekeeper Nell Regan found in the Crombie. Well, she got such a fit of laughin' she nearly crashed into a roundabout in Limerick. ''Tis no laughin' matter,' says I, 'poor Fr McGrath could be in real trouble if Nell goes to the bishop and tells him what she found.' The Mother laughed even louder. 'I'm sorry, Maurice,' says she, 'but I'm tryin' to imagine Nell Regan's face when she found the packets of condoms. She probably beat the walls of the presbytery with her fists. D'you know what's wrong with her? Jealousy. She's ragin' mad that Fr McGrath might be involved with a woman other than herself.' I told the Mother she was all wrong. 'Nell Regan is a nun in all but name,' says I.

'Now, listen to me,' says she. 'Any woman who sees Nell in action will tell you she's head over heels in love with the PP.' 'Ah for God's sake, Mother,' says I, 'you're watchin' too many soaps.' 'Hold on a second,' says she, 'I have evidence as well as intuition to back up my opinions. Do you remember when Fr McGrath was laid up with shingles for six weeks last year? Well the local women used to call in with all kinds of cards, food, flowers and cakes, and I know for a fact he never got any of them. Mary Costigan in the post office has land behind the presbytery and when Fr McGrath was sick she noticed smoke regularly comin' from his garden. One evenin' when the burnin' started she went over to the ditch to have a look and there was Nell Regan throwin' cards, homemade cakes, black puddin's, tarts and all kinds of scones into a ragin' fire and she cursin' like a trooper sayin': "Those interferin' auld bitches. I'll burn them before they get near my man. I'll mind him from them auld biddies." So there,' concluded the Mother, ''Tisn't the state of Fr McGrath's morality that's botherin' Nell Regan. 'Tis the fact that some other woman might have wiped her eye. Nell has her mind made up that he's playin' away from home and she's out there burnin' with vengeance. Hell hath no fury and all that.'

When we got back to Killdicken the place was alive with rumours. Nell's fury was already at work. Accordin' to these rumours Fr McGrath was havin' a lusty affair with a twenty-six-year-old woman from Clonmel and the bishop had given him until the weekend to finish with her. The Mother got the first of it when we stopped at Gleeson's shop. Later on, I went to the post office and was ushered in to the back office by a pale Lilly Mac, who repeated this slanderous fiction as absolute fact. In Lilly's version the twenty-six-year-old is married with two small children. I went to Tom Walshe's for a pint and Tom called me aside. His account of the so-called scandal involved the PP and 'a twenty-six-year-old separated woman in Clonmel'. By the time I got home and compared notes with the Mother, the twenty-six-year-old was married, single, separated, divorced, a foreigner, the daughter of a well-known businessman, a primary teacher and a cleaner in one of the hotels.

Poor Fr McGrath is in an awful mess and I'm the only one who can get him out of it. But I can't do anythin' without settin' off more explosions. How do I tell people that the items in Fr McGrath's overcoat weren't his and weren't mine, even though I had the coat in my possession when they might have been put there? The whole parish would be winkin', noddin' and nudgin' one another. Even Madge Quigley would be implicated. Though a fella might be innocent, confession can often be safer than denial. It reminds me of the story of an American governor who claimed that his electoral opponent, who was also a man, wore women's underwear. The governor's advisers told him he couldn't make such claims without evidence. 'Ah,' he replied, 'just watch him deny it.' God direct me.

DOIN' THE DOG ON IT

Thankfully, the saga about Fr McGrath and the woman in Clonmel is over. In the pub on Thursday night Sergeant Miller put a swift end to the rumours. He heard Pa Cantillon make some smart remark about the PP bein' a busy man of late and rounded on him like an Alsatian. In full uniform he announced to the whole pub that there was no truth in the vicious rumours about the priest. 'I'm warnin' ye all now,' he shouted, 'if I hear one more word of this I'm reportin' it to the man himself. If he takes my advice he'll see the slander mongers in court.' Once the sergeant was finished there wasn't another word about it. The bishop put his weight behind the PP on Friday when he made him a Canon. Meanwhile, Nell Regan, the housekeeper, withdrew her resignation and is back at work. In time, Canon McGrath and myself will iron out our little misunderstandin'.

Anyway, the parish is back to normal. Killdicken is like all small places: while we have our big moments, it's the minor outbreaks of tomfoolery and roguery that keep us from gettin' too sensible or goin' totally mad. One subject that never fails to infuriate and entertain people around here is the subject of dogs. Sheepdogs, greyhounds, mongrels and mutts can arouse all kinds of passions. For instance, in the townland of Cossatrasna the locals take their dogs so seriously that every canine creature carries the surname of its owner. There's Shep O'Brien, Lassie Ryan, Rex Cregan, Sheeba Gleeson and Bran Dillon. The most remarkable hound in the place is a Great Dane called Hector Houlihan.

In that particular townland the birth of a litter of pups draws as big a crowd as a wake. The neighbours gather around once a bitch produces and the entire conversation will be sure to centre on the identity of the father. Everyone will have an opinion on the matter. 'Well,' someone might say as they examine the newborns, 'most of 'em have the head of the Ryans but them two small fellas in the corner have the wobbly arse of the Dillons.' That would be contradicted. 'I'm tellin' you, them are Cregan ears. There isn't a Cregan with a straight ear since they had an outbreak of the mange twenty-five years ago.' 'Erra, go way outta that,' someone else would chime in, 'them flat feet are O'Briens. Sure, O'Briens spend half their time swimming in bog holes, they've feet like ducks.'

But things didn't always run that smoothly. If the owners had notions about the breedin' and pedigree of their particular bitch, the birth of a litter could be a tryin' time. There would be hell to pay if progeny bore no resemblance to the dog that had been carefully selected to do the fatherin'. Families were known to fall out for years if a neighbour's dog was accused of graspin' an opportunity that had someone else's name on it.

One time Moll Gleeson, a local in Cossatrasna, had a fine collie bitch called Sheeba. This animal got more pamperin' and groomin' than the Buckingham Palace corgis. Moll was all talk about the pedigree of the dog she had lined up to satisfy the basic instincts of her precious bitch. She was on one leg for three days before Sheeba began to show signs of labour. The vet was on standby and the shed was set up like a delivery ward in the Coombe.

However, in the darkness of Sheeba's womb, disaster awaited Moll and her notions. When the first head appeared Moll nearly took a weakness; by the time the fourth head was out she nearly had to be put down. 'Oh Jesus Mary and Joseph, will you look at the four big feckin' Houlihan heads on them!' she screamed. 'I'm goin' straight over to face that Houlihan crowd and their horse of a dog, that cursed Hector.' Turnin' to her husband she ordered, 'Have that litter of mongrels drowned before I come back.'

When Moll arrived at Houlihans' front door, one word borrowed another and eventually she was ordered to leave before they set the bould Hector on her. The families haven't spoken since. In fact, a few years later when Fine Gael selected Moll to run in the local elections, the Houlihans, who had been Fine Gaelers for generations, became loyal supporters of my good self. Their Hector might have delivered a litter of mongrels to Moll but his momentary dalliance with her Sheeba delivers a litter of fifteen votes to me at every election.

What brought me to the subject of man's best friend in the first place was an incident in the pub a few nights ago. Along with his few pints and his fags, Tom Cantwell loves dogs. He claims that one day they will make his fortune for him. Of late, he has been all talk about this marvellous golden retriever bitch he bought. 'I'll tell ye, lads,' he'd say as he sang her praises, 'her pups will see me comfortable for many a winter.' Well, when the pups arrived they were of very dubious parentage. Some were black, some brown and more were spotted. A very dejected Tom came into the pub not long after the birth. He blamed Pa Quirke's dog for the sneak attack on his beautiful retriever bitch. 'Of course,' says I to him, 'that's a postman's dog for you. Like their owners they never knock twice.' 'Well,' says Cantwell, 'This fella only needed to knock once and he had the damage done.' 'What breed of dog is he anyway?' I enquired. 'A Dana,' replied Cantwell. 'A Dana?' says I. 'What kind of a dog is a Dana?' 'All kinds of feckin' everythin',' retorted Cantwell as he stared despondently into his pint.

A TASTE OF THE MELTIN' POT

I was greatly relieved that there was no St Patrick's Day parade in the parish this year. At a meetin' a few months ago Percy Pipplemoth Davis, my eco-friendly councillor colleague, suggested that the parish should host a 'multicultural *céilí*' instead. He made a speech burstin' with rockers of words that nearly choked him. 'Twas a feckin' multi-cultural experience just listenin' to him because we couldn't understand half what he was sayin'. Anyway, in one of the more memorable phrases of the night he encouraged us to 'wrap the green flag around every class, colour and creed in the parish in an intercultural extravaganza that would be the envy of the country.' If there's an Orangeman in the parish he won't be too happy with being wrapped in that particular colour.

Most people were sure his proposal wouldn't work. The reaction of Tom Walshe, the publican, was typical when he said, 'For years locals won't go near the hall and now we're expectin' foreigners to fill the feckin' place.' In fairness to Pipplemoth, he worked like a devil organisin' the event. He went to buildin' sites, factories, hotels and restaurants and any place you'd find foreign workers. He visited every asylum-seeker and refugee for twenty miles and more than that, he got a representative from every club in the parish to sit on the organisin' committee.

The hoor didn't ask *me* to sit on the committee. Pipplemoth is turnin' out to be as crafty as the FFers. When I challenged him on my exclusion, 'twas like playin' handball against a haystack. 'Now, Maurice,' says he, 'this *céilí* must be seen a people's event and so you'll agree the involvement of one councillor is more than sufficient. I'm sure you're glad to be spared yet another series of meetings.' He might be a woolly-jumpered sandal-wearer, but he's no fool. He won't share the stage with the competition. I couldn't give a monkey's curse. After the *céilí* they might think Percy is a great fella, but wait till the next election. I'll be home and dry while he'll be rootin' around in the Shinners' knickers tryin' to scrape up a few transfers to drag him over the line.

With Paddy's night approachin', the excitement about the *céilí* was growin'. As well as dancin', there was goin' to be a selection of 'ethnic foods' served up. All through Patrick's Day the hall was a hive of activity with people of all shapes, makes, colours and sizes comin' and goin'. There were cars from Lithuania, Latvia, Poland and other faraway places. Tom Cantwell couldn't figure out what all the lefthand-drive vehicles were doin' in the village. The crowd in the pub convinced him that, since we started drivin' in kilometres Brussels now wanted us to drive at the other side of the road as well. They told him that people are already buyin' lefthand-drives to be ready for the changeover in January. He nearly had a stroke, cursin' Brussels and accusin' it of doin' what Hitler never got around to.

Of course, not everyone was happy with the notion of the multicultural *céilí*. One particular individual, who shall remain nameless, ranted and raved about 'these blow-ins dilutin' the purity of our heritage'. He attacked auld Pipplemoth in the post office durin' the week and told him he had some cheek hijackin' our national feastday with the aid of these 'ungodly hordes'. It didn't stop Pipplemoth. In fairness to Sergeant Miller, he took the man aside and warned him to keep his bitterness to himself.

At half-seven on Paddy's night the queue outside the hall was a mile long. The nations of the earth seemed to have descended on Killdicken as the main street was full of men in turbans and cloaks and gorgeous women in Nigerian national dress. The smells in the hall were like the smell from the bakin' box the Mother pulled out every year to make the Christmas cake. There was spicy stuff from Africa and China that would put the hair standin' on your head, along with sausages, cheeses and bread from eastern Europe. Closer to home there was hotpot from England and, of course, there was bacon and cabbage representin' our native cuisine. Needless to say, we all made pigs of ourselves.

The night wouldn't have been complete without a delay. At nine o'clock there was no sign of Pipplemoth or the band. The other members of the committee were gettin' worried. Finally, he arrived in style, dressed like the priest who invaded the Olympic marathon, and in a convoy of two vans with about fourteen Travellers. He announced that he had brought the best *céilí* band in the country and so he had. The dancin' went on until mornin'. Our foreign friends brought their own instruments and joined in with the band. The *craic* was mighty. Poor auld Tom Walshe put his back out tryin' to do the Cossack dance with a bunch of Ukrainians. The night closed with a Siege of Ennis that nearly demolished the hall.

On the way home the Mother and myself spotted the man who had accused Pipplemoth of dilutin' our heritage. He was stupid drunk as he attempted to open his front door. When it finally opened and he fell in, the Mother looked at me and commented, 'If that's our heritage, it could certainly do with a bit of dilution.'

The followin' day I went to Tom Walshe's for the post mortem. Accordin' to everyone it was the best night in the village in decades. Tom Cantwell who was half-asleep at the end of the counter, lifted his head to add his tuppence worth to the review. 'Well, I'm a walkin', talkin' international experience,' says he. 'I woke up this mornin' with a head like the North Pole, a throat like the Sahara and, after all that hot spicy food, I've a tail-end like the Japanese flag.'

ONE FuNERAL AND A WEDDIN'

Camilla and Charles postponed their weddin' for the Pope's funeral but not Superquinn and Dixie Ryan. 'Twould take more than the pontiff's obsequies to stop those nuptials.

The Mother and myself spent the mornin' of the weddin' glued to the telly lookin' at the papal funeral. I was bowled over by the pomp and ceremony. The heavenly strains of the Sistine Choir were no preparation for what I had to endure in Honetyne church that afternoon.

I arrived at the church around two o'clock to find Dixie pacin' the yard and smokin' three fags at the one time. He looked like a man facin' the electric chair. His cousin and best man, Jimmy 'The Stick' Ryan, wasn't doin' much to help. The Stick is a hungry-lookin', cantankerous scarecrow of a man. When he isn't pullin' on a fag he's wipin' the non-stop drip from the end of his nose. As I passed he was stampin' out a fag and shakin' his head at Dixie, sayin, 'Hadn't you a grand life till you met her?'

I went into the church and sat beside Pa Cantillon, Pa Quirke and their wives. The women were of the opinion that Superquinn wouldn't be a minute late. 'Breda Quinn will be here at half-two on the button,' predicted Trisha Cantillon.

By three o'clock there was still no sign of the bride and the crowd was gettin' fidgety. Another fifteen minutes passed before we heard the clippa cloppa of a horse and the sound of excited conversation echoin' up the aisle. The best man wasn't too impressed with Superquinn's punctuality. 'What kept you?' he barked. 'Only for me, Dixie would have done a runner.' 'Listen here, you gobdaw,' snapped the beautiful bride, 'the only one doin' a runner this mornin' was this lunatic of a horse. As soon as we left the house he bolted. I've been up and down the main street of Killdicken fourteen times. 'Twas like the feckin' Grand National.' 'Well,' says The Stick, ''tis time now to straighten yourself and face Becher's Brook.' He turned to Dixie. 'Now, Dix,' says he, 'either you head to the altar or you let that mad hoor of a horse take you off into the sunset.' With an air of resignation Dixie made his way up the aisle and the musicians got the nod to strike up.

Pee Hogan and the Blue Boys were organised to play the music in the church and in the hotel. Superquinn had obviously negotiated an all-in deal. 'Twas a good job the bishop wasn't listenin'. I go to enough weddin's to know what's allowed and what isn't and to my ears there was no difference between what Pee and the boys played in the church and what they play in Walshe's on Friday nights. Obviously Canon McGrath decided not to interfere with the choice of music and gambled on there bein' no Vatican spies around.

As the shadow of Superquinn appeared at the church door the first few bars of Tammy Wynette's 'Stand by Your Man' rang out from the gallery.

Hogan was at his melodramatic best as his voice quivered at all the right moments. I had to take a look back to make sure that he wasn't in drag for the performance. He certainly sounded like someone in a blonde wig and a sparkly dress.

Superquinn was given away by an uncle from Fethard, the owner and pilot of the runaway horse and trap. The poor man looked as if he had just come through downtown Baghdad. He got her to the altar and made his escape just as 'Stand by Your Man' climaxed with a big finish. Pee held the last note for five minutes while the drummer walloped the bejapers out of the drum kit. Poor Moll Gleeson's hearin' aid was screechin' like a siren at last crash of the cymbal.

Everyone breathed a sigh of relief when the song finished. Canon McGrath welcomed the people and asked Dixie and Breda to light the candles. At that point Pee and the boys launched into a loud and ropey rendition of 'Come On, Baby, Light My Fire'. There wasn't a dry eye in the church – for all the wrong reasons.

The ceremony continued with no major hiccup until the music started again. Just after the vows and the exchange of rings, Canon McGrath invited the congregation to give the newly-married couple a round of applause. From the gallery we heard Pee count in the band with 'A-wan, a-two, a wan, two, three,' and they proceeded to belt out a few choruses of Cliff Richard's 'Congratulations'.

For incidental music Pee had brought along a local box player, The Ticker Wickham. Now, Ticker has a repertoire of three tunes: 'Slievenamon', 'The Galtee Mountain Boy', and 'The Boys from the County Armagh'. Whenever there was a lull in proceedin's you'd hear a husky Pee callin', 'Ticker, Ticker, a few tunes.' Ticker grew in confidence as the ceremony went on. Durin' the signin' of the register he decided to have a second run at 'The Boys from the County Armagh' and threw in a few words of encouragement: 'Keep your partners for a last round of the house. Look into her eyes, hold on to her hips and you'd never know your luck. 'Tis my own Irish home, far across de fooooam.' Even Canon McGrath shook uncontrollably.

Just before the final song the main fuse blew, renderin' Pee and the band soundless. Ticker was about to step into the breach but Superquinn had had enough. 'Ticker,' she shouted, 'if you play one more note on that mellojun I'll tear it to pieces and make you ate it.' The weddin' party went down the aisle in silence. A dignified end to a most unceremonious event.

THESE WALLS HAVE EARS

It is often said that if houses could talk they'd tell great stories. We own such a house on the main street in Killdicken. At one time it was home to our family and our business, but, after rentin' it for a few years, the Mother recently decided to renovate it and sell. We went down the other day to look around the place and, sure enough, every room has a tale to tell.

Originally the front room housed my grandfather's cobbler's shop but my father very wisely opted not to practise the family craft. Given that he had trouble lacin' his shoes 'twas sort of obvious he'd have trouble makin' a pair. He turned the ground floor into a shoe shop while himself and the Mother lived upstairs. When I came along, herself demanded more space so they bought the house we now live in. After the father died the Mother closed the shop altogether. She reckoned there was more to be made collectin' rent than sellin' shoes.

Over the years the place has had a most chequered rental history. In its time it was a chip shop, an antique shop, a hairdresser's salon, a video library, a health food shop and a vet's surgery. The most remarkable in a series of remarkable clients was Buddy Sweetman, the vet. The poor man hated his profession, havin' been hounded into it by an ambitious father and a mother with notions. He spent a good few years haulin' himself through the farmyards of South Tipp before he decided that pets and poodles were easier to deal with than shitty cows, scuttery sheep and mad horses.

The last straw in workin' with large animals came for Buddy durin' a post-natal internal examination of a spirited young cow. The farmer had the animal held in a halter while his son had her jammed up against a stone wall. Buddy was up to his oxter in the cow when the farmer got a fit of sneezin' and the startled animal took off with Buddy in tow. She crossed three farms with the unfortunate vet hangin' out of her tail-end. He eventually managed to extricate himself when she ran out of fuel and stopped for a refill in a stream that flows through the next townland. At this stage a posse of locals on foot, on tractors and on quads were followin' the demented cow and her reluctant passenger. They came on Buddy sittin' on the ground, scratched, bruised and covered in bodily fluids of all descriptions. The cow was back on the run. 'How did you manage to hang on?' asked the farmer. 'I think I had her by the tonsils,' replied Buddy as he flexed the hand that did the holdin'. The followin' day he phoned the Mother, rented our premises and turned to the relative safety of treatin' small animals.

However, nothin' is simple. Buddy soon discovered that while pets might be easy to handle, their owners are a hundred times more cantankerous than any farmer. These pet lovers were drivin' him to distraction. As he got more and more frustrated he began to make simple mistakes. Things came to a head when he confused the treatment intended for a pedigree King Charles with the treatment meant for a randy terrier of dubious origin. He castrated the King Charles and de-wormed the terrier. The mix-up only became apparent when the King Charles developed a voracious appetite for food and a total indifference to bitches. He came to prefer a biscuit to a bitch any day. Meanwhile the terrier continued to attach himself to anythin' that looked vaguely canine.

The owner of the King Charles lost the rag entirely when she discovered what had happened. She came to Buddy's surgery and told him she'd sue him for every penny he had if she didn't get satisfaction. 'Mark my words, if I had my way, I'd have your faculties removed and pickled in a jar,' she railed. True to form, Buddy put the problem on the long finger in the hope that it would go away.

The woman got tired of writin' and phonin' until one Friday mornin' she arrived accompanied by her son, a solicitor based in Dublin. As she strode into the surgery she declared: 'Mr Sweetman, it seems the law is the only way to deal with you. This is my son, Benjamin, the solicitor in the family.

I'll let him deal with you from now on, but let me assure you that I will not stop until I am satisfied legally, morally and financially.' Well, to cut a long story short, while Benjamin and Buddy were tryin' to reach a settlement didn't they fall for one another and run off to America together! They are now married and live in Los Angeles where they have a very successful pet litigation business. Benjamin's mother mightn't have got her satisfaction, but by all accounts the two boys are extremely satisfied with their lot.

When Buddy eloped he owed the Mother two months' rent and left the premises in an awful state. There were enough medicines and powders thrown around the place to start a biological war. Well, about a year later didn't the Mother get a lovely letter from Buddy with a cheque for two thousand dollars towards the rent and the clean-up. 'A dacent man,' says she.

Sittin' on the remains of two chairs in the old house, the Mother and myself had great fun reminiscin'. 'Isn't it strange how things work out?' she mused. 'Little did Buddy realise as he removed the gearbox from the King Charles that this little procedure would bring him love and a new life in the new world.' I suppose you could say he's as lucky as a cut cat.

MORE PARISH NOTES

Mary Moloney is sick again and I reluctantly agreed to do the local notes for the *Weekly Eyeopener*. I always get into trouble writin' these but I get great pleasure from it.

Honetyne Ploughing

The Honetyne Ploughing championships had a record entry last weekend. Unfortunately, the event coincided with monsoon rainfall and at the time of going to print, five of the nine competitors are still trying to recover their tractors. Another three are totally unaccounted for and are presumed lost in the mud. One machine escaped unscathed, having failed to start.

The delay in recovering the stricken tractors is due mainly to the imposition of a recovery fee by the organisers. Bob Singleton, a competitor from Roscrea, hasn't been able to get at his Fordson Major since three o'clock on Sunday when he had to abandon it at the height of the downpour. It remains up to its axels in mud as Bob refuses to pay the recovery fee. 'It cost me sixty euros to enter this Mickey Mouse contest,' declared a furious Bob. ''Twas like feckin' Flanders out there on Sunday. Now they want a hundred and fifty to pull me out. That's nearly more than the blasted tractor and plough are worth. The crowd that organised this are nothin' more than gangsters and blackguards.' Meanwhile, the Secretary of the Honetyne Ploughing Club, Mickey Mulligan, is adamant that the fees will not be waived. 'If they won't pay up, the tractors will rust in the mud,' he stated. 'We might even turn the place into a sculpture park and make money out of it every Sunday. Most of them auld tractors and their owners are museum pieces anyway.'

Shooting

Best wishes to Tommy Carthy, Chairman of the Glengooley Gun Club who is recovering in hospital after a shooting accident. The incident occurred during a clay-pigeon shoot in Budnanossal. It appears that Mr Carthy took a violent fit of sneezing which dislodged his false teeth and sent them flying through the air. Tim Scanlon, a competitor who had mislaid his spectacles, mistook the flying false teeth for a clay pigeon and fired both barrels. Mr Carthy has now a permanent pierced ear and a shorter nose than the one he came to Budnanossal with. Mr Scanlon, who was quite shaken by the event, says that Tommy is a lucky man. Tommy remarked that having a pellet in his left ear and half his nose shot off isn't his idea of luck.

Sailor's Knot Position Leads to Legal Tangle

A local drama is attracting huge attention in Clonmel district court. Throngs from Killdicken and Glengooley are crowdin' into the tiny courtroom where yoga teacher Kimin Yo Cleary is being sued by Killdicken woman Minnie Murphy. Mrs Murphy claims she is crippled with backache as a result of injuries sustained in the course of a yoga class conducted by Kimin Yo.

Judge Terence Shanahan had to adjourn proceedings soon after Cleary took the stand. When asked by Terence Cregan, Mrs Murphy's solicitor, to explain the origin of his name, Mr Cleary replied that it was a family nickname given him by his younger brother. When his mother would call him in for his meals she'd shout, 'Come in, ya hoor.' His baby brother thought the older brother's name was 'Comin Yore' and it stuck as a nick-name. When he trained in yoga he adopted it and changed it slightly to Kimin Yo. 'It sounds kinda oriental, sir,' explained Cleary. 'Indeed,' replied the solicitor, 'it is somewhat more exotic than "Come in ya hoor".' At this point not even the judge could control himself. He adjourned for ten minutes.

When proceedings reconvened, Mrs Murphy's solicitor reminded Cleary of his client's claim that she put her back out while attempting the sailor's knot position in his class. He put it to Cleary that this yoga position isn't particularly safe or suitable for 'a woman in late middle age carrying considerable ballast'. The neighbours had to restrain Minnie Murphy from attacking her own legal representative. Luckily, neither Mr Cregan nor the judge spotted the potential fracas and he continued to question Kimin Yo. 'Could you describe the "sailor's knot position" for the court, Mr Cleary?' he asked. 'That'd be fierce hard,' replied Cleary. 'Could you demonstrate it for us, then?' asked the smooth-talking legal eagle. Cleary looked at the judge, who nodded, and so Cleary left the witness box, got down on the floor of the court where he proceeded to twist himself into contortions.

After staring in amazement at what Cleary had done to himself, the Judge asked him to return to the witness box. However, there was no stir out of the contorted Kimin Yo. 'Mr Cleary, please untangle yourself and return to the witness box at once,' instructed the judge. From somewhere under his oxter, a painful-sounding Kimin Yo informed the judge that he couldn't move. He was locked in a general spasm. An ambulance had to be called and the case was adjourned for a month.

Car-boot Sale Shut Down

The annual Killdicken car-boot sale in aid of Kill-Gool-Tyne Community Alert was closed by Gardaí last Saturday. In a surprise swoop on the event Gardaí seized a wide range of potted plants. Despite the protests of the organisers, Sergeant Miller insisted the Gardaí were acting on good information. He claimed that illegal substances were being peddled in the form of 'innocent plants'. There was outrage throughout the community at the heavy-handed tactics employed by the guards. Even Sergeant Miller's wife, Winnie, was horrified. 'My fella wouldn't know a pissabed from a poinsettia,' she declared. 'They might well be askin' Ian Paisley to name the Kilkenny hurlin' team as askin' my husband to identify any of those plants.' Gardaí are refusing to disclose the results of tests done on the seized plants.

KAMIKAZE CORRESPONDENT

Poor Mary Moloney has a bad dose so I'm still in harness writin' the parish notes for the *Weekly Eyeopener*. Last week's efforts got me into fierce trouble with the Honetyne Ploughin' Club. The number of abusive phone calls and text messages I got led me to believe that everyone in Honetyne was a member of the club. While some threatened to canvass against me at the next election, others threatened to plough me into the bog the next time I appeared anywhere near the place. I was kinda taken aback by the onslaught, but my contacts in the locality told me not to worry. Accordin' to Pa Quirke, the postman, the Honetyne Ploughin' Club is like a small farmer's herd: it's made up of big-bellied white-heads.

More seriously, Sergeant Miller isn't talkin' to me. He wasn't impressed by my account of the guards' raid on the Community Alert car-boot sale. I've warned the Mother to be careful of the speedin' and parkin' as she's now a legitimate target for the local forces of the law.

The strange thing about writin' the parish notes is that when the *Eyeopener* comes out on Wednesday mornin's I'm afraid of my life to answer the phone or the door. I know in my heart that what I've written is goin' to drive someone mad. However, when I sit down to write next week's notes, the devilment gets the better of me and away I go again.

Glengooley Fashion Show

On Friday night a huge crowd turned up at St Jude's Hall for the Annual Glengooley GAA Fashion Show. Clothes were supplied by local drapers while club members, their spouses and children did the modelling. The event was broadcast live on the local pirate radio station, The Sticks FM, with commentary by the master of bullology, Willy De Wig Ryan.

Things went fine until De Wig remarked that some of the models were made for the catwalk. Unfortunately he went on to say that others were only fit to drive cattle down boreens. Despite loud booing from the crowd the show continued. However, De Wig lost the run of himself again during the beach-wear section. As the models sashayed down the catwalk in their Tramore gear, De Wig commented that there were enough spare tyres on display to keep Eddie Jordan's Formula 1 team on the road for a few seasons. This was too much for Moll Gleeson, local FG councillor and chief organiser. She charged out from behind the curtain with a mannequin under her arm and lunged at De Wig. She met him in the chest with the mannequin's head and sent his hairpiece flyin'. All hell broke loose but De Wig continued to broadcast as he fended off furious Glengooleyites. A tape of the event is now sellin' like hotcakes. It is presumed that the fracas will not result in legal action; De Wig says he will make more out of the tapes than he would out of any claim.

Tidy Towns

Hopes of a Tidy Towns award for Killdicken received a huge setback this week. The County Council announced that it intends to proceed immediately with major sewerage and drainage works in the village. Tom Walshe, Community Council Chairman, is furious. 'The one time we want the village to look well, it will look like a bomb site. Those council officials are about as useful as fart in a space suit,' he thundered.

Popular local councillor, Maurice Hickey, is known to be working night and day to have the works postponed until after the Tidy Towns adjudication. 'We are looking for everyone's cooperation in this,' commented a concerned Councillor Hickey. 'We all know that our sewerage system is under strain and something needs to be done. However, a Tidy Towns award would work wonders for our little village.'

The Councillor has proposed what he calls the 'Hickey Roadmap for Resolution'. 'If the council agrees to postpone the works until the autumn, local people should use the sewerage facilities sparingly. I would appeal to them to reflect before they relieve themselves and ask, "Do I really need to go now? Could I hold on till tomorrow?"' Councillor Hickey went on to encourage people to think outside the box when making crucial decisions about their bodily functions. 'Twould be great if people could use open country when watering the horse and even better if they could confine a full sit-down performance to every second day. We might also ask residents on the two sides of the street to alternate their movements. One side could perform on Mondays, Wednesdays and Fridays and the other side on Tuesdays, Thursdays and Saturdays. Everyone could do the business on Sundays.'

Council officials are said to be reviewing the Hickey Roadmap while the Community Council is willing to give it a shot. However, true to form, Councillor Percy Pipplemoth Davis dismissed the Hickey plan as 'A North Korean solution for a South Tipperary problem'.

Parish Lotto

With this week's jackpot standing at a miserly €2.67, Canon McGrath appealed to people to renew their support for the lotto. Contributions declined after it emerged that the main beneficiaries of last year's fund, Killdicken Pitch and Putt Club, used the money to purchase three golf carts for their nine-hole course. After numerous collisions involving the three vehicles, only one cart is now allowed on the course at any time. Lotto sales collapsed entirely when the Pitch and Putt Club applied for a further grant to expand the playing area in order to accommodate the golf carts.

Postmistress Lilly Mac spoke for many when she commented: 'It's like lookin' for a loan to build an extension because you bought a suite of furniture that's too big for the house. Fools and their money are easily parted. Well, the Pitch and Putt Club has just run out of fools in Killdicken. They must think they're running the feckin' K Club.'

ICA TO GAA – TWO PILLARS OF THE COMMUNITY

Mary Moloney is getting the hip done. Once again I must take on the onerous task of being chief news correspondent for Killdicken, Glengooley and Honetyne.

ICA Walk

The Annual Irish Countrywomen's Association (ICA) Slievenamon walk took place on Sunday. A big crowd of women left for the mountain but there was great concern when five failed to return at the appointed time. As dusk was falling, a worried Guild President, Moll Gleeson, called in the rescue services. The Civil Defence had just arrived in force when Harry the Hippie drove into the carpark carrying the five missing women in the back of his camper van. The women were in mighty form – even Lizzie Whelan, who hasn't smiled in forty-five years, was grinning from ear to ear.

A furious Moll demanded to know what kept them. Nell Regan, housekeeper to Canon McGrath, recounted their ordeal. She explained that as they passed Harry the Hippie's cabin they got the smell of fresh baking. 'We were parched for a cup of tea,' said Nell, 'and when we stopped to ask Harry what was in the oven he invited us in. He treated us to some beautiful herbal tea and the finest scones we ever tasted.' She went on to explain how the visit turned into something of a hooley. 'After the tea we sang a few songs and ate a few more of the lovely scones,' she recalled. 'Then Harry produced the squeeze-box and, sure, we tore into a Ballycommon set and the day passed us by completely.'

Moll Gleeson wasn't one bit impressed. 'It sounds like *Dancing at* feckin' *Lughnasa*,' she thundered. The more she lambasted the offending women, the more they roared laughing. Moll nearly went mad entirely when Nell advised her to 'Take a walk on the wild side', and proceeded to hand out Harry the Hippie's scones to all and sundry. Within ten minutes the whole place was swinging. The Civil Defence led the bus down the mountain with blue lights flashing, horns blaring and sirens wailing while Moll led the busload of women in a way-out version of 'Slievenamon'. Harry has been offered a stall in a prime location at the ICA cake sale in two weeks' time. As they say in the westerns, there's more than flour in them there scones.

Brussels Trip

Independent MEP Riobáird Mac an Sceach is hosting a trip to Brussels from June the 20th to June the 24th. Flying from Dublin to Amsterdam, the group will spend two exhilarating nights in this exciting city. Then it's off to Brussels on Wednesday for a visit to the EU after which the group returns to lively Amsterdam for the last two nights. Mr Mac an Sceach thinks it is important for constituents to get a feel for continental life as well as the EU institutions.

Those interested should contact Councillor Maurice Hickey or Riobáird's mother, Maisie, in Fethard. The cost of the trip will depend on numbers. Mr Mac an Sceach advises people not to worry about cost. 'Just contact Maurice or my mother and they won't see you stuck.'

The Late Mick Higgins

Glengooley turned out in great numbers last Monday to say goodbye to the late Mick Higgins. Mick was Chairman of the local GAA club from 1969 to 1999. In the early years he oversaw the suspension of all Glengooley teams from county competitions. By 1974, the club's medal hopes were entirely pinned on the performance of the under eights. With their suspension in 1975 for the kidnap of a referee, the club was without a team, but training and recruiting continued. With the readmission of the club to county competitions in 1978, there followed a golden era.

Mick believed that the most important asset the club had was its ferocious reputation. He was proved right. After some bruising encounters in early stages of the '79 championship the Glen hurlers found themselves in the county junior final after a remarkable series of walk-overs and no-shows. Having taken the junior title, the same pattern repeated itself during the intermediate championship of 1980, which they won. Mick Higgins was hailed as the hero when they turned senior in 1981. Despite all attempts on and off the pitch, they failed to take senior glory until centenary year, 1984. Then a remarkable series of flooded pitches and cattle damage led to an October county final, which the Glen won with eleven men and a crowd of hysterical supporters. They held the senior title on four occasions over the next few years. Mick Higgins was the giant in Glengooley during this period.

In latter years, bitter in-fighting led to a decline in the Glen fortunes. Mick found himself isolated in the clubhouse and was eventually ousted as Chairman in 1999 when the club built a new clubhouse at the other end of the pitch. He is survived by his faithful Alsatian, Savage.

THERE'S ALWAYS SOMETHIN' QUARE IN THIS PLACE

Safe Swimming Lessons

With the sun making an occasional appearance, it's time to take the plunge. In anticipation of the day we'll have our own pool, the annual Killdicken Dry Swimming School will open in the community hall on Saturday next. Classes will be held on Saturday mornings between ten am and eleven thirty am. Sessions for children will take place upstairs in the canteen area while adult lessons will happen in the main hall.

Launching the school, Tom Walshe, Chairman of the Community Council said that it been a major success last year. 'Up to forty people got certificates in swimming skills last summer and I understand that a significant number transferred to water swimming at Dromtrasna bridge later in the year.' Mr Walshe went on to say that dry swimming is a very safe way to learn the skill. 'It is risk free. We hadn't one swimming accident in the hall all last summer. It is especially suitable for people with a fear of the water,' declared Mr Walshe. 'As long as you can keep one leg under you and can hop, you'll learn all you need to know.'

New Organisation Accused of People-poaching

There is increasing friction between Honetyne ICA and the newly formed Active Retirement Group. Guild President, Maude Reidy, claims the new organisation is poaching her members. In a statement she accused Hannah Grimes, founder member of the Active Retirement, of sour grapes. 'She only founded the group because she failed to be elected President of the ICA guild here in Honetyne. This new organisation is supposed to serve older people, but in reality it's nothing more than a vehicle for the organiser's ego trips. That woman has no respect for democracy.'

Hannah Grimes totally rejects what she describes as the slanderous accusations made by Ms Reidy. 'Maude Reidy has about as much respect for democracy as Robert Mugabe. For the past fourteen years she has rigged every election in the ICA. She takes a celebrity chef approach to the ballot box – here's a result I prepared earlier.'

Tempers are frayed in Honetyne but both sides are said to be considering an offer of mediation made by popular local Councillor, Maurice Hickey.

There 'Twas and 'Twas Gone

Clonmel Gardaí are anxious to talk to anyone who might have witnessed the removal of a speed camera and tripod from outside Higgins's gate on the Honetyne Road. The disappearance took place between twelve noon and 12.30pm on Monday week last. Gardaí manning a speed trap at the location had gone to round up loose cattle and found the camera missing on their return.

High-scoring Tournament

Local soccer is locked in crisis. As the season ended, Teerawadra, Glengooley and Killdicken found themselves at the bottom of the first division with one of the three facing relegation. Teerawadra was ahead on goal difference before the last fixture involving Glengooley and Killdicken. A particularly high-scoring game between the neighbouring clubs ended in a draw with a final score of 27 all. Teerawadra manager, Mattie Stapleton, is crying foul after his team was relegated. He claims the game was fixed to keep his club out.

Both Glengooley and Killdicken have denied fixing their match, blaming goalkeeper problems on the day for the high score. It appears the Glengooley goal-man had hamstring problems while the Killdicken keeper had the runs. According to Stapleton, Teerawadra intend to take this issue to the highest possible level. Killdicken manager, Pa Quirke, isn't worried. 'I don't care if they take their case to the top of Keeper Hill, it still won't make them good enough for the bigtime,' commented a confident Quirke.

THE POLITICS OF THE LAST OPPORTUNITY

Mary Moloney is home from hospital and is writin' the parish notes again.

I'm back to council business. I had no sooner returned to the day job than I learned a hard lesson: while journalism might sharpen the skills of observation, it doesn't help you spot an opportunity for makin' political hay.

Summer is the time for fairs and festivals. Last year we had the International Jew's Harp Summer School. It was a total disaster and so I thought 'twould be politically wise to avoid the organisation of this year's event. Anyway, I found myself hauled in to a meetin' at the parish hall on Tuesday night. It had been decided a few months earlier to organise the Killdicken Old Time Waltzin' Festival. As usual, they made the decision in February but it didn't strike anyone to do anything about it until June. There was hell to pay at the meetin' when it emerged that nothin' had been done. The blame game took off into full flight. Lilly Mac and Sean Mac Feochadáin were like the leaders of a lynch mob. They wanted to find out who was to blame and see him bleed.

Lilly Mac told the chairman, Tom Walshe, that he wouldn't run a henhouse. He responded sayin' he had successfully run his family business for forty years, 'Family business? Is that what you call it?' says Lilly. 'That place was lovely when your mother had it, but you've turned it into a shebeen. How did we ever think you could run the Community Council?'

This was turnin' out to be a most entertainin' meetin'. Mac Feochadáin was lookin' for a paper trail. He wanted to know the whereabouts of the minutes with a record of the decision on the old-time waltzin' festival. The only minutes Tom has are the ones on his watch. 'Who will provide the music for this festival?' demanded Mac Feochadáin. 'You can't waltz without music. Or are we going to become famous for silent waltzing the way we've become famous for dry swimming? Killdicken is the laughing stock of the country because of your hair-brained ideas, *a chathaoirleach.*'

It was great to watch Walshe sizzlin' like a rasher. I was totally distracted by my enjoyment of the proceedin's and my pleasure at Walshe's discomfort. Like a flash, that hoor of a Percy Pipplemoth Davis jumped on the passin' political wagon with a rescue plan in hand. He suggested that the waltzin' competition could have a two- or three-week build up if a series of heats was organised. Each parish in the county could be asked to put in a pair of waltzers. The whole thing could culminate in a grand finale on the last night of the festival. He proposed that Comhaltas be asked to provide the music. Everyone went into orbit with delight at Pipplemoth's suggestion, Tom Walshe's bacon was saved, the lynch mob was called off and Pipplemoth's back was nearly broken with all the slappin' he got.

I was enjoyin' the spectacle so much I missed the boat completely. As the crowd left, I must have looked like Father Jack, sittin' there with a stupid grin on me face. Tom Walshe flew past with a bundle of papers and grunted, 'Hickey, you were a great feckin' help.' He was followed by Lilly Mac who didn't put a tooth in it: 'Hi, Councillor Hickey. You better make up your mind whether you're a spectator or a player in this parish. If you don't tog out soon, Pipplemoth will have the next election to himself.' My father always said that the politics of the last opportunity would beat you at least once a year. Hopefully, this is it for the year.

BARBECUE BLITZ

One thing about modern Ireland I can't understand is the barbecue. People with the finest kitchens you ever saw are spendin' the summer in the backyard burnin' good meat over an open fire. An uncle of mine in America says that the difference between the Irish and the Yanks is that the Irish eat inside and relieve themselves outside while the Yanks eat in the open and go inside to water the horse. We have turned into Yanks, but it's a pity we haven't the weather to go with our notions.

The lunacy of the Irish barbecue was brought home to me on one particular occasion last summer. A local family, full of jeeps and new money, was christenin' a child. To celebrate the event, the whole parish

was invited to a barbecue in their huge palazzo-gombeeno of a house.

The proud parents weren't blessed with a good day. It poured rain and the multitudes of guests, who should have been swannin' around the lawn, were confined to the house. I, along with forty others, was standin' in an idle kitchen that would feed half of Africa. Meanwhile the parents of the newly-baptised child were outside in the yard huddled under an umbrella fryin' sausages and burgers on a barbecue grill. People have been put away for less.

I'm sorry to say that here in Killdicken the curse of the outdoor grill is infectin' all aspects of life. Last month the Graveyard Committee, that bastion of traditional Killdicken society, announced that its annual fundraiser would take the form of a barbecue in the graveyard. Now, it's one thing to hold a barbecue, but the decision to hold it in the graveyard bate Banagher. Let me tell you, when I die the last thing I want is some hungry hoor sittin' on my gravestone drippin' tomato ketchup on me while he slobbers into a quarter-pounder. The prospect is enough to make a fella promise to do a bit of hauntin' after he crosses over.

Anyway, on Friday evenin' we all turned up at the cemetery where Canon McGrath kicked off the event with 'Grace Before Meals'. Anyone lookin' at us from the outside would be forgiven for thinkin' we were about to dig up the bones of our ancestors and make soup.

Madge McInerney, Pa Cantillon and Lilly Mac set up the barbecue near the republican plot where there's plenty of room. The grill was a homemade, half-barrel effort compliments of Cantillon's angle grinder and welder. Unfortunately, Pa loaded in too much charcoal with the result that Madge and Lilly were burnin' all before them. Even the bullocks in the next field were in danger of being medium- to well-done.

It was decided to remove a few shovels of charcoal to help the grill cool down. Unfortunately, in the course of the operation, some hot coals fell from a shovel and rolled in under a loose grave-slab. Well, about two minutes later, an explosion ripped through the ground, sendin' sods of earth, food and tupperware flyin' in all directions. Miraculously, no-one was hurt, but the scene looked like somethin' from a horror film. People were walkin' around covered in raw burgers, sausages and chicken pieces while tomato sauce ran off them. Ambulances and fire brigades arrived from four counties but, mercifully, all we needed was a good wash.

Thanks to the Killdicken Graveyard Committee, the barbecue has taken its place in Irish history. It delivered the first public and verifiable act of decommissionin' in a renewed peace process.

CLERICAL CHANGES

We had a most welcome development here in the parish last week. We have a new Church of Ireland minister, the Reverend Whistletweel. Our last minister, the Reverend Terry Larchfield, was ill for a long time and retired over a year ago. Everyone in the parish was delighted when the new minister was appointed and crowds went along to St Bartholomew's in Glengooley last Friday evenin' for the installation. To say that Protestant, Catholic and Dissenter had turned up to pray together would be an exaggeration – we were all there to have a good look. Nell Regan, Canon McGrath's housekeeper and sacristan, was there to get the full of her eyes of the minister's wife. She's always suspicious of female competition in clerical circles.

As we waited in the church, there was all kinds of chat about who the new man was. Some said he was comin' from the North, others said he was from Cork, and someone else heard it for a fact that he was from England. By the time the organist struck up the openin' hymn, the crowd was gone mad with curiosity. As the procession made its way up the church, everyone in the congregation nearly got permanent neck damage tryin' to get a glimpse of the new man.

Whatever about neck damage, there was an outbreak of lock-jaw when it emerged that the new man was a woman. All eyes became fixed on the tall, elegant, grey-headed figure walkin' up the aisle just ahead of the bishop. When his Lordship introduced the Reverend Winifred Whistletweel as the new pastor, there was a thunderous round of applause. Nell Regan buckled at the knees and had to be supported by those around her. Canon McGrath might be delighted with his new counterpart, but that's more than can be said for Nell. She's been spittin' fire ever since she recovered from the initial shock. The prospect of havin' to serve tea to a woman in a clerical collar is enough to give her shingles.

After the service there were light refreshments in the garden at the newly refurbished rectory. Everyone behaved themselves till it came time for the photographs. There was more jostlin' among the councillors tryin' to be pictured beside the Reverend Winifred than you'd have in a scrum. Moll Gleeson pulled the Mná na hÉireann card, thinkin' the new rector was her property, while Pipplemoth was tryin' to let on he owned the place. We all know well that he doesn't darken the door of church, chapel nor meetin' house.

When things drew to a close, the Reverend Winifred stood at the gate shakin' hands with her guests and thankin' them for the welcome. Well, didn't auld Pipplemoth position himself at the other side of the gate and, in a brazen attempt to milk every drop of political advantage from the event, proceeded to shake hands with all an' sundry and thank them for comin'. He wasn't there too long when the Reverend Winifred spotted what was goin' on. After she finished talkin' to Lilly Mac she strode across to Pipplemoth, shook his hand and in a boomin' Donegal accent exclaimed: 'Wonderful to meet you, Councillor Davis. I trust I'll see you in the pews frequently. Now run along and do your canvassing somewhere else.' He took off like a frightened rabbit, the little hooreen.

When it came my turn to shake hands, she had a big welcome for me. 'Ah, Maurice, the very man,' says she. 'I was told that if I want to find out anything about this place I should–' I interrupted her. 'I know,' says I. 'You were told you should talk to me.' 'No, actually,' she replied. 'I was told I should talk to your Mother. When you want to know everything, you ask a woman. Could you arrange a meeting for me?'

That fairly punctured my balloon. Mná na hÉireann are on the march again.

THE HEAT IS ON

The Killdicken Old-Time Waltzin' Festival is beginnin' to pick up speed. As I told ye a few weeks ago, the main event will be the grand finale in which finalists drawn from a series of local heats will compete for the grand prize. The first of these was held in Honetyne on Saturday last and 'twas a disaster.

Things went wrong from the very start. They charged €10 a head admission and that put everyone in bad form. Mickey Mulligan of the Honetyne Ploughing Club, a man with all the charm of a furze bush, was on the door. Anyone who complained about the price was told to 'Eff off' and come back if they found cheaper entertainment.

At half-nine, with the hall about a third full of disgruntled punters, Mistress of Ceremonies Moll Gleeson decided no-one else was comin'. The waltzers were ordered to take the floor.

Eight couples were competin' for two places. For the first part of the heat each couple waltzed on their own. Then, all eight couples danced together. This was followed by an 'Excuse me' dance and the heat concluded with a brief individual dance.

The atmosphere wasn't great, but it got even worse when Madge McInerney started the music. She had a lone Foster and Allen album and a CD player that must have been through the two gulf wars. 'Old Flames Can't Hold a Candle to You', the chosen track for the individual waltzes, had more scratches than a monkey's arse. It skipped, hopped and jumped all over the place. The waltzers did their best, but 'twas like tryin' to ice-skate on galvanise. Every time the CD jumped, even the most graceful dancers looked as if they got a sudden root in the backside. 'Twas very unfair, but hilarious.

Pa Cantillon was in knots. He sidled up to me and whispered: 'By God, Maurice, this was well worth the ten euro. I'd say a lot of the auld flames on the floor will hold more than a candle to Madge if she doesn't straighten the music.' 'You're right,' says I. ''Tis a blow-lamp they'll be holdin' to her.' The tracks for the next set weren't quite as scratched as 'The Flames' but they had their ropey moments.

When it came to the 'Excuse me' dance, 'twas back to kangaroo music. 'For Twenty One Years is a Mighty Long Time,' sang a hippity-hoppity Foster and Allen. The song proved to be a long and cruel sentence for the unfortunate dancers as it skipped and jumped while they tried to execute seamless changes of partners. They were like relay runners crashin' into one another. The whole thing came to a sudden end when the electricity meter ran out and the power went. Not one of the committee had change for the meter so I was delegated to go around among the dancers with my hand out and collect as many euro coins as I could get. I was never as embarrassed in my life. This waltzin' festival is turnin' into a major fiasco.

As a worried Moll made her way to the stage to announce the break and the raffle, I whispered a few words of encouragement to her. 'Sure, 'tis over now,' says I, 'nothin' else can go wrong.' 'Just wait and see,' she growled.

After the break, she introduced the adjudicator, a very scuttered Willy De Wig Ryan of The Sticks FM. He started his adjudication by comparin' the dancers to loose spuds rollin' around an empty trailer. He went on to say that some of the male waltzers would make great show-jumpers if only they had a second pair of legs. He concluded with the observation that tractors pickin' up round bales on the side of a hill would have more grace than some of the dancin' he endured that evenin'.

He refused to put anyone through to the next round, tore up his notes and fell off the stage makin' smithereens of Madge McInerney's CD player. Such was the uproar, the Festival Committee agreed to re-run the heat. So ended another night in our quiet little rural parish.

NOTIONS, LOTIONS, DOGS AND HORSES

Since people started gettin' the bit of money they're gone mad. Have you heard the ads for pet insurance on the radio? I nearly choked on my soft-boiled egg the other mornin' when I heard this man tellin' me that his 'comprehensive pet care insurance plan' would 'take the worry out of my pet's medical needs'. Now, when I was a young fella, the nearest thing to pets anyone had were dogs and cats. These weren't insured against anythin'. In fact, the only thing they were sure of was regular verbal abuse, such as: 'Get out of my way you little hoor or I'll skin you alive.'

I don't want to go back to the hungry days of the seventies and eighties, but I do think that the good times are drivin' us beyond ourselves. I was down at the school the day it closed for the summer. It's a great day to be seen around because everyone is in good form with the holidays stretchin' out before them. After goin' down I could see no-one and no-one could see me. I spent my time duckin' in and out between big jeeps driven by cross-lookin' women in sunglasses. You'd imagine 'twas the mart you were at and not the school.

The remarkable thing about the owners of these jeeps is that the vast majority of them have no more than a half-acre of land, most of which is taken up by their house. Maybe they have farms in the Alps or the Magillycuddyreeks. Most certainly we don't have the terrain, the weather or the road conditions around here to merit these monsters. I was givin' out about it in the pub a few nights later when Tom Cantwell informed me that these vehicles are now regarded as 'fashion items'. 'Is that what they are?' says I. 'There was a time when people wore such things. Obviously, nowadays it's not a fashion item unless you can sit into it.'

More than anythin' else what bates Banagher about this new wealth is the amount of money spent on potions and lotions. There's a fella I know who used to be a salesman for a builder's supplier. He inherited a few acres near Clonmel and before long he transmogrified into a 'developer'. He has three or four estates under his belt at this stage, along with a few million quid. He was a grand fella. Loved his pint, his curry chips and the greyhounds. I met him at a weddin' last week and he's a different man. He had a tan that Albert Reynolds would envy, a black head of hair on him the like of which you wouldn't see on a twenty-year-old and he smelt like a perfume factory. He made a big show of tellin' me that he was rushin' off to the races, he had a 'promising mare' runnin' in the 5.30 at the Junction. When I said I'd go with him, I could see the wife wasn't too happy at the prospect of sharin' the winner's enclosure with me. She needn't have worried, their 'promising mare' obviously never promised anyone she'd come out of a startin' gate.

While we were waitin' to meet the trainer, it started to pour out of the heavens. Well, didn't the black head of my developer friend begin to run down his fawn Crombie while his tan began to drip off the top of his nose. The wife nearly hit me when I suggested she get an umbrella before her husband melted into his shoes.

As I made my way back to the weddin' in a taxi, I began to wonder if the whole country might be in danger of a similar meltdown.

THE LAST LAUGH

When I was a young fella we were always told that mockin' is catchin'. I found out recently that there's a lot of truth in that auld sayin'.

I was in the pub on Thursday evenin' when who should come in but Dixie Ryan, Superquinn's new husband. He'd just had the hips done and the poor hoor was crippled. A few of us were sittin' at the counter when he clattered through the door with his walkin' sticks. 'By God,' says Pa Quirke, 'Superquinn is some woman. Ye're hardly married two months and she has you banjaxed.' Dixie ignored the dig. 'Give me a pint and a small one, Tom,' he said to the publican, 'and no guff.' 'Do you know somethin'?' says Tom, ignorin' the instructions. 'When people talk about the pressures of marriage they talk about financial pressure, emotional pressure and psychological pressure, but they never talk about the physical pressure. Marriage can put huge physical pressure on a man that's not used to it. Here you are, Dixie, hardly down from the altar and the two hips collapse under the pressure.'

Dixie began to shake with temper. 'Listen, ye shower of mockers,' he shouted. 'This operation was booked before ever I got married.' 'So you had intended to do the damage?' interjected Tom Cantwell. 'That's a premeditated injury. I hope the VHI don't get to hear of it or they won't pay for the plastic arse they're after puttin' under you.' I thought Dixie would explode. I was enjoyin' every minute of it.

Pa Cantillon was next to add his tuppenceworth. 'Lads, if the damage done to the hips is anythin' to go by, the bed must be fit for the dump. I'd go so far as to say the foundations of the house must be affected.' 'Now, now,' interrupted the publican, 'enough is enough. Give the man a break.' Things quietened down until the door flew open and in strode Pipplemoth Davis in ridin' boots and jollipers. When he saw Dixie with the two sticks, he raised his glass to him. 'Richard, my good man, I see she's broken you in. Marvellous, marvellous, there's hope for all of us, isn't that right, Councillor Maurice?' That hoor never fails to get the dig at me.

The followin' mornin' the Mother woke me early. She was on a mission to clean up the back yard and had me pullin' weeds for the whole day. When she called me for the supper I couldn't straighten myself. My back was locked in a spasm. After half-an-hour spent tryin' to straighten me she put me into the car and took me to Gerda Van Hoosen, a Dutch physio with a practice in Killdicken.

Gerda, a small, wiry woman with the strength of a pony, met me at the door. She brought me into a treatment room, told me to undress to the waist, and left. When she returned she mentioned that the patient in the next room was a friend of mine. 'He advised me to do a good job on you,' she added. With that she got me down on the floor, put one hand under my chin, stuck her knee into the small of my back and pulled. I roared like an ass. When she had me straightened she turned me over on my back and got me to pump my legs as if I was cyclin' a bike. I was in total agony.

She went out to the other patient and came back smilin'. 'I have just finished with your friend, Mr Dixie Ryan,' she announced. 'He told me you probably got your injury from being a naughty boy. Now, Councillor, there can be none of that for about six weeks. The rest will do you good, ya, ya?' 'Ya, ya,' says I, 'the rest will be great and the weeds will be delighted.'

BODY TALK

Even after Gerda Van Hoosen straightened me out I was still not a hundred percent, so I went to see Dr Doherty, who told me that all the manipulations of all the Gerdas in the world wouldn't solve my back pain. 'The problem with your back,' says he, 'is caused by your front. Until you lose about two stone off that huge belly of yours, you'll have trouble. You see, Maurice,' says he, 'you're like someone in a constant state of advanced pregnancy. Have you ever seen a woman about eight months gone? She's forever puttin' her hand to the small of her back for a bit of support and ease. At least she has the comfort of knowin' that in a few weeks she'll have delivered. You have nothin' to deliver. In fact, it's more likely that the mountain below your chest will get even bigger and you'll either keel over or burst.'

After that talkin' to I was fit for coronary care. Dr Doherty made an appointment for me with a nutritionist in Clonmel and the Mother drove me in the followin' day. On the journey, I got yet another lecture from herself about my lifestyle. 'How many times do I have to tell you that you're flushin' a fortune and your health down the toilet in Walshe's auld shebeen? What's more, Sticky Stakelum's chip wagon and every grease bucket in the country loves to see you and your likes comin', loaded to the gills with porter and ready to devour any kind of saturated scutter they pull out of a barrel of boilin' grease? No wonder you're in the state you're in.' She was on a roll and she wasn't about to stop.

'Now, let me tell you,' she continued, 'as soon as we go home, the fryin' pan is goin' into the bin. No more greasy breakfasts for you. After that, I'm not drivin' you to any meetin' within three miles of the house. You can walk. What's more, I intend warnin' Tom Walshe that if anythin' happens your health because of drink, I'll sue the bony arse off him.' Thankfully we had arrived at the health clinic before she had time to declare a national disaster.

The nutritionist asked me a thousand questions about my weekly lifestyle: what I ate, how much exercise I took and what I drank. As I spoke, she typed the information into a computer. When I finished she took one look at it and said: 'Mr Hickey, this is the most potent coronary cocktail I have ever seen in my professional career. I'm not so much surprised that you're overweight, I'm just surprised you're still alive.' After that she measured me and weighed me. She then multiplied one by the other and divided them by somethin' else to get my BMI, my body mass index. I was reminded of a limerick I heard a few years ago:

A mathematician named Hall
Was enormously fat and quite small,
The sum of his weight,
Plus his ticker times eight
Measured three-fifths of five-eighths of feck-all.

She finished her calculations and told me that a man carryin' my weight should be at least six foot six and not scrapin' five foot. She said she'd send a proposed diet to my doctor.

When I got back to the car the Mother was dyin' to know how I got on. 'Well,' says she, 'what did she say?' 'She told me I'm fine,' says I, 'except I'll have to do somethin' about my height.'

ONE HUNGRY HICKEY

My recent visit to the nutritionist has had a sudden and massive impact on my life. She sent a diet to Dr Doherty who passed it on and told me to stick to it or die. As I read through the contents I could feel the pangs of hunger rise up in the pit of my stomach. I'll fade away into one leg of my trousers if I take this on. Have a look at it and you'll agree that neither man nor beast could be expected to survive on these scraps. I call it the 'Hungry Hickey Express Diet'. It operates on a three-day cycle – as soon as you've finished one round of misery you've to turn and face it all again:

Day 1   **Breakfast** *(The Lough Derg Jumbo)*
1 slice of brown toast with a scraping of margarine
1 cup of black tea, no milk or sugar

Lunch *(The Bugs Bunny Special)*
2 medium carrots (raw)
2 medium slices of turnip (raw)
1 small portion of natural yoghurt

Dinner *(well, the smell of it)*
1 boiled potato (no salt or butter)
1 grilled lamb cutlet
1 small portion of broccoli

Dessert *(lovely, feckin' lovely)*
1 marietta biscuit
1 cup of black tea, no milk or sugar

No alcohol, plenty of water
(Is this part of the diet or a description of the mid-Atlantic?)

Day 2   **Breakfast** *(The Miss Piggy Deluxe)*

1 bowl of bran in skimmed milk

1 cup of black tea, no milk or sugar

Lunch *(The Slug's Delight)*

1 small portion of lettuce

1 tomato

1 small apple

Dinner *(The One-legged Chicken)*

1 boiled potato

1 chicken leg

1 small portion of broccoli

Dessert *(I couldn't, I'm stuffed)*

1 cream cracker

No alcohol, plenty of water

(That sounds like summer in Ballymena.)

Day 3   **Breakfast** *(of bitterness)*

1 grapefruit *(for feck's sake!)*

1 cup of black tea, no milk or sugar

Lunch *(aeroboard and cardboard)*

1 small portion of cottage cheese

2 rye crackers

1 half banana

Dinner *(A Double Blandy)*

1 portion of boiled rice

1 small tin of tuna in brine

1 small portion of garden peas

Dessert

1 plum *(sheer gluttony)*

No alcohol, plenty of water
(A description of my bladder.)

I decided that takin' on a new project like this should be put off for a few weeks at least. A fella would need a few fine days behind him before he could face into this misery. I was about to put the sheet of paper into my back pocket when the phone rang in the hall. When I returned from answerin' it I found the Mother with the glasses on top of her nose and she readin' through the diet. 'Now,' says she, 'that'll straighten you. We might as well start immediately. I have some brown bread for the toast, I could rise to a scrapin' of margarine and, sure, we have buckets of black tea. Sit down there, Maurice, and enjoy the first meal of the rest of your life.'

She has taken to enforcin' the diet to the letter. The whole parish has been warned not to feed me. Tom Walshe refuses to serve me alcohol, Sticky Stakelum will only let me near his chip wagon for the smell and the shops won't serve me as much as a lollipop.

Two nights ago I hid around the corner from the chip wagon and gave young Quirke €10 to get me a quarter pounder, a battered sausage and a curry chip. As I waited with my tongue out, the young fella stuck his head around the corner and shouted, 'Hey, Maurice, do ya want sauce on the burger?' I knew the game was up. He came back with my tenner and told me Sticky was afraid my Mother would boil him in his own oil if he fed me. I've no immediate plans to meet St Peter but if I don't eat soon, I'll have to pencil him in.

DANCE TILL YOU DROP

Last Friday saw the launch of the Killdicken Old Time Waltzin' Festival. I took a break from preparations and spent the afternoon in Walshe's, drinkin' water and watchin' the show-jumpin' from the RDS. A well-oiled Tom Cantwell was commentatin' from the end of the bar. Every time a horse knocked a pole or ploughed into a fence he'd shout, 'Take him home and feed him.'

I had to go home early but there was no feedin' for me. I was on the verge of malnutrition, thanks to that hoor of a diet. I also had to report for community duty at the Festival Office. Festivities were supposed to kick off with open-air dancin', but a bunch of Pa Cantillon's yearlin's broke out durin' the Aga Khan and left their trademark all over the street. When we went to hose it down the water pressure collapsed, so we got a load of sand and covered it. To add to our problems, the sky opened.

Moll Gleeson, the Festival Chairperson, decided to move things indoors. Percy Pipplemoth Davis was furious. He was adamant that we should 'have the whole community waltzing gaily up and down the main street.' 'If people dance in that cesspool of rain, sand and cowshite,' declared Moll, ''twill look like a feckin' mud-wrestlin' festival.' She told Pipplemoth he could dance as gaily as he liked in the scutter.

The highlight of the festival was to be the grand finale of the waltzin' competition on Saturday night. Ten couples had reached the final. My Mother and her boyfriend, Dan from Chicago, had come through to represent Killdicken, but unfortunately, Dan got a dose of the 'flu. I was called up as first sub. Now, when I waltz I do so with all the grace of an ice-skatin' duck. Luckily, as part of the weekend there were ballroom dancin' classes in the hall on the Saturday mornin' and so the Mother sent me down. An instructress tried for two hours to get me to waltz without trippin' over her or myself, but I hadn't one clear round. When she eventually gave up she asked me to recommend a good chiropodist.

Let me remind you that I was goin' through all these exertions and me still on that hoor of a diet. I was famished, but all I could have was a cup of water and a small apple.

As I went into the hall that night I met Tom Walshe, who commented that I looked somewhat the worse for wear. 'Why wouldn't I,' says I, 'and my belly wrapped around my backbone for the want of a bit of dacent grub? What's more, I have to dance in the feckin' competition in Dan Quigley's place.' 'Come back to me in five minutes,' whispered Walshe. 'I'll have somethin' for you.' When I went back he handed me a small bottle of spring water. 'Try that,' he said with a wink. I took off the cap and put the bottle to my head. 'Twas the grandest drop of poteen I ever tasted.

When it came time for myself and the Mother to take the floor, I was in great form. We glided around like two auld smoothies. Pee Hogan and the Blue Boys were beltin' out 'Newport Town' and I was flyin' it. The crowd from Killdicken was cheerin' like mad and so I decided to lead the Mother on a lap of honour. There's no doubt but pride comes before a fall. Halfway round the hall, the poteen struck and sent the place spinnin' out of control. I collapsed in a heap. Meanwhile the Mother landed in Tom Walshe's arms.

I woke to find Dr Doherty shinin' a torch in my eyes while Canon McGrath whispered an Act of Contrition in my ear. The next voice I heard was that of Tom Cantwell shoutin', 'Take him home and feed him.' Good man, Tom.

The followin' mornin' I woke to the sweet smell of a fry. The Mother had the pan full of sausages, rashers, puddin's and eggs. I spent an hour eatin' and I felt great. I was ready to plough. The Mother told me she never wanted to hear the word diet again, we both agreed that it's better for life to be short and happy than long and miserable. The diet is in the bin and I'm back at the table.

THE HEART AND THE HOSPITAL

This week I starred in my own hospital soap opera. Since my old friend Dixie Ryan and my sparrin' partner Breda Quinn (Superquinn) got married everyone knows I've had little or no contact with them. That was until last week when they overtook myself and the Mother at speed on the Clonmel road. 'Huh!' grunted the Mother. 'Since he married that one he tears around the place like a greyhound with a sore backside. She has him nearly killed.' With that we came around a bend and almost crashed into their car and it stopped dead in the middle of the road. The front doors were open and Superquinn appeared to be tryin' to drag Dixie out of the driver's seat. 'Look,' says the Mother, 'he was obviously goin' too slow for her.' 'No,' says I, 'there's somethin' wrong.' I went up to the car to find Dixie had collapsed behind the wheel. 'He's gone, he's gone, he's gone!' panted a breathless Superquinn as we laid him down on the side of the road.

The Mother took over operations and told me to call an ambulance. She then got down on her knees beside Dixie and with one hand on top of the other began to pump his chest as if she was tryin' to close an overloaded suitcase. 'What happened?' she asked Superquinn, who was on her knees at the other side of Dixie. 'We were hurryin' back to meet the accountant and he complained of a pain in his chest. The next thing I knew he slammed on the brakes and slumped over the steerin' wheel.'

There was no mobile phone signal so the Mother decided we'd have to take him to Clonmel ourselves. She kept pumpin' his chest and when he began to breathe again we prepared to carry him to her car. As we lifted him he broke wind quite loudly, promptin' a swift rebuke from Superquinn, 'For God's sake, Richard, control yourself.' 'By God,' says I, 'I thought you'd be used to his eloquence by now.' 'Shut up, the pair of ye,' snapped the Mother. 'Where there's life there's hope. Any sign of life is welcome, from whatever end it comes.' I was tempted to say somethin' about an ill wind, but thought better of it. We stretched Dixie out on the reclined passenger seat, while myself and Superquinn packed into what was left of the back seat. The Mother took off like Michael Schumacher, with the undercarriage of the Micra knockin' sparks off the road.

As soon as we got to Accident and Emergency, Dixie was wheeled off to Intensive Care. The Mother and myself were about to leave when Superquinn started cryin' and asked if I'd stay with her. I agreed, so we sat in the waitin' room drinkin' coffee and talkin'. I recounted stories of the many excursions I undertook with Dixie and the various scrapes we got into. The conversation eventually got around to discussin' our own ill-fated relationship. Superquinn agreed with me that we were lucky to escape one another. 'If you had married me,' says I, 'we'd both be in Intensive Care by now.' 'No,' she responded. 'You'd be in Intensive Care and I'd be in a padded cell.'

We were in knots laughin' when a very severe-lookin' consultant appeared. 'Mrs Ryan,' he intoned crossly, 'you may be interested to know that your husband is recovering. If you're finished having fun with your friend, you might like to see him.' I thought Superquinn would devour him. But no, she turned and gave me a big smather of a kiss. 'Wait here, Honey,' says she, 'I won't be a minute.' With that she took the stunned consultant by the arm, 'Now, doctor darling, be a dear and take me to my poor sick husband.' 'Twas great to be back on good terms with Superquinn and Dixie.

KILLDICKEN NOTES

While Mary Moloney is soakin' up the sun in Ballybunion, I'm saddled with her bit of scribblin' for the local paper.

Waltzing Festival

The first Killdicken Old Time Waltzin' Festival was deemed a resounding success by all concerned. However, like everything else in Killdicken, controversy haunted the event. Ten couples danced in the finals and, to the great delight of the vast majority of the people, a most popular and unusual dancing partnership emerged as winners. The packed community hall went wild when chairman of the judges, RTÉ's John Creedon, announced that Canon McGrath and the Reverend Winifred Whistletweel had waltzed their way to victory.

No sooner had their Reverences accepted the Golden Trotter Award than the recriminations began. Runners up, Cissy and Tom Mangan of Honetyne, were not one bit happy with the result. They accused the judges of being blinded by the celebrity status of the winning couple while turning a blind eye to their 'dodgy' dancing. Third-placed Tim and Regina Furlong of Teerawadra were visibly upset at their placing and their prize. 'It's bad enough to come third,' declared a furious Regina, 'but to be handed a voucher for lunch in Tom Walshe's shebeen adds insult to injury. They might as well have given us a bag of Taytos and a can of Fanta.'

The Reverend Winifred and Canon McGrath are over the moon with their win. However, everyone is wondering what they will do with their prize: a weekend for two in Tramore.

Community Motoring Scheme Brought to a Halt

Judge Maurice Cruthers had harsh words for members of six Cossatrasna families who appeared before him in Clonmel District Court last Thursday. James Ryan, Mick O'Brien, Richard Cregan and Bernie Dillon pleaded guilty to driving without tax, insurance and NCT certification at Cossatrasna on 8 April 2005. Mary Houlihan pleaded guilty to the charge of failing to display a current tax, insurance and NCT disc on the same date, while Sean Gleeson pleaded guilty to displaying incorrect tax, insurance and NCT discs in Clonmel, also on the same date.

According to Sergeant Miller of Killdicken the people in Cossatrasna had invented their own community motoring scheme. Under the scheme, the neighbours identified one car in the townland, which they taxed, insured and got tested for the NCT. As Mary Houlihan possessed the car that attracted the lowest road tax, a Daihatsu Charade (950cc), this was the chosen vehicle for all official documentation. Sergeant Miller explained to the court that when driving around the locality, the neighbours did so without discs of any kind. However, if they were driving to Clonmel or further afield, they would borrow the discs from Mary Houlihan and give them back on their return to the safety of Cossatrasna.

Judge Cruthers declared himself to be flabbergasted at what he called 'this community scam'. Addressing the defendants directly he said: 'There is an uncanny similarity between the name of your townland, Cossatrasna, and a name used by the Mafia, "Cosa Nostra". We cannot stand by and allow every townland in the place to turn itself into a lawless little Sicily.' He fined each of the defendants €1,000 and ordered them to attend ten civics classes to be delivered by Sergeant Miller. Everyone agreed that Sergeant Miller got the heaviest sentence of the day.

Jersey Mystery

Killdicken GAA is anxious to hear from anyone with information on the whereabouts of its Junior B hurling jerseys. The entire kit went missing last

Friday night from Millie Moran's pub in Shronefodda. Mixie Dunne, club chairman, is also anxious to trace four sets of false teeth, five sets of contact lenses and assorted personal underwear that disappeared from the Killdicken dressing room at Shronefodda GAA grounds earlier that evening. Is there nothing safe?

PUB TALK

You'll remember that I was off the drink while I was on that hoor of a diet. That didn't stop me goin' to Walshe's most nights for a few pints of Adam's ale. 'Twas a real education to sit there and listen as the drink took the conversation from sense to nonsense to pure baloney.

Many's the mornin' after a night before I'd swear to the Mother that I'd never sit through scutter like that again. She'd put me in my place fairly lively. 'Don't you be gettin' up on your high horse,' she'd say. 'Over the years you've contributed more than your share of hot air to the history of pub talk, and I'm sure you've a lot more left in you.' 'Tis true for her.

It doesn't take much to get conversation goin' in a public house. In recent years, the telly is the most common jump-lead for such banter. I was in Walshe's one night in the company of Pa Quirke, Tom Cantwell, Pa Cantillon and Tom Walshe himself. There was somethin' on the telly about the royal family of Monaco. Royalty became the topic of the moment, with no shortage of comment on royal exploits in the stable, on the ski slope and in the bedroom.

It was all sensible enough until the topic was eventually abandoned for another. Pub talk is a bit like a badly-disciplined huntin' dog: it follows every hare that rises. However, as we know, hares run in circles and so does bar conversation. About two hours and a few gallons later, the topic of royals was revisited with particular attention to the history of madness that affects most royal households. At this stage Tom Cantwell came into his own. 'That's all caused by lead poisonin',' he declared, with a sideways nod of the head. 'You see, every royal palace is constantly being painted. Just before their highnesses visit each one, the painters have to make sure the place is spankin' new for them. If they're invited to open a community hall or a school or visit a hospital, the last man to leave before the royals arrive is the painter. Now, years ago, one of the main ingredients in paint was lead, and lead can have awful effects. Sure, any painter you ever knew either died young or went mad. So it is with the royals. Those that don't die young, go mad from lead poisonin'.' Cantwell concluded his thesis with another sideways nod of his head.

'Well, do you know somethin'?' chimed in Quirke, 'You're damn right. There isn't one royal that can walk straight. They're worn out from pullin' all that lead around in their veins. I mean have you ever seen a royal runnin'? You won't because they can't. They can just about pull their arses after them.' Cantillon decided to add his tuppence worth and came at the topic from an equestrian angle. 'Sure, they say,' says he, 'that Prince Charles has to get a new horse every six months for playin' polo. The horses do be killed from carryin' him around.'

Cantwell, now fully fuelled by a gallon and a half of porter, re-entered the discussion with a dramatic revelation. 'Do ye remember the auld Queen Mother?' he asked. 'Well, she was walkin' with lead. They say her teeth were lethal altogether. It's a little-known fact that the people around her wore bulletproof vests at all times in case she sneezed and a tooth came loose. Sure 'twould kill a man at twenty paces.' As they all nodded knowingly at this last bit of lunacy I decided 'twas time to go home to the safety of my own house and into the care my own lead-free Mother.

SNATCHIN' DEFEAT FROM THE JAWS OF VICTORY

I found out durin' the week that the high moral ground is only a few paces from a big drop.

It all started when I opened the *Weekly Eyeopener* on Wednesday and found Killdicken at the bottom of a litter survey and at the top of the news. 'Kill-dirty-dicken' screamed the headline over a picture of our main street and it submerged under burger papers, chip bags, bottles and cans.

This litter survey of the county had been undertaken by my colleague Pipplemoth Davis and his woolly-jumpered friends. They had chosen to inspect Killdicken on the mornin' after the Old Time Waltzin' Festival. Why wouldn't the place be dirty? There had been over two thousand people in the village the night before. To crown it all, Pipplemoth used the survey to attack *me*. He accused me of bein' 'a central part of the litter problem' with my campaign to bring back the plastic bag.

Well, I rang Tony McGrath, a reporter with the *Eyeopener* and accused Pipplemoth of organisin' the Killdicken inspection on the day he knew the village would look its worst. I said he was willin' to sacrifice the good name of Killdicken for the sake of a few cheap political points scored at my expense. When McGrath asked me if I had reconsidered my attitude to the ban on plastic bags I told him I had not. 'If the people of Killdicken and our visitors had plastic bags on the weekend in question,' says I, 'they'd have been able to take home their own litter.' I was on the high moral ground, I had Pipplemoth on the run and should have stopped there. But no, I lost the run of myself and expanded on my theme.

'Do you know another thing, Tony?' says I. 'The disappearance of the plastic bag has had more side-effects than people admit. I'll bet you that there are a lot more women on blood-pressure tablets since that feckin' ban came in. If you're ever in a supermarket queue on a Friday you'll see what I'm talkin' about. At least one in every five women who arrives at the check-out with her trolley-load of groceries will be heard to cry out, "Jesus, Mary and Joseph, I left the feckin' shoppin' bags in the car." With that, these unfit women become like heifers in bad need of the bull. They jump over whatever chain or barrier is in their way and take off runnin' for the carpark. They return five minutes later in an even worse state, with one hand longer than the other. The bags are inevitably buried under the calf nuts that were picked up at the Co-op or they're covered in oil and grease from the last hydraulic hose that burst doin' the silage. These poor distraught women then have to go searchin' for someone who might know where to get a few boxes. They're inevitably landed with cardboard monstrosities as big as pallets that wouldn't fit into a trailer. These poor misfortunes are seen leavin' the supermarket, hangin' on to trolleys piled high with wobblin' boxes. Now, Tony,' says I to the reporter, 'this plastic-bag issue is not just about litter, 'tis a huge women's health issue and no-one but me is talkin' about it.'

I was sure I had done a great day's work for women and my community, and couldn't wait for this week's paper to arrive. Arrive it did, and I've been in hidin' since. The first one on the phone on Wednesday mornin' was Willy De Wig Ryan from the Sticks FM. 'Have you seen de headline in d'*Eyeopener*?' he asked. 'No,' says I. 'Let me read it to you,' says he. '"Women Shoppers Like Heifers in Need of Bull, Says Hickey".' I hung up and got the Mother to drive me to the cousin in Kilkenny.

HATE MALE

I have drawn the anger of Mná na hÉireann down on me. Thank God I went to Kilkenny for a few days to lie low. My mobile phone collapsed under the weight of the messages and it seems the e-mail system in County Hall packed up due to the volume of stuff comin' to my address. Luckily, after the Mother dropped me in Kilkenny, she went on to the aunt in Dublin. She wasn't at home for the hate mail either.

On Tuesday I decided to face my public and took the bus back to Killdicken. The first person I met was the postman, Pa Quirke. 'It's like Valentine's Day for you, Maurice,' he shouted across the street. 'You're gettin' a full bag of post these days.' When I got home I could hardly open the door with the amount of letters jammed behind it. It took ten minutes to gather them up and put them on the kitchen table. I decided to make tay before I faced into them, but after readin' the first one I needed a drop of the quare stuff.

The abuse I got in one letter after another had to be read to be believed. Here is a taste of it.

Tyrawadra
21st Century

How does one address a chauvinist like you? I'll try 'Oink!'
Oink Councillor Hickey,
I have put up with my share of insults over the years but the last grunt from your particular pigsty is among the lowest.
I am a woman like those you describe in your interview. Many a time I arrive at the check-out with a full trolley only to discover that my 'bags for life' are in the car, which is in the carpark. And yes, I do abandon trolley and children to make a mad dash to get them. You see, the €1.50 it will cost me to buy your much-beloved plastic bags is money I don't come by too easily. Unlike you, I don't get expenses for picking my own nits.
As for acting like a 'heifer in bad need of the bull' and jumping over chains, let me tell you, the particular bull in my life wouldn't entice me to jump over much. More than likely, while I'm struggling with a full trolley and three exhausted children on a Friday evening, he's at a watering hole with other males of the species celebrating his hunting and gathering. By the time he gets home the only one to jump at him is the dog.
They say that people get the public representatives they deserve. Do I deserve a chauvinist like you? I can't even think of a sow that would deserve you. She most certainly would spend a lot of her life in 'dire need' of decent male companionship.
Oink, Oink.
A Trolley Sister

That was mild compared to some epistles that I got. The short ones were the most dangerous.

Hickey

If this heifer happens to meet you on the road, by the time she's finished with you, 'tisn't a bull she'll be needing but a panel beater. You'll be in bad need of an ambulance.

Furious,
Fidelma

The last one I read before goin' to bed and coverin' my head was a sort of a large postcard. On the front was a picture of a dinosaur with a cut-out of my head pasted onto the top of his long neck. At the back was a one-line question: *How are things in Jurassic Park?*

A RING OF FIRE

When Pa Cantillon gets drunk he hangs on to conversation with the aid of auld sayin's and proverbs. As soon as his brain is too sozzled to think for itself it falls back on a store of these things, and more often than not they come out arseways. He has been known to deliver extraordinary pearls of wisdom such as: ''Tis a long bend that doesn't have a turn,' or: ''Tis a long turn that doesn't have a road.' A drunken Cantillon version of one auld sayin' sums up my current situation: 'God never closes one door without shuttin' another.'

I don't have to remind ye that I got into awful trouble with Mná na hÉireann recently when I compared them to what my Limerick cousins might call 'ramblin' heifers'. I got such a mountain of poisonous letters from disgruntled members of the sisterhood, that disposin' of them became a problem. Would I hire a skip? 'Twas too dangerous to put them in the wheelie bin. What if the local media got a hold of them? I decided there was nothin' for it but to burn them in the back yard.

By Thursday, the flow of letters was down to a trickle. At that stage I had ten full black bags. 'Twas time to destroy the evidence. After the breakfast I took an auld barrel from the shed, piled the letters into it and set fire to the lot. It was just lightin' when the phone rang and I went in to answer it. Tinky Ryan, undertaker and entrepreneur from Budnanossal, was on about the cost of emission controls at his sawmill. Little did I realise that while I was listenin' to Tinky's problems, the emissions from my own back garden were incineratin' my political career.

The unattended fire had taken off in earnest and, to make matters worse, a wind rose and carried burnin' bits of paper all over the village. Unfortunately, May Gleeson, my neighbour and first cousin of my fellow councillor, Moll Gleeson of Fine Gael, had a line of washin' out since the evenin' before. When my smoulderin' embers alighted on a pair of May's dry undies there was instantaneous combustion. One fiery knickers led to another and, in seconds, the washin' line was a towerin' inferno.

As soon as May and the garden hose got her blazin' lingerie under control, she phoned the Council fire wardens. There happened to be one on duty in the locality. I had just hung up from Tinky when I heard a rap on the door. I opened it to be confronted by a man in an unfamiliar uniform. He wasn't a guard and he wasn't a postman. If he was a traffic warden, then he had wandered far from the kind of civilised place that has illegal parkin', traffic jams and drug problems.

Before I had time to enquire if he was lost, he cleared his throat and, with all the certainty of a sergeant arrivin' in a pub after hours, he declared, 'I have reason to believe that you are illegally disposing of waste material by burning it on this property.' Now, he was standin' at my front door with a full view out the back door to where the letters from my incensed female constituents were blazin' like an Iraqi oilfield. He might as well have said, 'Sir, I have reason to believe you have a rectum in your trousers.'

The upshot of the whole thing is, I am to be taken to court by the environmental section of my own county council. I am to be charged with illegally burnin' rubbish. How can I survive this politically?

All I can think of is one particularly convoluted pearl of wisdom that fell from the lips of a very drunk Pa Cantillon on the night Ireland drew nil–nil with Liechtenstein. As we gazed in total disbelief at the television, he declared, 'There's no ill wind like your own ill wind.'

But what was I goin' to do about the public disaster that was about to befall me in the form of an ill wind generated by my own council? I chatted to Cantwell about it – he's a cuter hoor than all of them put together. 'Listen,' says he, 'why don't you ring the County Manager and tell him you're goin' to the press about this heavy-handed interference in people's lives. The last thing he'll want is a public campaign against his new litter wardens driven by you, given your campaign on the plastic bags.'

Sure enough, I rang the manager and he was only too willin' to negotiate. He agreed to tell the wardens to go easy with the pen if I would tell my constituents to go easy with the box of matches.

As Pa Cantillon might say, 'You scratch your back and I'll scratch my own.

A REAL LIVE CONSULTANT

Community Council chairman, Tom Walshe, is under fierce pressure. The Community Council has a matter of weeks to spend five grand it got from the regional tourism office to hire a walkin' consultant to develop walks on Crookdeedy, our local mountain. I made a few phone calls to mountainy colleagues in Wicklow who recommended one particular expert, Terry Hollow. For someone supposed to be an expert on hills, the name didn't inspire great confidence. Anyway the person was hired and last Saturday there was a gatherin' at Pa Cantillon's yard in preparation to climb the mountain.

Myself and Tom Walshe waited for the consultant at the community hall in case he'd get lost on the way to Cantillon's. We were lookin' out for a Mercedes or a four-by-four, when a yellow motorbike, ridden by a figure in full yellow leather and matchin' helmet, roared down the street. Tom looked at me and grunted: 'The last feckin' thing we need today are these feckin' bikers. This is probably the first of a swarm.'

The bike pulled in beside us and a perfectly proportioned figure in tight leather dismounted. The helmet was removed and the most beautiful locks of blonde hair you ever saw fell in waves down on the shoulders of a gorgeous young woman. She shook the mane like one of them young wans in a shampoo ad and turned to us. 'I'm looking for Councillor Hickey,' says she. Jaysus, I nearly fainted. The finest woman ever to ride into the parish was lookin' for *me*. 'Actually, in fact, I'm Councillor Hickey,' I grunted. She stretched out the hand and gave me a big smile. 'Hi Councillor, I'm Terry Hollow, the walking consultant. I believe you have a mountain for me to climb.' 'Begod I have,' says I. Without thinkin', I added, 'And I wouldn't mind bein' the mountain if 'twas you was doin' the climbin'.' 'I beg your pardon, what did you say?' she asked. 'Oh I just said I hope you don't mind the bit of climbin'.' Tom Walshe was starin' at me and, if looks could kill, I'd be brown bread.

'Let's go, then,' she declared and took off at a sprint. By the time Walshe and myself caught up with her she was at Cantillon's gate. We were fecked, but she was just warmed up. As we made our way towards the crowd in the yard I put my foot in it again. 'If I was in them leathers I'd be sweatin' like a horse,' says I. 'Don't worry, Councillor Hickey,' she shot back, 'by the end of the day you'll certainly be sweating, but not in these leathers.'

Well, she took us around Crookdeedy at breakneck speed. By the time 'twas over, Moll Gleeson had enough ladders in her stockin's to equip the fire brigade, Lilly Mac lost a wellie in the muck and I had a severe dose of erosion in my undercarriage. Ms Hollow was none too impressed with our mountain. She said there was more interestin' things to be seen in a housin' estate in Clonmel. She thought the route was more like an assault course than a walkin' path.

Pa Cantillon invited everyone in for tea. By the time the crowd left he was cleaned out of tea, ham sandwiches, Vaseline and Band Aids. To my delight, Ms Hollow asked me to accompany her back to her bike. I forgot about my wounded undercarriage as the foolishness of the hopeful male overtook me. Off I trotted after the vision in yellow leather. When we got to the bike she unzipped her jacket and pulled out an envelope. 'My invoice, Councillor Hickey. I trust you won't sweat too much over it.' With that, she mounted her machine and, like any consultant worth her salt, she left me holdin' the bill.

RADIO GAG(A)

There's public uproar around here at the moment. Last week our local radio station, The Sticks FM, sacked its most popular and controversial personality, Willy De Wig Ryan. De Wig is a radio legend in these parts and while he'd drive you mad, you have to listen to him. Up to last Thursday he presented 'De Top of de Egg', the mornin' talk show on The Sticks. De Wig loved to describe the show as 'De programme dat laves no yoke unpoked.' Unfortunately, he poked the wrong yokes once too often.

As a broadcaster, he was the loosest cannon you ever came across. He used the burnin' issues of the day as an excuse for a bit of gallery. He had no interest in facts, figures, policies or promises. Once he got you in front of the microphone he could ask you anythin' or say anythin'.

A few weeks ago I found myself on 'De Top of De Egg' to talk about the lack of jobs in Killdicken. Just as I arrived at the studio he was finishin' a telephone interview on men's health with a local GP. The conversation concluded with a discussion on prostate cancer and the tell-tale signs men should look out for if things aren't right in that department.

As soon as De Wig started to introduce me I knew I was in trouble. 'Now, listeners, I'm jined by one of my favourite local politicians. His fadder was at it and his fadder before him was at it and now Councillor Maurice is at it: I'm talking about local politics, of course. Ye all tink I was talking about d'udder ting, but sure, maybe dey were all at dat too.' This interview was turnin' out to be a bad idea. I was sweatin' when De Wig turned to me: 'Councillor Maurice, I know dat you're very cross about de lack of job opportunities locally, but I was just talkin' to De Doc Doherty about men's helt and d'auld prostate, maybe we could begin with a few words about dat? Do you get d'auld undercarriage checked out frequently?' I nearly died. 'I suppose,' I stuttered, 'I don't have a check-up as often as I should.' 'Well now, Councillor Maurice,' interrupted De Wig, 'after my little conversation wit De Doc Doherty I'd be in a fair position to give a diagnosis if you'll answer a few questions.'

My heart passed my prostate like a bullet as it sank to my boots. Willy De Wig was liable to ask me to put my crown jewels up on the table. Lucky 'twas only live radio and not live telly. 'Now, Councillor Maurice,' continued De Wig, 'when you're answerin' de call of nature would you describe your performance as a power-hose in full flow or a lakin' tap drippin'?' He didn't stop there. 'In other words,' he continued, 'would you overshoot a five-bar gate or would you just spatter your boots? Now, let me tell you, if you're in the boot-spatterin' department, you'd want to be makin' plans to mount de ramp and have de gearbox looked at. 'Tis as simple as dat.' Lucky for me the eleven o'clock news put an end to the interview and I escaped.

However, De Wig himself didn't escape as easily. He was on air givin' out yards about de legal profession when a well-connected barrister phoned in to defend it. After lettin' him talk for a few minutes, De Wig interrupted with a question, 'Tell me, sir, as an outsider, what do you tink of de human race?' De Wig got his walkin' papers the followin' day.

PEOPLE POWER

If I'm ever sacked from the council I hope my constituents are half as loyal to me as Willy De Wig Ryan's listeners are to him. The people are up in arms since he got his marchin' papers from the The Sticks FM after sailin' too close to the wind.

As a broadcaster, De Wig viewed his guests and listeners as fair game for entertainment. But he was playin' with fire. You see, The Sticks FM is a locally-owned pirate station and lately the owners have been puttin' out feelers about legalisin' the operation. 'Twas easy to threaten them with bein' shut down and that's exactly what happened when De Wig got on the wrong side of a few powerful people.

After he was sacked, there was a 'public outcry', as they say in the media. One thing led to another and a protest meetin' was organised for the Community Centre in Killdicken. The place was thronged. They came in cars, tractors, bikes, Honda 50s and walkin' frames. Everyone who was anyone, includin' my good self, addressed the gatherin'. No heroic defender of free speech, from Cúchulainn to Martin Luther King, was left in peace by the speakers. One by one they were dragged out to give weight to the case for the reinstatement of Willy De Wig Ryan. Never in the history of speechifyin' were so many dead celebrities enlisted to assist in the salvation of such a looderamawn. When a certain contributor quoted Saddam Hussein in support of the cause, Chairman Tom Walshe decided 'twas time to call a halt.

It was agreed that a protest march would be no good. You see, The Sticks FM is broadcast from a caravan behind a disused shop in Honetyne. If there was a protest march to the location, the guards would have no option but to act and 'twould be the end of The Sticks FM.

A campaign of public agitation was proposed. Lilly Mac suggested a boycott of advertisin' on the station. 'Hit them where it hurts,' she exclaimed. 'Hit them in the pocket. No one should advertise with them till Willy is back on the air. That includes the death notices. The crowd at The Sticks FM know that if we have no funerals to listen for we'll tune in to that long skoorloon who took Marian Finucane's job – what's his name, Brian Rubsidy.'

Nell Regan, Canon McGrath's housekeeper, offered to nobble the death notices. She said she'd get the Canon's sick list and ask everyone on it to leave instructions that their death was not to be broadcast on The Sticks FM unless Willy De Wig was back on the air.

There's a powerful campaign under full steam. Nell is policin' the ban on death notices like the Gestapo. The crowd at The Sticks got cute and would phone the funeral homes for the names of the dead and the times of the arrangements. If they did, Nell's contacts tipped her off and she'd ring the radio station threatenin' them with bein' haunted by the disturbed souls of Willy De Wig's deceased fans.

De Wig Ryan is surely a big hit with the women. The ICA have had

T-shirts printed bearin' all kinds of slogans such as: 'De Wig is De Only Wan'; 'The Ryan Line is Broken: Bring Him Back'; 'No Wig: No Wadio'. However, the campaign is havin' unexpected side-effects. A few nights ago, the ICA had a specialist speaker booked to give them a talk on dealin' with the menopause. When he turned to face his audience he made umpteen attempts to get started and failed. It's hard to blame the man. How do you talk about the menopause to a crowd of women arrayed in front of you in T-shirts emblazoned with the slogan, 'Bring Back Willy'.

THE NUCLEAR OPTION

The campaign to reinstate De Wig to the local pirate station took one step forward, moved kinda sideways and exploded. Station bosses at The Sticks FM weren't long realisin' that the people had turned off and weren't turnin' back on. The phonelines were as quiet as a monastery, the ads were dryin' up and the station wasn't gettin' the smell of a funeral.

I was in the scratcher on Wednesday mornin' when the Mother came home from Mass with the news that De Wig was back on the radio. While 'twas a relief that the tomfoolery of the campaign was over, my stomach turned when I heard how the thing was solved. It emerged that a deal was brokered by none other than that hoor of a councillor to share an electoral area with, Percy Pipplemoth Davis. He'd use his own mother to get publicity. I was furious. After my high-profile presence throughout the campaign, on comes this slithery, slythery snake who didn't raise a finger, and here he was, about to take all the credit. I shouldn't have worried my head. Pipplemoth is too cute for his own good – I suppose you could say he's so crooked he regularly snares himself in his own nets.

The delight that De Wig was back soon turned to disgust when the details of the 'Pipplemoth Deal' became known. De Wig's mornin' programme, 'De Top of de Egg', was to be dropped. Instead he was goin' to be on air from midnight to two in the mornin' with a programme called 'The Scrapin's of the Bag'. 'Only the owls and the bats will be listenin' to the poor hoor,' declared a furious Superquinn, who had put her considerable weight behind the campaign.

People were still recoverin' from the news of De Wig's late-night banishment when they were hit with another mallet as they tuned in to The Sticks the followin' mornin'. Everyone was anxious to know what was bein' broadcast in place of De Wig. Well, you could almost hear the sound of radio sets bein' fired out kitchen windows as the new show took to the airwaves. 'Good morrow, good people and welcome to "The Lark and the Pipplemoth", your all-new daily feast of fine radio. Percy Pipplemoth Davis here and I'll be with you every morning to butter your scones and deepen the aroma of your morning coffee.'

There was total outrage. 'Did you hear that?' gasped the Mother. 'He'll deepen the aroma of our mornin' coffee, I ask you? The only aroma deepenin' around here is the smell from that rotten, dirty, double-crossin' hoor. If someone doesn't put him off the air, I will. I'll drive my little Micra through the side of that caravan they call a studio.' 'Twas time to act before people started to take the law into their own hands. Whatever about survivin' Pipplemoth's schemes, I would be in deep political trouble if the Mother ended up in Mountjoy for takin' out the opposition.

There's one thing about Pipplemoth that can't be denied, he has a neck that's as tough as a jockey's undercarriage. The phonelines to the station were red from abusive phone calls but he kept broadcastin' regardless. People were so annoyed, I was afraid they'd lynch Pipplemoth. I ran out to the Honetyne road and thumbed a lift to the station on the Co-op milk lorry.

I was too late. Pa Cantillon had the radio on in his tractor as he drove out to spread a load of slurry. When he heard Pipplemoth announcin' his new show he drove straight to Honetyne, backed his load of slurry into where the broadcast caravan was parked and blasted the radio station to kingdom come. I don't know if 'twas a misprint or not, but the headline in the *Eyeopener* said it all: 'Pirate Radio Station Shite Down by Farmer'.

A-RAMBLIN' I WILL GO

The tradition of ramblin' to the neighbours still goes on around here, especially in the winter months. On the night I don't have a meetin' there's many a warm fire to ramble to where there's great tea and better stories.

I do love an auld ramble. November to Christmas is a great time for it because many of the pub regulars give up the drink for the month and stay off it till the 8th of December. Rather than put themselves in temptation's way, they avoid the high stool by visitin' the neighbours.

Like everythin' else, the tradition isn't without its drawbacks. In ramblin' houses where there's mountains of talk, small stories often develop very long legs. I know of a man who was in hospital with an ingrown toenail. I heard it for a fact at a ramblin' house that he was dyin'. With the authority of a surgeon someone said: 'The doctors took one look at the toe and said there was nothin' they could do for it. He was sent home to die. All that's left for him is the measurin' tape and the rosary beads.'

Within half an hour the man was dead and buried, the will was read, the relations were fightin' and the land divided. When the supposed corpse turned up at a ramblin' house a few nights later everyone told him how well he looked. Not one of them was embarrassed at the misdiagnosis and the grim prognosis they arrived at concernin' his health and longevity. Barefaced, they told him they knew he'd pull out of it because his people were always made of tough stuff. Then, without battin' an eyelid, they turned their attention to the next juicy bit of news.

A few years ago, I myself was the subject of a ramblin' house rumour. I have always suffered with my back. In fact, my difficulty with holdin' down a normal job stems from this. I can't take too much sittin' or standin'. The

Mother thinks 'tis roguery. 'Isn't it a wonder, Maurice,' she says, 'that the only position you can remain in for any length of time is on the flat of your back. And isn't it a medical wonder that the hours you spend on a high stool don't affect it?'

She wasn't impressed when I suggested that she might be in denial about my condition. She told me that if she was as lazy as me 'tisn't in denial she'd be but in the Suir.

Anyway, a few years ago the back got so bad I had to attend a woman physiotherapist in Clonmel. Didn't Pa Quirke spot me goin' in to the clinic a few evenin's when he was comin' out from Clonmel after deliverin' to the post office. Now, Pa is a great friend of mine, but he's a hoor for news and a woeful gossip.

Late one night in a certain ramblin' house he told the hushed crowd that I was a regular visitor to a massage parlour in a local town. Now, Quirke might be a divil for news, but Pa Cantillon is worse, especially in winter when he has little to do. In fairness to Cantillon, he informed me on the quiet as to what they were all sayin' about me. I knew well he only told me because he wanted to hear all the gory details on the so-called massage parlour. I was furious, but pretended nothin'. With a wink and a nod, I encouraged him to experience it for himself. All he had to do was ring and make an appointment for 'muscle treatment'.

When I met him a few nights later at a crowded ramblin' house he was like a fella that had spent six months holdin' a jack-hammer. He shouted across the room at me: 'Hickey, that's no massage parlour you go to. 'Tis a feckin' torture chamber.' Ramblin' houses are great places to start and finish stories.

SELF-DESTRUCTION

My advisers tell me I need a political jump-start. I was in Tom Walshe's one evenin' in the company of my 'inner circle' – Walshe himself, Pa Cantillon, Pa Quirke and Tom Cantwell. The Mother describes them as 'the usual dose'.

Anyway, Walshe was behind the counter flickin' through the *Weekly*

Eyeopener. 'Begod, Maurice,' says he, 'there isn't one photograph of you in the paper and there's three of your Mother. She's doin' more to hold on to the family seat than you are.' 'True for you, Tom.' adds Quirke. 'Hickey, you're not makin' the runnin' on anythin' around here. You won't feel the next election comin' and you'll be expectin' us to bang on doors and get votes from people who'll look blankly at us and ask, "Maurice who?"'

'The farmin' vote is turnin' kinda green,' says Cantillon. 'You might have noticed we're gettin' fierce concerned about the Brazilian rain forest. Percy Pipplemoth could get a lot of support inside the farm gate.'

'You need a major issue to hang your political hat on,' declared Tom Cantwell. 'Find somethin' that will grab the headlines and go for it.'

This was like havin' your school report read out in public: Must do better.

With my head spinnin' from the avalanche of comment and advice, I finished my drink and walked home. I was no sooner in the door than the phone rang and within seconds I realised I had the 'major issue' Cantwell told me I needed.

Madge McInerney of Community Alert was on the line tellin' me that her cousin Mag Cahill, who lives on our local hill, Crookdeedy, is driven to distraction. 'In the black dark of early mornin', truckloads of fellas are drivin' into the forest stealin' Christmas trees,' whispered Madge. 'It's a disgrace. No-one is doin' anythin' about it. The forestry looks like a bombsite.'

The followin' day Madge took me to meet cousin Mag, as strong and determined a human bein' as you are likely to meet. Not only did she give me an account of the stealin' of the Christmas trees, she gave me a disk of photographs recordin' the thieves, the thievin' and the destruction. She could get no joy out of Coillte, the council or the guards. I promised to help. With the photographs in my pocket I came down the hill determined to show Walshe and Cantwell and all them feckers that Councillor Maurice Hickey was alive and kickin'.

I called a public meetin' for Monday night in the Community Centre. I prepared a mighty speech for the occasion and asked Cantwell to bring his laptop and projector to shine the photos onto the wall. Such a crowd turned up I was beginnin' to dream about a run for the Dáil.

I opened proceedin's with a picture show of the thieves and the destruction. I then launched a blisterin' attack: 'These devastaters of our forests are terrorisin' the community and usin' the Christmas season for naked profit. Where are the guards when you want 'em? Where is Coillte? It is time to protect our people and our forests from the greed of these profiteers.' The crowd nearly brought the roof down with the round of applause. As soon as the clappin' ended a man stood up and introduced himself as a representative of Coillte. I felt the tongue stickin' to my mouth as he explained that the 'thieves' in the photos were Coillte workers and the Christmas tree operation is entirely legitimate and above board.

I tried to rescue myself sayin' I was delighted with the clarification and relieved that the people of Crookdeedy could sleep safe in their beds. The crowd left in silence. Those who didn't glare at me stared at the ground. As Cantwell passed he looked at me from under his eyebrows. 'I suggested that you should find somethin' to hang your political hat on, not somethin' to swing your political neck from,' says he.

LORD, WON'T YOU BUY ME A MERCEDES BENZ

Durin' the week we buried one of our great characters, Tim Canty. 'Twas appropriate that he passed away near budget day as he was famous for his live commentary on ministerial budget speeches.

Since retirin' from the council twenty-five years ago, Tim went to Walshe's every day at three o'clock where he drank two pints and two small ones. As soon as he had those finished he went home. When RTÉ started doin' live broadcasts of the budget, a few of us would gather in the said public house to listen in and comfort one another in the face of the impendin' hardship. But more than anythin' we gathered to experience

Tim's reaction.

He was a dyed-in-the-wool Blueshirt and whenever Fine Gael were in power his commentary on the budget would be more positive than anythin' a top-notch spin doctor could produce. Even if the minister put a pound on the pint and a fiver on the fags, Tim would nod and say, 'Good man, good man, the country has to pay its way, good man.' Of course, tax hikes on the usual items brought roars of protest from the rest of us, but Tim would call for order and respect. He was like our own Ceann Comhairle.

However, when a Fianna Fáil government was deliverin' its budget, Tim had a different tune. With each announcement he'd have a new name for the misfortunate minister: 'You hoor; you mane hoor; you hoor's ghost; you robbin' b*****d.'

Of course, to add to his annoyance, we'd be demandin' order and respect for the man in ministerial office. Eventually Tim would stand up and hit the counter a wallop. 'He's no Finance Minister, he's just a robbin', thievin' son of a hoor's ghost who's takin' the bit of grub out of the mouths of hungry children to put petrol into his big, black, shiny marysheedy.'

That's all we wanted to hear: Tim's assault on the 'big, black, shiny ministerial marysheedy.' We'd collapse laughin' and he'd hit the counter another belt of his fist, finish his drink and turn to us with a dire warnin': 'Well ye might laugh, but when he and his likes drive past ye, blindin' ye with dust, I hope ye realise 'tis yer own money that's puttin' petrol into the very thing that's blindin' ye,' (and we'd all join in for the last line) 'that big, black, shiny marysheedy.'

In the lead-up to the latest budget, everyone knew 'twas goin' to be a sort of a Gay Byrne affair 'with somethin' for everyone in the audience'. We were dyin' to see Tim's reaction. Sure enough, he was in the pub as Brian Cowen got to his feet. With every bit of good news Tim just stared at the telly shakin' his head, proclaimin' ruination for the nation: 'Merciful God, he'll break the country'; 'There'll be nothin' left for the children.'

When the hike in the old-age pension was announced he had enough of

Cowen's generosity. 'What do we want it for?' he shouted at the telly. 'When we were young enough to spend it ye wouldn't give it to us.' Tom Walshe called order for the minister, but Tim was on his feet. 'He's no minister. He's more like the prodigal son squanderin' our hard-earned money on auld fellas with notions and young wans with too many children. Ye'll all pay for this yet. When the hungry days come back ye'll be scratchin' empty bellies while he's drivin' around the bogs of Offaly in his' (we all joined in the chorus) 'big, black, shiny marysheedy.'

Sadly, Tim got sick and died two days after the budget. There were more than a few smirks on our faces as we followed him to Poulnenave graveyard, and he stretched out in Tinky Ryan's new hearse: a big, black, shiny ...

HIGH DRAMA AND HILL-STARTS

The Christmas was what you might call an event of two halves. Drink, that great loosener of the tongue, played its part in both halves, with mixed results.

I'll start with the beginnin'. As had been arranged, Madge Quigley and her Uncle Dan from Chicago arrived for the dinner on Christmas day. You'll recall that himself and the Mother hit it big at the Sheepman's Ball. We got through the soup, the turkey and the puddin' without incident, but myself and Dan had been helpin' ourselves to the few jars along the way. As we tucked in to the Christmas cake he dropped a bombshell. You could say the truth seeped out through the liquor.

He declared that ''twould be a great idea if himself and the Mother got married and moved into our house.' Myself and the Mother were fairly stunned by that, but we were flattened completely when he went on to suggest that ''twould be the icin' on the cake if Madge and myself were to put our shoes under the one bed – in her place.'

I needn't tell you I sobered up fairly lively. Talk of nuptials is enough to bring any bachelor to his senses, but the prospect of an arranged marriage could drive a man into exile. The Mother wasn't impressed at all. She said nothin' but started clearin' the table with all the subtlety of a bulldozer. After the wash-up she strongly suggested that Madge and Dan should be gettin' on the road before it started to freeze. Indeed, the Mother herself was generatin' enough frost to bring on another ice age.

Once they had left she turned on the telly and parked herself in the armchair with the air of a woman who had sorted things out in her head. 'That's the end of that,' says she. ''Twas worth feedin' the pair of them to get to the bottom of their schemin'. Uncle Dan can feck off back to the Windy City and blow all he likes.' So much for the first half.

The second half of my eventful Christmas happened on St Stephen's Day when I found myself huntin' the wren with a crowd from the pub. We had a mighty time travellin' between houses and hostelries in the three parishes. 'Twas better than a month's canvassin'.

At about nine o'clock that night we ended up with Willy De Wig Ryan, live on air at The Sticks FM. The drop of drink had loosened all tongues and De Wig got more than he bargained for. As usual he was ollagonin' about how things have changed, how the auld neighbourliness is gone and only for traditions like huntin' the wren, Mother Ireland would be dead.

He was lamentin' the disappearance of cars that needed pushin' and tractors that only started on hills when a lubricated Pa Cantillon stopped him in his tracks. 'That reminds me of a story about your father,' says Pa to De Wig. 'What story is that?' asked De Wig. 'Well,' says Pa, 'your father was a well-known bandsman in this area. He even had his own showband.' 'Dat's right,' chimed in De Wig, 'Billyboy Ryan and De Lonesome Riders.' 'They were lonesome enough in that department all right,' continued Cantillon. 'Billyboy, your father, was fairly long in the tooth and not in great health when he married your mother, a younger woman. Isn't that right?' says he, checkin' his facts with De Wig. 'Dat's right,' says De Wig, who was beginnin' to get worried about where the story was goin'. Well he might.

'Well,' says Cantillon. 'Auld May Cantwell was in the post office when news came that your mother was in the family way.' 'Begod,' she said, 'that young missus must have parked Billyboy on the side of a hill. Sure he hasn't started off the button in years.' There was a big 'Yo ho' live on The Sticks FM as a redfaced Willy De Wig called for a commercial break.

DRUIDS, DIGGERS AND DESPERATE VIRGINS

I find it fierce hard to get goin' after the Christmas. A kick in the backside is the only thing to get me started. Such a kick arrived last Wednesday. I was just out of the scratcher when I got a call on the mobile that there was trouble over on the Honetyne Road.

You might remember that in April I made great political hay announcin' that a scheme of forty council houses was planned for Killdicken. The work was to begin in August at a site at Kyletalahan on the said Honetyne Road. However, that hoor of a colleague of mine, Councillor Percy Pipplemoth Davis, launched a campaign of objection that delayed everythin'.

He claimed the proposed site with its grove of trees was an ancient Druidic place of worship and there was evidence that human sacrifice had taken place there. It seems our Celtic ancestors were partial to the sacrifice of the odd virgin. In the course of a radio interview with Willy De Wig Ryan he vowed that the council would have to cut him in half before he'd let them touch a tree in Kyletalahan. I'm not sure about the status of Pipplemoth's virginity, but I'd have no objection if he wanted to have a go at bein' sacrificed. And he nearly did.

When my mobile rang on Wednesday mornin' 'twas Pa Cantillon. 'You better get your fat backside over here to Kyletalahan fairly lively,' says he. 'There's a line of bulldozers and diggers tryin' to get into the wood to start work on the council houses. Pipplemoth has chained himself to a tree and

is holdin' everythin' up. There's all kinds of media here.'

The Mother drove me straight to the Honetyne Road. When I got there the place was like a circus. Pipplemoth was sittin' on the branch of beech tree about fifteen feet above the ground. He had a chain around his belly and around the branch. Willy De Wig Ryan was hoisted up in the front bucket of a JCB conductin' an interview with him for The Sticks FM. An RTÉ camera crew and an interviewer were standin' on the roof of a van waitin' their turn to talk to Pipplemoth.

Mickey Mullins, the contractor, a bad-tempered man at the best of times, was at the foot of the tree wieldin' a chainsaw and shoutin', 'Come down, you mad b*****d, before I cut the perch out from under your cantankerous arse.'

Things looked like they could get nasty until Sergeant Miller arrived and him stuffed into a Fiat Punto. Once he squeezed himself out of the sardine tin they call a squad car, he ordered everyone to get off the site so he could begin 'negotiations with the protestor'.

He instructed Willy De Wig to get himself down from the bucket of the JCB, but unfortunately the driver was nowhere to be found. Mickey Mullins immediately volunteered to help and climbed into the cab where he proceeded to tip the front bucket, sendin' a desperate De Wig plungin' into the beech tree. De Wig grabbed Pipplemoth as he fell and the two tumbled together. However, Pipplemoth's chain prevented them from hittin' the ground and they finished up swingin' in mid-air like a pair of frightened monkeys.

An ambulance was called, the injured parties were taken to hospital and the protest was over. Or so we thought. Along with the County Manager who had arrived on the scene, I adjourned to Tom Walshe's for a stiffener. We were no sooner parked at the counter than a purple-faced Mickey Mullins burst through the door. 'I'm cursed. I'm cursed,' he bellowed. 'How can a fella make a bob when he's surrounded by lunatic environmentalists and nit-pickin' pen-pushers. The feckin' health and safety crowd have arrived now and closed the site. I should have swung the bucket of the JCB at that nut-case of a Pipplemonth and sacrificed the last virgin in Killdicken.'

THE WINDS OF CHANGE

The housin' development at Kyletalahan is held up. The site is sealed off with yella tape followin' the protest by Pipplemoth. Himself and Willy De Wig were taken to hospital, but released with only minor bruisin'. It seems De Wig refused treatment, claimin' he was fine. Of course, he has a thing for wearin' women's undies, and God only knows what kind of a contraption he had on.

Anyway, 'tis amazin' the kinds of things that are holdin' up buildin' projects around the country. The Port Tunnel and the Luas had their moments and here in Killdicken our own little development is held up, of course, by rumours of sacrificial virgins.

Tom Walshe, our local publican and Chairman of the Community Council, is ragin' over it. He spends his days behind the counter givin' lectures to anyone who'll listen. I suppose you could say he has a vested interest given that the housin' development is within walkin' distance of the village and would bring him a whole new crop of customers.

'We wouldn't be such a laughin' stock if 'twas held up because of drainage problems or somethin',' he declares, 'but to be held up because of quare things that might have happened in Kyletalahan when Adam was no more than a boy – that makes the whole village look ridiculous.' 'True for you,' agreed Tom Cantwell. 'But, sure, 'tis the health and safety crowd is the latest problem after De Wig brought Pipplemoth tumblin' out of the tree.' 'Now,' says Walshe, 'that's one pair of virgins that could do with havin' a match put to them. They'd be no loss.'

Postman Pa Quirke had just arrived after finishin' his rounds. Quirke, like many an eejit at this time of the year, thinks he can mend his ways. He's drinkin' only water. January is miserable enough without these public displays of self-denial. After the first sip from his glass of grey bubbles he decided to add his tuppence worth to the discussion. 'I think 'tis important to find out what kind of people inhabited this place before us. Remember them two fellas they found in bogs in Meath and Offaly? They're thousands of years old and 'tis fierce interestin' to hear what they were like and even what they had for their breakfast. If they ended up buried by the bucket of a JCB we'd never know these things.'

He might as well have thrown a petrol bomb over the counter at Tom Walshe. 'That's the blasted problem with this country,' Tom shouted. 'We're always lookin' back at the great things the people before us did. As far as I'm concerned the people who went before us made a total hames of a lot of things. Look at the railways. In the thirties, forties and fifties they closed most of them to save a few hundred pounds. Now we're spendin' billions openin' them again.'

Tom was on a roll and there was no stoppin' him. 'Do you know somethin' else?' he continued. 'Durin' the 1987 general election Charlie Haughey was passin' through this village and he came in here to relieve himself. The local FFers arrived ahead of him like a bunch of CIA men to make sure he got a clear run at the jacks. He left after he had his business done and that was the end of it. But now, at the rate things are goin', if I ever want to remodel this premises and knock that jacks I'm liable to have a delegation of FFers demandin' the place be preserved because Charlie Haughey once broke wind in that esteemed spot.'

With that, Cantwell hit the counter a belt of his fist and shouted: 'Good man yerself, Tom. That's it. Keep lookin' forward, and may the wind behind you always be your own.'

MAD DOGS AND IRISHMEN

Is it me or is it the rest of the world that's gone cracked? I can't understand how we heap all kinds of praise on people who badly need to keep takin' the tablets. I'm thinkin' of the two fellas who tried to cross the Atlantic in a rowboat. Did no-one tell them that if they went to Shannon and got on a plane they'd arrive at the other side in the full of their health, well rested and safe as houses? And if 'twas fear of flyin' that was at them, doesn't the *Queen Mary* sail from Southampton fairly frequently? But, sure, maybe they were in a bit of a rush and couldn't wait for the next sailin'.

Anyway, after the pair were plucked out of the water and brought to Spain by their Spanish rescuers it became clear that fear of flyin' wasn't their problem at all. As soon as they came ashore they hopped on a plane and flew home. Now, you'd expect their brush with the grim reaper would have led them to conclude that crossin' the ocean in a tub isn't a good idea. But no, not these boys. They announced they were hittin' for the rowboat again. If I was a friend of theirs I'd have cancelled the welcome home party and organised a security van and a pair of padded cells for them. After that, I'd put them pickin' stones. If 'tis hardship they want, it might as well be useful hardship.

These endurance junkies are everywhere. I was listenin' to the radio the other day and heard a fella boastin' about runnin' marathons at the North Pole, the South Pole and the Sahara desert. A total martyr for misery, this character was plannin' another long-distance trudge through some other god-forsaken place. Not only that, he had the cheek to put out an appeal for a sponsor to pay for his habit.

The world has more than enough hardship without people spendin' money goin' out lookin' for it. A few nights ago I was watchin' a programme on the telly about rickshaw drivers and men who haul loads for a livin' in Bangladesh. For a pittance these poor misfortunes spend their days doin' the work of draft horses and then die of exhaustion in their forties. Meanwhile, here we are at this side of the globe rollin' out red carpets for looderamawns who have nothin' better to do than inflict hardship on themselves because they seem to like it.

I have a suggestion about what should be done with people who declare a fondness for endurance and misery. Any man or woman who declares an intention to circumnavigate the world in a shoppin' trolley lined with plastic bags, or climb the Himalayas in Wellington boots usin' baler twine for rope, or cross the Gobi desert with one hand tied behind their back and their left ear stapled to the right cheek of their arse, I suggest that such people should be handed over to the United Nations. The UN could send them to a place that suits the kind of hardship they like and let them do somethin' useful with their addiction.

I made this suggestion at a council meetin' last week. I was givin' out that while there's no money to be had for repairin' the roads, there's fortunes bein' spent rescuin' mad hoors who do mad things. I got great support from everyone except Percy Pipplemoth Davis who claimed that the people I was complainin' about raise lots of money for charity. 'In fact,' he declared, 'I myself intend to climb Kilimanjaro in April to raise funds for the Irish Wolfhound Preservation Society. I'll be calling on all of you for your support.'

When he approached me with his sponsorship card I told him I wouldn't contribute to his junket, even if he climbed the mountain in flip-flops and a bikini, with an Irish Wolfhound draped around his neck.

FAREWELL TO DIXIE

It's been a sad week around these parts. My auld friend and travellin' companion, Dixie Ryan, passed away. He wasn't well these last couple of months and, thankfully, I got to see a lot of him before he coughed his last. 'Twas the fags put an end to him; the poor misfortune had a pair of lungs like tar barrels from the cursed things. His missus, Breda Quinn (Superquinn), nursed him at home and had an open door for anyone who wanted to visit. Even me.

You'll remember that the Mother tried to set me up with Breda in Lisdoonvarna a few years ago. Dixie drove me to the ambush but, between the jigs and the reels, 'twas he ended up with Superquinn. I came home on me own. There was a lot of frost between us for a good while after that until our little episode in the hospital, but since he got sick there's been a great thaw. I'm glad of it. I'd hate for him to have died and we not to have made up.

In the years before he married Superquinn we toured the country together. There wasn't a festival or a fair that was spared our presence. We did the Listowel races, the Willie Clancy, the coursin' in Clounanna, Puck Fair, Lisdoonvarna, the Ballinasloe horse fair, the Trip to Tipp, the Pope's visit and the fair of Cahermee. Since he got hitched, he barely got beyond the turf shed.

I remember one year, the Mother wanted us to go to Lough Derg to do a bit of penance for our sins. I hadn't a notion of goin' and tried every excuse to get out of it, but the Mother was determined to send me for a spiritual worm-dose. To my amazement, wasn't she being aided and abetted by the bould Dixie. I couldn't figure out why he was so agreeable to take on such a long journey in his banger of a Hillman Avenger. That yoke was a bigger threat to public safety than Sellafield.

Anyway, the day of departure to Lough Derg came and Dixie arrived in the Avenger. When I went to put my stuff in the boot I was kinda surprised to see 'twas loaded with sausages, rashers and puddin's, along with campin' gear, a fryin' pan and a kettle. 'I thought 'twas only bread and water was allowed in this place,' says I. 'Keep your mouth shut and hop in,' ordered Dixie.

As soon as we were out of sight he announced we were goin' to Sligo to the Ballisodare Folk Festival. All my Christmasses had come together. I loved the bit of hairy folk music, and the thoughts of seein' Planxty, the Bothy Band and Paul Brady was better than goin' to heaven. 'Ballisodare is only a stone's throw from Lough Derg,' says Dixie. 'When we get back you can tell the Mother the sermons were preached by a Fr Christopher Moore and confessions were heard by a very understandin' man, Fr Lunny.' We had a mighty weekend. Once we landed home the Mother interrogated us. In particular, she asked if we did the pilgrimage barefoot. 'Barefoot, Missus?' says Dixie. 'If we'd had the chance we'd have done it bareback.'

Sittin' beside his sick bed over the last few weeks we talked for Ireland. We went back over every trip and every session, to the point where I could nearly taste the porter, smell the fags and hear the rattle and splutter out of his auld cars. We had it all said when, at six o'clock last Friday evenin', poor auld Dixie passed away with only myself and Superquinn in the room.

She gave him the finest wake you ever saw. 'Twas lovely, 'twas gas crack and 'twas sad, very sad. Sayin' goodbye to Dixie, I suppose I said goodbye to the madness of the youth of us. Life is a quare thing.

MAGIC MUSHAROONS

Since he died, everythin' puts me in mind of poor auld Dixie Ryan. Even the ban on magic mushrooms (or musharoons as we call them around here) brings back memories. Himself and myself had an encounter with them yokes that I won't forget.

You see, Dixie was always buyin' and sellin'. Whenever you'd meet him he'd want to show you his latest purchase, which could be anythin' from moondust to Mongolian mareshite. 'That's the best of stuff,' he'd say, even though he wouldn't have a clue what 'twas for.

I remember as a young fella he bought a horsebox load of what looked like individually wrapped balloons. He took myself and Pa Quirke home to view these luxury inflatables, but hadn't his grandmother come on them and was busy blowin' them up for the youngsters. Dixie made out there was a killin' to be made at the school sellin' the things to the junior classes.

We were in the process of plannin' our profitable venture when Dr Doherty drove into the yard to see Granny Ryan. His eyes nearly fell out of his head when he got a close look at one of the balloons. 'Where did you get these things?' he demanded. 'I bought them, Doctor,' says Dixie. 'For what?' asked the doctor. 'For twenty pound,' answered Dixie, openin' the door of the horsebox. 'I'll give you thirty for the lot. Put them in my car.' 'You'll give me fifty,' says Dixie. 'You'll take thirty or I'll tell the guards,' barked auld Doherty. 'Those balloons are banned in this country, they give people backache. Now put them in my car at once.'

Within months of the doctor takin' the 'balloons' the birth rate in the locality fell dramatically. He quietly rationed out the things to women with big families and active husbands. A secret code developed to conceal the Killdicken family plannin' strategy. When a woman found herself in the family way for the third or fourth time 'twould be suggested to her that she might get herself 'a few balloons from Dr Johnny'.

Gettin' back to the magic musharoons – if the market demanded product, Dixie would supply. One time I was givin' him a hand to deliver a bull to Mary Kate Cleary in Budnanossal. Mary Kate was married to Jelly Cleary, a quiet auld misfortune. His full name was Jeremiah Lawrence, his mother called him JL, but when he went to school he became known as Jelly.

As we unloaded the bull, Dixie remarked that the animal would have no problems in the fatherin' department. ''Tis a pity I can't say the same about me own male specimen,' declared Mary Kate. 'Jelly by name and jelly by nature. I've tried every sort of coaxiorum and you might as well be attemptin' to raise the *Titanic*.' 'Begod,' says Dixie, 'I know a fella up in Slievenamon who's forever collectin' wild musharoons. He claims they can cure every ill known to man.' 'Well, Dixie,' says Mary Kate, 'get me a handful of them things and 'twill be worth more to you than the sale of the bull.'

Dixie delivered the magic musharoons, but in his excitement at makin' easy money he forgot to warn Mary Kate to administer the yokes in small doses. I was havin' a pint with him when he realised his mistake and we took off for Budnanossal like the hammers of hell. We were too late. We arrived to find Jelly perched on top of the hay-barn, naked as the day he was born and screechin' like a crow. Mary Kate was wanderin' around the haggard in an overcoat and not much else.

She turned on Dixie. 'What kind of feckin' stuff did you give me, Dixie Ryan? That mad hoor thinks he's an exotic bird and here's me stuck to the ground with the world of a want on me. Them musharoons are magic, all right. They've turned my fella into the first cousin of a cockatoo.'

That was the last I heard of magic musharoons till now.

CAUGHT IN THE NITRATES NET

'Tis lovely to see the stretch in the evenin's; you'd be tempted to think 'tis nearly summer. That could be a fatal mistake. There's many a man took off his coat at the first peep of sunshine and found himself in a shroud soon after. Anyway, spring is great; a time of singin' birds, leppin' lambs and lanky calves. Thanks be to God I can admire them all from a distance. I wouldn't fancy havin' to tend to the creatures every day. To be honest, I don't know how farmers do it. 'Tis true they have land and assets and all that, but spendin' your days from October to April workin' in muck and scutter is not my idea of a picnic. Even the tidiest farmer is forever tryin' to keep ahead of the shite.

Now, all the recent complainin' about nitrates is drivin' these mud-spattered misfortunes mad. They're bein' accused of poisonin' their land with fertiliser. And who is doin' the accusin' but fellas who spend hours in traffic jams spewin' out fumes on their way to air-conditioned offices.

I know this environmental crowd only too well. Haven't I spent the bones of two years fightin' them over the plastic bags? I can tell you that the ban on plastic bags is causin' more waste than anyone will admit. Every day you'll see women comin' out of Gleeson's shop and they tryin' to balance mountains of messages in their bare arms. You'd never risk salutin' one of them because if she moved a muscle it could bring the mountain totterin' down around her. Not a day goes by but there's a few dozen eggs, a few cartons of milk and various other foodstuffs plastered on to the street, all dropped by misfortunate women in bad need of a plastic bag or two.

One mornin' Moll Gleeson was goin' in to get her paper, all decked out in her best finery. She met May Cantillon comin' out with a load of messages. 'Good Morning, May,' shouted Moll. May tried to get a look at who was salutin' her and, if she did, her load came apart. The first thing to hit the ground was a bottle of tomato sauce that burst like a hand-grenade sendin' lumps of red ketchup in all directions. Moll's full-length white coat took a direct hit and looked like somethin' that had escaped from the butcher's stall. The same lady had supported the ban on plastic bags and now she was payin' the price. We're all payin' the price with every dozen eggs and carton of milk that goes down the drain.

The plastic bag ban is a foal from the same stable as the nitrates business. I was in Tom Walshe's the other night and poor auld Pa Cantillon was beside himself with worry about it. 'I've worn out more tyres than a rally driver drawin' and spreadin' artificial manure, all on the advice of them hoors of agricultural instructors. Now the same shower will have me jailed if a manure bag is found in my yard – there's a total ban on it,' he moaned. 'Isn't it the groundwater and the fish they're worried about?' enquired Tom Walshe. 'I'd be worried about the fish myself,' piped up Tom Cantwell. 'Over the years they've gotten used to havin' a certain amount of nitrates in the water. They'll have awful withdrawal symptoms. I'll tell you, within a few weeks of this directive comin' into law there'll be fish leppin' sky high out of the rivers to see if there's any sign of a fella spreadin' an auld bag of 10-10-20. They'll be strung out for want of a bit of nitrogen.'

'Begod, you're right,' says I. 'The next thing the department will come up with is a nitrates treatment scheme. The farmers will be given small bags of fertiliser to spread near the rivers to keep the fish from gettin' the shakes. A sort of a hair-of-the-dog approach.'

No-one disagreed with me. We've gotten used to lunacy.

THROUGH THE CHAIR

As ye well know, the councillor's life is made up of meetin's, meetin's and more meetin's. If I got a euro for every one I attend I could retire early. Things wouldn't be too bad if there was somethin' to show for them, but there's little enough beyond a shine on the arse of your trousers. I was in an office in County Hall durin' the week and spotted a great poster that said everythin' about these gatherin's: 'When all the meetings are over we might get some work done.' And that's a fact.

I'll give ye a taste of one of the fifteen meetin's I attended last week.

Monday night 'twas the St Patrick's Day Parade Committee at the Community Hall in Killdicken. A new committee took over after last year's multi-cultural *céilí*. At the top table there was Chairwoman, Councillor Moll Gleeson, Secretary Lilly Mac (Postmistress), Treasurer Nell Regan (Sacristan and Housekeeper to Canon McGrath), PRO Breda Quinn Ryan (Superquinn). The Chairwoman, with her glasses perched at the end of her nose, asked Lilly Mac to read the minutes of the last meetin'. That went fine and all was plain sailin' until it came to Nell Regan's Treasurer's report durin' which it emerged that last year's Paddy's Day event, the multi-cultural céilí, had incurred a loss of €43.50.

Nell had no sooner finished her report than Percy Pipplemoth Davis was on his feet. He demanded to know how a profit of €12.50, announced in April 2005, had turned into loss of €43.50. 'Well, through the Chair,' explained Nell, as she rooted around in a big brown envelope, 'it went on a doctor's bill and medicine for Madge McInerney.' 'Through the Chair,' 'twas Pipplemoth again, 'What are we at, paying people's medical bills?'

'Ah here they are,' declared Nell, and she passed a few slips of paper to the Chairwoman. Moll read out the contents: 'One receipt for €35.00 from Dr Doherty in respect of attending Madge McInerney and a receipt for €21.00 from Fitzgerald's pharmacy in respect of antacid tablets and syrup.' 'Through the Chair,' says Nell, 'if I may explain the background. You will all remember that during the *céilí*, people were serving a variety of ethnic foods. Mary Hayes from Glennabuddybugga brought along a strong lamb curry she made herself, but nobody would chance it. Madge McInerney felt sorry for her and ate a plateful, with fairly severe consequences.'

'Through the Chair,' interrupted Superquinn, 'isn't it well I remember it. Mary Hayes left us with a whole pot of the stuff sayin' we could serve it to the people at the end of the night. We nearly had to call in the army bomb disposal unit to get rid of it. When myself and my lovely Dixie spilled it out on the grass behind the hall it burned all before it. 'Twas as good as Round-up. God only knows what it did to Madge's insides.'

'But, through the Chair,' came back Pipplemoth, 'who agreed to pay Madge McInerney's medical bills? Surely we are completely exposed in the event of litigation? Does this mean that if we organise a parade this year and if I wear my shoes out marching up and down main street, I can go in to Clonmel, buy a new pair of Guccis and send the bill to the Killdicken St Patrick's Day Parade Committee? This is ridiculous.'

At that stage, Chairwoman Moll Gleeson pulled the glasses further down on her nose and tore into Percy: 'Councillor Pipplemoth Davis, buying shoes for you would indeed be ridiculous, seeing that your feet spend most of their time in your mouth. Madge McInerney is fully recovered and I am sure that taking this committee to law would be the last thing on her decent mind. Only cantankerous cranks like yourself get involved in that sort of thing.'

A major row took between Moll and Pipplemoth, and the meetin' was abandoned. With about three weeks to go, there is still nothin' done about the Paddy's Day parade. God give me patience.

CONVENTIONITIS

I'm feelin' very left out of things at the moment. Councillors from the political parties are runnin' around like headless chickens wonderin' who will get the nod to run in the general election. The local media are full of it, with the result that an independent councillor like myself would want to appear naked in the council chamber before he'd get a bit of coverage.

A few weeks ago, I was moanin' to Superquinn about bein' squeezed out of the news by this rash of election conventions. She appointed herself my PR guru and, since then, if I as much as break wind, she'll send out a press release.

But I might as well be breakin' wind for all the attention the radio or the papers give me. On the other hand, every sneeze made by prospective Dáil candidates is carried in full, with pages of pictures and columns of comment.

Councillor Peter Treacy of Fianna Fáil has put his hat in the ring for the umpteenth time. Peter has a dry-stock farm over in Budnanossal, but I'd say he hasn't seen a beast of any kind since he was elected to the council. Before that he was up to his ears in the IFA and spent all day every day at meetin's about farmers' issues. Meanwhile, back at the ranch, his neighbours were puttin' up with Peter's own farmin' issues – his stock could be found wanderin' everywhere. When it came to a choice between doin' a bit of fencin' or drivin' to a meetin', the meetin' always won. When Peter ran for the council the wife had enough of his antics. She took over the farm and the place is thrivin' since. Rumour has it she gives him an allowance on condition he stays away from the farmyard.

Peter is mad anxious to have a go at a Dáil seat and has at least three mobile phones in full flight at the one time. He organised the local paper to do a big profile of him down on the farm last week, but the wife refused to be photographed with him. She told him she wouldn't be involved in hidin' the fact that he's a lazy hoor.

The photographer wanted a picture of 'Peter the farmer' in action, and so the prospective TD picked up a four-prong fork and started forkin' silage. In his attempts to impress, he put out his back and will be in traction for the next six weeks. He's hopin' for a sympathy vote.

Councillor Moll Gleeson was lookin' for the Blueshirt nod and lost the run of herself entirely. She thought she was feckin' Hillary Clinton. She had a hairdo that was as golden as a bale of straw and as stiff as a motorbike helmet. No matter where there was a crowd, she was to be found pesterin' them goin' in and comin' out. She had at least eight photographs in the papers two weeks ago.

However, she crash-landed at the convention in Glengooley. The husband, Christy, dropped her at the parish hall and went off to park the car. On his way back he called in to Mick Brennan's for a few pints and by the time he got to the convention a defeated Moll met him at the door with the mascara runnin' down her face like molten lava. She was eliminated at the first count – and she nearly eliminated Christy with her handbag for failin' to turn up to vote for her.

That hoor of a Percy Pipplemoth Davis is runnin' for the Greens. He barely scraped through their convention, winnin' by one vote. It seems he brought two aunts out from the nursin' home who nearly nobbled his chances by votin' against him.

Readin' the local papers this week was depressin'. Councillor Maurice Hickey might as well not exist. I was cryin' into my tea on Wednesday mornin' when Superquinn came in. 'What are you ullagonin' about?' she asked. 'If you can't beat 'em, join 'em. Sure, you need no party convention.'

Why didn't I think of that? All I have to do is call a few of my cronies together and tell them I'm runnin' in the general election. I'll make my decision whenever I feel like it. Now, that's my kind of democracy.

ARTISTIC TEMPERS

People get upset over the quarest of things. Listenin' to Joe Duffy some days you'd think we aren't happy unless we have somethin' to give out about. However, let me tell you, here in our exclusive corner of the country, we are very choosy about the things that upset us. We'll cope with potholes, pollution and pestilence, but don't upset our artistic sensibilities.

It's not just any auld art form that can upset us. Dubliners have been known to get excited over what happens on the Abbey stage, and in Milan the locals have rioted because of what appeared on stage at La Scala, but here in South Tipp, we loves or hates the auld bit of sculpture.

To put you in the picture, the current County Development Plan provides for the erection of sculpture pieces in every village in the county. I have no memory of

discussin' this in the council, but, I suppose, we were all so busy fightin' over housin', plannin' and roads we took no notice of the art section in the aforementioned plan.

But now the sculptures are comin' home to roost in the villages. A public art committee, made up of a small group of councillors and their cronies, commissioned the works and decided where they were to be to be erected. Percy Pipplemoth Davis chaired the committee, so you can imagine the kind of contraptions that are descendin' on the unsuspectin' people of South Tipp. There is uproar.

The crowd in Glengooley are gone mad altogether. You see, the sculptures are specifically created for each village and are supposed to take account of the legends, traditions and crafts of the locality. Now, Glengooley had a thrivin' bacon factory from 1890 to 1972, with the whole area bein' well known for pork and puddin's and rashers. In fact, you'd still be told there's no pig's head like a Glengooley pig's head.

In the last month or so, council workers arrived and put up hoardin' around an open area in the middle of the village. When the hoardin' was taken away it revealed a statue depictin' two pigs supposed to be rollin' in mud. However, the pair are lyin' on their sides facin' one another as if engaged in what might be called 'pillow talk'. That's bad enough, but the work is entitled, 'Will we roll around or what?' Locals have threatened to get a bulldozer to the statue, with the result that Sergeant Miller is patrollin' the place mornin', noon and night.

Of course, the crowd from Killdicken is takin' great delight in the Glengooley work of art. Anyone from 'the Glen' is now called 'Babe', and last Sunday things got so hot, a soccer match between Glengooley Rovers and Killdicken FC had to be abandoned before it started. As the Glen team lined up for the photograph, the crowd from Killdicken began to chant:

> This little piggy went to the market,
> This little piggy stayed at home,
> This little piggy went to Glengooley
> And never again felt alone.

The Glen supporters launched an attack on the Killdicken contingent and the teams left the pitch to join in the row. The whole thing turned into a typical Tyrone–Dublin encounter, all because of a work of art. It's makin' national headlines. RTÉ is comin' down to explore how sport and art are crossin' over to create such excitement. There's nothin' to explore. 'Tis just a case of two parishes that have hated one another since Adam was a boy findin' another excuse for a scrap.

The smirk was soon wiped from Killdicken faces with the appearance of our own piece of art. It depicts a man with his legs stretched out on the ground, restin' on one elbow and surrounded by sheep. The Glen crowd have christened it 'The Killdicken Harem'. More trouble. And more money wasted and not a pothole filled.

SPARED THE PAIN

I was blue in the face from the blasted plannin' for St Patrick's Day. Expectations were high, but bursts of imagination in Killdicken are as frequent as volcanoes on Slievenamon.

I'd love to get away for Paddy's Day. How is it that every other hoor of a public representative in the country gets to take the salute in places like Manhattan and Buenos Aires? A fancy dress parade in Honetyne is as exotic as it gets around here. Anyway, as it turns out I was spared the torture of the Killdicken parade by two rows and a cold hall.

Durin' the umpteenth meetin' about the parade last week we nearly died of exposure. The hall was as cold as Shackleton's arse. What misery community groups put themselves through in the name of public enjoyment. If you were to stand back and look at us huddled in that cold, half-lit barn, you'd imagine we were preparin' for a wake.

There's nothin' like discomfort to concentrate the mind. We weren't twenty minutes on our backsides when all signs of argument disappeared. We'd have agreed to spend six months in jail in return for an end to the meetin' and the chance to go home for an extra pair of socks. A combination of agreement and surrender made us put up our hands and opt for a traditional parade. It was agreed to invite the Irish Dancin' school, the Comhaltas band, the vintage maniacs and any sort of a yoke that would look colourful and different.

As soon as the meetin' ended I headed straight for Tom Walshe's and nearly jumped into the stove as I waited for him to get me a hot toddy. He had been at the meetin' as well and I never saw him take a drink in his own bar except that night. He came out with two hot one's and went back for two more without takin' a bob from me. We both agreed that we never wanted to see the inside of the parish hall again.

We weren't to have our wish. The followin' night, Chairwoman Moll Gleeson called an emergency meetin'. There was a crisis. Ms McEnery, the dancin' teacher, didn't know there was goin' to be a parade and wouldn't be around to supervise her dancers. 'Besides,' she told Moll Gleeson, 'I have no intention of asking the children to risk double pneumonia in their little costumes while you and your likes are wrapped up like Eskimos in furs and sheepskins.' Moll didn't fill us in on the rest of the conversation, but I imagine she won't be getting the number one in the McEnery household the next time she appears on a ballot paper.

Worse news was to come. The local Comhaltas group split up after an unmerciful row in Shronefodda. It seems they were playin' in the local Scór competition and Mattie Clancy, on the concertina, had a few pints on the way to the hall. He got the runnin' order mixed up and by the time they finished playin' their set they didn't know if they were comin' or goin'. They were to start the set with 'The Broken Promise', followed by the 'Maid from Moyganny', 'The Chicken's Stitches' and 'The Canon's Brass Bed'. As he smiled and wiggled his head, Mattie went in and out of the tunes like an untethered goat.

Durin' the row that followed, he admitted his guilt and caused even greater commotion. 'Oh yes, yes, yes,' he exclaimed. 'Now I see where I went wrong. I took off after the "Maid from Moyganny" and followed her straight into the "Canon's Brass Bed", and, sure, that was the end of us.' That was the end of the Comhaltas group too. When it emerged that they failed to get through to the County Scór for the first time in twenty-five years, the guards had to be called to protect Mattie.

That was also the end of parade plans for this year. Thanks be to God. We had one quick meetin' after that and it was decided that Killdicken would have to do without a parade. What a relief. However, I was just about to plan a nice and easy Paddy's Day for myself when along came an invitation to be Grand Marshal at the Teerawadra effort. For feck's sake, Grand Marshal? I'll have to walk, there won't even be the comfort of sittin' on the stand. Is there no relief from public torture?

THE GOD-HELP-US FACTOR

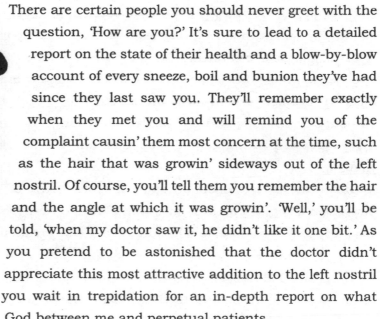

There are certain people you should never greet with the question, 'How are you?' It's sure to lead to a detailed report on the state of their health and a blow-by-blow account of every sneeze, boil and bunion they've had since they last saw you. They'll remember exactly when they met you and will remind you of the complaint causin' them most concern at the time, such as the hair that was growin' sideways out of the left nostril. Of course, you'll tell them you remember the hair and the angle at which it was growin'. 'Well,' you'll be told, 'when my doctor saw it, he didn't like it one bit.' As you pretend to be astonished that the doctor didn't appreciate this most attractive addition to the left nostril you wait in trepidation for an in-depth report on what happened next. God between me and perpetual patients.

This hardy weather brings out droves of health reporters. You can see them comin' a mile off in Crombie coats with the collars turned up and their chins buried in the folds of paisley scarves. A council colleague, Richard O'Regan, is a renowned health reporter and the greatest pain in the neck you're ever likely to meet. Before retirin' to Teerawadra he had a drapery shop in Carrick-on-Suir. In his rag-trade days the women of two counties loved him and wouldn't let their husbands buy a new suit from anyone else. 'Twas said that O'Regan had the ear of every woman and the measure of every inside leg in Waterford and South Tipp. After he sold the shop and retired he was approached by the Pee Dees to run for the council and won a soft auld seat. Despite all predictions to the contrary he held on to it.

I could never figure out how he got elected. When he's not moanin' about the chills he gets at funerals he's blamin' damp community halls for aggravatin' his sinus and plastic chairs for givin' him piles.

However, I discovered recently where the hoor gets his support. When Dixie Ryan was sick he had a path worn to his bedside. I came to the conclusion that he's a kind of a homin' pigeon when it comes to sick people: he finds his way to them no matter where they are. His targets include those who are genuinely unwell and others, like himself, who are not happy unless they have some sort of medical condition. He's constantly on the phone to his fellow-sufferers comparin' notes about doctors, chemists, treatments and the price of ointment.

O'Regan's whole life is a search for sickness and sympathy, and come election time this search takes on an added intensity. He puts out the rumour that 'Poor Richard isn't well and is in danger of losin' the seat.' The story spreads like wildfire and they come out in ambulances to vote for him.

Durin' the last election he spun the best yarn of all time. I was canvassin' a house where one of his fan-club had worn her knees up to her backside prayin' for him. In the course of our conversation she says to me: 'Maurice, you're so lucky and blessed to have your health. Look at poor Richard. God help us, he can't canvass at all. Sure he can barely stand since he got the vertigo up the Eiffel tower durin' the Meals-on-Wheels excursion to Paris.' 'Not to mention,' says I, 'what he picked up durin' his little excursion down Pigalle.'

Richard is the only man I know who gets elected from the comfort of his own bed. Much as I'd like to, I'd never get away with it. Maybe I should join the health reporters myself and put out regular bulletins on every shiver and sniffle that I get. After seein' the bould O'Regan in action, there's a lot to be said for the 'God-help-us' factor.

CANINE CONSIDERATIONS

Did you ever think about the strange relationship between dogs and humans? Am I right in thinkin' that people are losin' the run of themselves about pets in general and dogs in particular? Between groomin' parlours, medicines and pet insurance, people are spendin' the health budget of a small African country on their mutts. Years ago, a visit from an under-employed Guard might force you into buyin' a dog licence, but, aside from that, the only thing the animal was sure to get was a regular kick in the arse. Nowadays, not only do you need a licence, you may also need to keep records of vet visits and shots. The only shot ever given to a dog around here came down the barrel of a gun.

That reminds me of Pa Quirke's father, who had a great cure for four-legged friends with a graw for chasin' bicycles and cars. He'd take the shot out of a cartridge and replace it with wheat. One blast of hard grain up the west end and any chasin' dog would be guaranteed to retire immediately from that particular pursuit. Auld Quirke and his remedy were in demand in the four parishes. However, it was a dangerous kind of a cure that ran a constant risk of what the Yanks might call 'collateral damage'.

One time, Auld Quirke was asked by Gleesons in Honetyne to quieten their maraudin' sheepdog. He prepared his weapon, took up his position and waited for the offendin' dog. The same animal could smell a bicycle comin' a half-mile away. An unsuspectin' Madge McInerney was happily pedallin' her High Nellie towards the village, totally unaware of the ambush she was cyclin' into. The dog crouched behind the front wall like a tiger waitin' to pounce, while Auld Quirke, weapon at the ready, hid behind a bush at the opposite side of the road. As soon as the dog took off, Quirke let fly with the shotgun and tumbled him into a ball of yelpin' fur. Poor

Madge, thinkin' she was next, headed straight for a clump of briars where she lay, hangin' onto her beloved High Nellie for dear life. Mrs Gleeson nearly died of embarrassment when she found her neighbour in the ditch, frightened out of her wits, and all because of their mad dog.

Anyway, Gleesons' mutt gave up the chasin' and Madge was happy she could cycle the Honetyne road in peace.

Around the same time, a stray dog attached himself to the Hickey household and nearly caused our whole family to be wiped out. He took to terrorisin' every man, woman and child that passed within a hundred yards of our door. The father decided to administer Auld Quirke's treatment himself but, unfortunately, his efforts at doctorin' the shotgun cartridge went all wrong. He removed everythin', includin' the gunpowder, but, try as he might, he couldn't get it to work. Eventually he sent for Auld Quirke, and put the shot and gunpowder from his failed experiment into a jar, which he placed on the top shelf of the dresser.

A few months later, the Mother got a fit of spring-cleanin'. Everythin' she considered useless was taken out of cupboards, drawers and dressers and put into a pile in the middle of the kitchen floor. Once the big stuff was thrown out the rest was swept into the open hearth. Among the items that went from the dresser to the floor and eventually into the hearth were the shot and gunpowder. When this material encountered the hot coal an explosion ensued that sent pots, pans and ashes flyin' in all directions. The chimney didn't need to be cleaned for two years.

Luckily there were no casualties but the incident had a lastin' impact on family relationships. The Mother blamed the father for attempted manslaughter and named the dog as an accessory. From that day to the day he died, not a civil word passed between herself and the mongrel. If it happened nowadays, we'd probably end up in family therapy.

SPECTACULAR SERVICE

Easter reminds me of my altar-servin' days. Each year all the boys in second class were frogmarched to the church where the sacristan, Phonsie

Landy, put them through their paces like a Templemore drill sergeant.

He was an old soldier and treated the church as a barracks and had altar servers lined up for inspection twenty minutes before any ceremony began. We'd rush in to the sacristy, pull on our cassocks and wait for Phonsie to make his entrance. He'd stride through the door, shoutin', 'Fall in,' and we'd obey like commandos. With a stick in one hand and a wet facecloth in the other he'd walk up and down the line in search of dirt and untidiness.

Neither the stick nor the facecloth was ever misused. Phonsie was a decent sort of a tyrant. His bark was his bite as he commented on our appearance: 'Cantillon, you must have used that nose to dig spuds. Take this facecloth and relieve your dial of the dirt'; 'Hickey, that head is like a gorse bush. Stick it into the rain barrel and put some order on the wilderness.'

He reserved his harshest treatment for fellas with unpolished shoes. Like military people everywhere he was fierce particular about shoe-shine. If you came in with dirty footwear you could find yourself consigned to a long spell on the bench. This was disastrous, as it meant no free classes for funerals and no few bob from weddin's. There was also the shame you brought on the family with people lookin' at your parents as if they had been found guilty of neglect.

Whatever about footwear, the deadliest of mortal sins was to make a show of yourself durin' a ceremony. Three of us sinned so grievously we were never allowed back after committin' major 'spectaculars'.

Pa Quirke had his moment durin' a Mass celebratin' the completion of renovations at the church in Killdicken. A special collection was held and the PP gave instructions to Phonsie that the collected baskets were to be left at the back of the church. He didn't want the people gettin' a peep at how much he had gathered in case they took the foot off the pedal the next time the basket passed under their noses.

Quirke hadn't grasped this instruction so when the other servers deposited their baskets as instructed, he took it on himself to carry them all up to where he presumed they belonged. He teetered up the aisle, desperately tryin' to balance his wrigglin' tower of hard currency. As he reached the sanctuary he tripped and sent a tinklin' torrent of coin rainin' down on a furious PP. That ended Pa's days on the altar.

My moment came the day Fr Kelly dropped a piece of communion. With arm outstretched and paten in hand, I dived like Bjorn Borg to save the day, but in the process got my head stuck between two pillars of the altar rails. It took Dr Doherty and the blacksmith, Tim Hayes, an hour to free me. It took Phonsie five seconds to tell me I was decommissioned.

However, Mick Healy performed the spectacular of spectaculars durin' the 1968 Olympic games. We were all full up of pretendin' to be athletes, and Healy, who was built like a tank, thought the Russian hammer throwers were the business.

That summer our neighbour Kit Slattery died and her funeral took place at the height of Olympic fever. The funeral Mass progressed normally until after communion, when, as usual, the servers went to the sacristy to get ready the incense and holy water for the final farewell. While they waited to be called back to the altar, Healy decided to display his hammer-throwin' skills with the thurible. Round and around he swung the smokin' vessel until the door leadin' to the church swung open and in strode Phonsie. In terror, Mick let go and the thurible took off, straight through the door, out over the heads of the mourners and crashed through the window behind the gallery. Healy immediately joined the ranks of ex-altar-servers in early retirement.

A WEALTH OF MATERIAL

Mary Moloney is gettin' an ingrown toenail removed so here I am again writing the parish notes for the *Weekly Eyeopener*. This writin' job always gets me into trouble, but I love it. It's especially enjoyable when there's high jinks in the locality as this provides rich pickin's for the rovin' reporter.

Crisis at Glengooley Women's Group

An emergency meeting of Glengooley Women's Group broke up in disarray in the parish hall last Friday night. After a stormy meeting, founder members, Mary Kearney and Betty Ryan Hogan, led a walk-out, accusing the current committee of hijacking the organisation in the name of militant feminism. 'We founded this group to support women in the parish who wanted to meet and talk,' explains Mary. 'That crowd of bra-burners have destroyed everything. They think every woman is a desperate housewife, who should go nowhere without a cattle-prod. The last straw came when the topic "Men Are Pigs" was chosen as the motion for our annual debatin' competition. We knew nothing about it till we saw the posters plastered all over the four parishes.'

Current Chairperson of the Women's Group, Melissa Hayes Riordan, is relieved that the internal problems of the organisation are over. 'Now that the bun-makers and knitters have left we can get on with real women's issues,' declared Ms Hayes Riordan. Meanwhile Mary Kearney and Betty Ryan Hogan are in the process of setting up an alternative group. The new group is known locally as the 'Continuity ICA'.

Recycling Centre Closes

Locals in Honetyne are up in arms at the closure of the recycling facilities at the community centre. Council officials claim they had no option but close it. 'It was meant to be for bottles, cans and clothes, but everything was being dumped there,' declared an employee of the environmental section. 'In the last three weeks we removed the remnants of a piano, the chassis of a Zetor tractor and a donkey that was tied to the recycling bins. How and where were we supposed to recycle that animal?'

Local Boy Does Well

It isn't every day Killdicken makes it big in Australia, but thanks to Sylvester Quinn, the parish is all over the media Down Under. Sylvester, a native of Budnanossal, picked up first prize in the Australian National Flower Arranging finals. His mother, Minnie, was overcome with the news. She paid tribute to Sister Carpathia of the convent in Clonmel. 'Sr

Carpathia spotted Sylvester's talent at a young age and as soon as he was old enough she had him in the garden morning, noon and night. Thank God she made him stick to the flowers,' Minnie said. While his father, Mick, is delighted with his son's success, he reminded well-wishers that Sylvester is also 'a great man for the bit of weight-lifting'.

Canoeing Club

The Dribble Canoeing Club has postponed its inaugural paddle along the river Dribble. Postponing the event, PRO Chris Norris explained that unless there is a decent shower of rain soon they might have to move the club to a parish with a bigger river. He was disappointed that Canon McGrath wouldn't offer prayers for rain at Sunday Masses. The Canon remarked that praying for rain exposed him to the risk of being lynched by his congregation. If there are a few decent showers before Saturday night the inaugural paddle will take place at Moyganny Bridge at three pm on Sunday. Lifejackets must be worn.

Popular Band Releases First CD

Local band, Pee Hogan and the Blueboys, will launch their first CD, 'Hold Me Again in the Haybarn', in Walshe's Bar, Killdicken, on Sunday night. Well known on the wedding and cabaret circuit, this is the first venture by the Blueboys into the recording studio. Lead singer Pee Hogan is very excited about the debut album. 'I've been writin' auld songs for years and I'm thrilled to have them all together in the one place,' he said. While he thinks the title track would make a great single, his personal favourite is a song he wrote for his mother entitled, 'I Won't Find a Woman Who'll Mind Me Like You'.

OFF MY TROLLEY

Mary Moloney is still in hospital. In fact, the poor misfortune has gone from bad to worse, thanks to our health services. She spent three days inside the doors of the casualty department on a trolley, with her ingrowin' toenail cocked to the air and elements. Now, it might be the month of May, but our weather isn't even a distant cousin of summer. To add injury to insult, didn't Mary get frostbite on the toe. She went in with one complaint and ended up with two. I suppose that's what Mary Harney would call a bargain.

The poor woman is worried sick they might have to take the entire toe off when they get around to removin' the nail. Nell Regan says that if she's not attended to soon she might even lose the leg. Tom Cantwell makes out people are left stranded in casualty until there's somethin' major wrong with them to make it worthwhile operatin'. His father is the inspiration behind this theory – auld Cantwell didn't believe in takin' the car to be serviced until it was so crocked it had to be towed to the garage.

When I went to visit Mary on her trolley durin' the week I was buttonholed by all and sundry. The casualty department turned into a pyjama clinic. I had my notebook out and within a few minutes there was a queue of people in wheelchairs, on drips and carryin' slings waitin' to talk to me. 'Tis awful the things people have to go through before they get a bit of treatment. In fairness, the nurses and doctors are great. There's one nurse, Bridie Callinan from Budnanossal, stationed in casualty and she does the work of five. She attends to the patients' every need with bedpans, mugs of tay, drips and sangwiches. She even recharges their mobile phones for them.

One poor auld divil from Shronefodda was three days on a trolley and mad anxious to phone the neighbours to see how his greyhound did at the track. Unfortunately, the battery in his phone was dead, but someone told him to ask for Nurse Callinan and she'd sort him out. When she got round to him, he was in full flow, relievin' himself into a bed bottle. 'Do you want me to recharge that auld thing for you?' she shouted as she approached the bed. 'Ah no, nurse,' he replied sheepishly, ''tis gone beyond it. But I'd be obliged if you could recharge me mobile phone.' 'Don't worry,' says she, ''twas the mobile phone I was referrin' to. I never met a man yet who needed to have that other thing recharged. 'Tis in a permanent state of readiness with all of ye, no matter what vintage ye are. Where is that phone and we'll find out if your auld greyhound is goin' better than yourself.' 'Tis bits of humanity like that that keep people from goin' mad.

I nearly ended up as a permanent fixture in the hospital myself. I was two hours in the place before I eventually got talkin' to Mary Moloney. I found her in good enough form, but a poor woman on the trolley next to her was very uncomfortable. She was waitin' to be admitted for some kind of a 'woman's problem' and asked me to mind her trolley while she went to the loo. I obliged and stretched myself out on the contraption, pulled up a blanket and fell fast asleep. I was no sooner snorin' when two porters came along, looked at the chart on the trolley and wheeled me down to an examination room. I don't know how long I was there but I woke suddenly to the sound of a screamin' nurse. When she pulled back the blanket coverin' me she was faced with a woman's problem she hadn't seen before. Wasn't I the lucky boy to escape the clutches of our health services with all my bits in one piece?

THE MUNSTER MONSTER

Let me out from under this never-endin' Munster rugby scrum. Now, don't get me wrong, I'm as proud a Munsterman as the next fella, but I've had an overdose of rugby and rugby experts lately. I am delighted when they win. The best win of all time, of course, was that one against Biarritz in Cardiff and, like everyone in the province, I nearly had heart failure durin' the match. I walked the backyard for the last ten minutes in fear and trepidation that, like the Battle of Kinsale, the '98 Risin' and the Civil War, the misfortunate Gael would once again snatch defeat from the jaws of victory.

In fact, without any great knowledge of the sport, I had come to the conclusion that Limerick hurlin' and Munster rugby have a lot in common: great entertainment, great heroics and little silverware. I was beginnin' to believe that the Munster team was the teaser pony of the Heineken cup: it created a bit of excitement before the real stallions took over. I'm relieved I was proved wrong.

Aside from all that mopin', I know nothin' about rugby except that a try gets you five points, a conversion adds two to it and a penalty gets you three. For all I know, when it comes to rucks, mauls, scrum halfs, lock forwards and hookers, you could be talkin' about the internal workin's of a JCB or someone makin' a livin' on the streets of Amsterdam.

I'm afraid not everyone is as frank as myself about their knowledge of this rough sport for young gentlemen. I'm worn from listenin' to eejits who have transmogrified into clones of George Hook over the last two weeks. These are fellas who have been watchin' junior football and hurlin' for a generation and still know nothin'. The intricacies of rules governin' the square ball is beyond them – they're the clowns who call for the referee to be lynched for disallowin' a goal even when the full forward has been sittin' on the goalie for ten minutes before the ball comes near the square.

Years ago, people weren't a bit shy about displayin' their ignorance. The day Ireland won the Triple Crown in 1985 Tom Cantwell's father was in Walshe's pub holdin' onto the corner of the counter with one hand and to the remnants of his life with the other. When asked what he thought of the match, he declared: "Twould be a grand game if they would only pump up that auld ball. Sure, by the end of the match 'tis gone into a duck egg from them big lazy hoors lyin' down on it.' God be with the days of the honest man.

The Cardiff match and its aftermath have left me with serious questions about the mental state of the people of this country. The notions some people have got has to be seen to be believed. Some fellas are turnin' up to GAA matches in sheepskin coats and carryin' naggins of brandy, while others have developed the flattest Limerick accents you ever heard.

But what bates Banagher is the rash of rugby-style pet-names people have taken to givin' one another. The rugby crowd loves to rechristen their buddies with names you wouldn't give a pom dog. I went into the pub the other night and discovered the infection had spread to my own intimate circle of friends. Cantillon had become 'Canty', Quirke had become 'Quirky', Walshe had become 'Walshie' and Cantwell was now referred to as 'Wellie'. At first I chose to ignore this rugbification of titles until Tom Walshe addressed me as 'Hicksie'. I told him if he didn't ban these pet-names I'd bar myself from his premises.

I can't take much more of this Munster love-in. Thanks be to St Jude for the return of the Munster championship when Cork, Tipperary, Limerick, Clare, Waterford and Kerry revert to the natural state of mutual hatred that has existed between them since Adam was a gorsoon. As it was in the beginnin' …

NIGHTMARE NUPTIALS

There was a time when I went to at least one weddin' a month. Nowadays, they are few and far between. I suppose anyone my age with a bit of get up and go has got up and gone, so the weddin' invitations now come from relations who feel obliged to invite representatives of the 'Hickey crowd' to their do.

Generally, I go with the Mother, and she's great entertainment. As long as I'm sober enough to understand what she's sayin', there is no-one better to do a runnin' commentary in the church and the hotel. Last week we found ourselves on the plains of Kildare at the weddin' of a daughter of a first cousin of my father.

To be honest, neither the Mother nor myself was too excited about these particular nuptials. I wanted to go to a match in Shronefodda and the Mother wanted to tackle her garden. 'Twas the first dry Saturday we had since Easter and she nearly lost her reason at the prospect of missin' the chance to dig in. 'Tis like the Amazon,' she moaned. 'The river or the jungle?' I asked. 'Both,' she replied. 'Come on, we'll get on the road to this feckin' weddin' before I change me mind.'

When it comes to doin' her duty, the Mother is of the old school. She wouldn't entertain my suggestion that we develop 'car trouble' and phone our apologies. 'If your father was alive he'd be at that weddin' and I'll do what I think the man would want me to do.'

We got to the church in this lovely, quiet Kildare village. Now, it might have looked like rural Ireland, but after a few minutes we were in no doubt that we were in the 'commuter belt', mixin' with the 'beautiful people'. All the young wans were as blonde as Danes and poured into skimpy dresses that barely covered the essentials. Not one youngfella in the church had combed his hair. Every one of 'em looked as if he'd just pulled his head out of a barrel of axel grease.

Whatever about the young people, the mothers and fathers took batin'. There was fellas as auld as myself tryin' to look like teenagers in fancy sunglasses and bleached heads. The Mother was gobsmacked at the sight of middle-aged women showin' off bellies that should never see the light of day. We were sittin' near the back of the church and as these mature beauties made their way up the aisle the Mother kept up a particularly vicious runnin' commentary: 'By God, Maurice, there's enough spare tyres in this place to cover Pa Cantillon's silage pit twice over. Look at 'em – mutton dressed up as lamb – you'd need a lot of feckin' mint sauce to put a bit a flavour on some of them auld biddies.'

The ceremony itself had to be seen to be believed. Between lightin' candles, swappin' flowers, huggin' and kissin', I didn't know if 'twas the Academy Awards or a weddin' I was at. The Offertory procession was like somethin' out of *Little House on the Prairie*. They brought up his first soother, her first pair of shoes, the first medal he got for Irish dancin', the schoolbag she had on her first day at school, and on and on until I thought the Mother would have to be tied to the pew. 'By God,' she remarked, 'that priest is a lucky man disposable nappies were invented. They're about the only things belongin' to that pair that didn't find their way to the altar.'

Immediately after the ceremony she sent me to the car for the present. I returned to find her explainin' to the mother of the bride that she had to leave immediately as her son, the councillor, 'had an important meetin' with the county manager'.

As we took off for South Tipp I remarked that Daddy mightn't be pleased at her tellin' lies to his relations. 'Wherever he is,' says she, 'I'm sure he hasn't to put up with the kind of shite we put up with today.'

OVERHEATED

The heat has me killed. You can say what you like about hot summer days, but I'd give anythin' this minute for an east wind. Between sweatin' and pantin', I'm like an overfed dog on his last legs.

I was at a funeral in Honetyne last Thursday and thought I'd be joinin' the corpse on the road to kingdom come. There we were in the open air, with the midday sun beatin' down on us, and Canon McGrath prayin' like a hoor. The only one with a bit of shelter was the man in the coffin. I felt like climbin' in beside him when I heard the Canon announce he was goin' to lead us in the full rosary. That man loves the sun – he'd pray all day in the open air if the sun kept shinin'.

They say that in weather like this he spends his time in the back garden with little or nothin' on him. In fact, he wasn't long in the parish when a heatwave struck. One day Nell Regan, housekeeper and sacristan, unaware of his passion for sunbathin', came runnin' into the garden with news of a sick call. The full of her eyes of the PP in his nakedness was too much for her and she keeled over. The poor priest panicked and his cries for help reached the ears of our postman, Pa Quirke. When Pa arrived and saw the naked man standin' over a woman who appeared to be dead, he thought the worst. He grabbed a shovel, forced a terrified Fr McGrath into the garden shed and locked him in. He was about to phone the guards when Nell came around and explained everythin'.

After that, the PP grew a huge hedge around his back garden and fitted a doorbell that's as loud as a foghorn. He won't be surprised again.

Back to the swelterin' graveyard. I was on the verge of havin' a mirage by the time the prayin' finished. As I struggled towards the gate I was nearly run over by farmers rushin' back to their meadows and silage pits. How anyone could think of workin' in this weather I don't know. It's takin' every ounce of energy I have just to stay alive.

Clothin' is another big problem for a man like me in hot weather. Bad and all as the cold and wet are, at least all you have to do is cover yourself and no-one passes a remark on the garments you've chosen to keep the weather out.

Unfortunately, when the heat rises, you're forced to strip down to the near essentials in order to avoid meltdown. Now, in my case this is not a pleasant sight. The vision of me in a string vest and turned-up trousers is somethin' to behold. Cantwell says I'm like somethin' hangin' from a fishin' trawler at Killybegs.

Whatever about the summer attire, what really gets to me is the effect the heat has on my delicate places. Now, I know people might get cross at me for talkin' about such matters, but I'm told that the problems with men's health start with the fact that men don't talk about the things that ail them. One thing that ails me is the effect hot weather has on my undercarriage. In mechanical terms, I suppose you could say that the gearbox siezes up and becomes welded to the housin'. Geographically speakin', 'tis a 'down under' problem that occurs when your New Zealand starts rubbin' up against your Australia and they get very sore with one another. You end up walkin' like John Wayne and go through enough Vaseline to lubricate a self-propelled silage harvester.

For people like me, the heat is a mixed blessin', so when we have a regular Irish summer one Maurice Hickey won't be found complainin'. But when the sun bursts the rocks, have pity on sweaty men in string vests.

A HOT DRY SEASON

There's a drought in Killdicken. The Dribble has dried up and there's only water in the taps for two hours a day, an hour in the mornin' and an hour in the evenin'. We're gone back to shavin' out of mugs and people are usin' the same basin of water to wash up after the breakfast, dinner and supper. Rationin' was announced last Thursday and the people are up in arms since.

At Mass on Sunday, your nose would tell you the water shortage was beginnin' to bite. By the time the final blessin' came, the chapel smelt like an overcrowded tent in Ballybunion on a hot August weekend. The odour of hot bodies broke through all kinds of perfumes and aftershaves. You'd want to stay upwind of the fellas on the hurlin' and football teams, especially the dual players. They've had four matches, six trainin' sessions and no shower since the rationin' started. They're in danger of bein' closed down by the EPA.

I have to admit that the smell in the chapel took me back years. There was a time when the whiff of sweat was as much a part of nasal reality as the aroma of an open fire. In them times nobody was worried about the pong from their armpits or any other pit for that matter, 'twas all nature. I don't care what anyone says, but the traditional smell of the workin' man had its attractions. That mixture of sweat, porter and plain tobacco was as rich as anythin' that went up the nose of Marco Polo on the Spice Road. We've gone a long way from bein' at ease with the body as we try to perfect the body beautiful.

Anyway, as the water rationin' and the drought got worse, people began to get more and more irritable, especially the women. I couldn't go for the paper without bein' attacked. You'd swear I'd turned up the temperature and drank all the water myself. Dr Doherty told me the irritability was due to withdrawal symptoms from tay. In his estimation some of these women drink a gallon of tay a day and were now confined to two or three cups. He reckoned if the drought went on much longer a lot of marriage beds would come apart under the pressure from a combination of BO and the shakes.

I have to say the crisis has woken me up to the amount of water we waste these days. I know of people who never rise as much as a bead of sweat and still take at least one shower every day. Why they have to wash I'll never know. I remember years ago, there was many a hale and hearty auld person went to hospital for a small thing and ended up in Tinky Ryan's hearse. They wouldn't be two days in a ward when they'd catch their death. Why? Because Sister-in-Charge decided that the first thing they needed was a bath. The soakin' in soap and water washed away layers of natural insulation and they were swept by pneumonia soon after the first sneeze.

This current water shortage resulted in an emergency debate in the council chamber. Percy Pipplemoth Davis gave us a lecture on global warmin' that started with the last Ice Age and ended up at the next one. Moll Gleeson declared that our failure to provide a consistent supply of clean water is deprivin' people of their human right to a wash. I suggested that the modern obsession with the body beautiful is wastin' gallons of our basic natural resource and recommended that the daily shower be banned except for those who rise a sweat at their work.

I should have kept me mouth shut. Moll Gleeson replied that any use of water by me in pursuit of the body beautiful could certainly be regarded as waste of a natural resource. Councillor Peter Tracey remarked that if showers were confined to people who rise a sweat, then Maurice Hickey should never be allowed wash again.

POWDERS & POTIONS

There's a lot of talk about alternative remedies and complementary medicine. I have me doubts about it. Quare ones with every kind of a half-baked cure are settin' up shop and takin' money from people you'd imagine have more sense. Tom Walshe is a case in point; you'd think he'd have more sense, him bein' a publican. He badly needs a hip operation, it's as simple as that. He's goin' around like an overloaded council lorry with a broken spring, but will he have the hip seen to? No. He's gone to every therapist and 'ologist' in nine counties – meanwhile he's gettin' more bockety by the day.

Last week he went to this new 'ologist' who apparently massaged his 'aura' for him. 'What's your aura?' asked Cantillon. 'It's invisible,' says Tom. ''Tis like a full-body halo. You can't see it or touch it, but 'tis all around you, about an inch out from your skin. When that bit of you is out of gear you're in trouble.' 'So you had it massaged,' continued Cantillon. 'And tell me, did you feel it bein' massaged?' 'Oh no,' says Tom, 'she never laid a finger on me. She kind of waved her hands all round my body, about an inch out. I haven't felt as good in years.' 'And how much did that cost?' enquired Cantwell. 'A hundred and fifty euros,' replied Tom. 'Jaysus,' says Cantwell. 'You paid someone a hundred and fifty euros to wave at you! A fool and his money are easily parted.'

In fairness, these alternative remedies are nothin' new. There was a time when every parish had people with 'the cure' for particular ailments such as hoopin' cough, warts, corns, ringworm, lumbago or arthritis. Rarely you'd find someone with the cure for all complaints, but someone with 'the cure' for one was easy to come by.

There was a woman, Lizzie Tracey, in Glennabuddybugga, who had mighty cures for animals. No matter what the ailment – red water, hoose, worms, mastitis or scour – Lizzie was your woman. They said she had a garden that grew every herb and plant known to mankind.

She didn't do much work for human beings, except for men who needed a 'leg up', in the marital bed. Whatever she prescribed for the odd nervous stallion or the occasional lazy bull, she would divide by ten and give to any under-performin' man who summoned up the courage to darken her door. Whenever a man came to her with the cap rolled up in his fist, and all the appearance of a fella goin' to confession, she knew she had a client for her 'giddy-up treatment'. She'd play the fool with them until they declared what their business was.

I heard a story about a fella, Bill the Flat Cap Power from Shronefodda, who got married for a second time late in life and needed her services. He arrived with the cap in the fist and he lookin' up at her from under his eyebrows. 'I suppose, you've a fine bull that's fallen into a bit of flesh and needs a lift?' says she to him before he had a chance to open his mouth. 'Well, it's a stallion actually, Miss Tracey,' he replied. 'Oh is it, faith?' says she, 'and I suppose a fine stallion he is, too, well fitted out for the job, but kind of distracted.' 'Now you have it,' says he. 'And would this stallion have a notable pedigree?' she asked, with the devil in her eye. 'Oh indeed and he would, Miss Tracey. He's so well bred he wouldn't be seen talkin' to our likes.' 'Ha, ha,' says Lizzie, 'it's no wonder he can't do the deed if he's full to his throat with that kind of auld bigness. I don't know if I've anythin' for a stuck-up auld nag like that.'

Flat Cap panicked and admitted he wanted the dose for himself. After lookin' him up and down, Lizzie wasn't impressed. 'Listen,' says she, 'I heal the sick but I'm not great at raisin' the dead.'

Whatever she gave him worked because after the arrival of the seventh child his missus made smithereens of Lizzie's bottle and burned the bed.

A PLEA FROM THE BELLY

I love plain, ordinary grub. I'd live happily on a diet of spuds, bacon, cabbage, tay, brown bread and butter. But nowadays you might as well be tryin' to catch a corncrake as tryin' to find this kind of feedin' anywhere outside the safety of your own home.

When I'm in Clonmel for a council meetin' or anywhere else aside from home at feedin' time, 'tis feckin' impossible to find ordinary, dacent grub. 'Tis easier to get an outer-Mongolian moose wrap and Colombian coffee made from beans crushed by dancin' llamas and strained through crocodiles' teeth than it is to get a ham sangwich and a pot of tay.

I pity the poor pensioners who go to town to do their bit of shoppin' and hope to get a cup of tay and a bun before they go home. A lot of them have given up tryin'. They bring sangwiches and a flask rather than face the trendy cafés with menus that read like a zookeeper's grocery list.

I was in one of these places a few weeks ago, and I declare to God I thought I was on another planet. 'Twas as spotless as a clinic, with marble everywhere. You'd be afraid to sit down in case you'd ruin the place. A young waiter, dressed completely in black with blond hair greased into a solid ponytail, approached me. He shone like a wax model. 'Can I help you, sir?' he asked. 'Indeed and you can,' says I. 'I'll have a pot of tay and a few Marietta biscuits.' 'Now, sir,' says my waxen friend, 'in the line of teas we have Indian, Sri Lankan, Chinese, camomile, raspberry, almond and juniper.' 'Stop, stop, stop,' says I. 'Listen, when you make tay for yourself at home do you reach for the tay bags or the atlas?' 'Well, the tea bags, I suppose,' he replied. 'Very good,' says I. 'Now, spare me the geography lesson and the tour of the fruit and veg stall and make me a pot of tay, the kind your mother might make for you.'

'Yes, sir,' says he, 'and you also want a snack of some kind?' 'That's right,' says I, 'I want a few Marietta biscuits.' He looked at me blankly. I might as well have ordered a set of hen's teeth for all he knew about Mariettas. But he recovered well. 'Now, sir,' he continued, 'in the line of snacks we have ...' and he proceeded to rattle off a litany of tarts and flaps and flips and flops that sounded like a selection of physical jerks performed by Bulgarian gymnasts. 'Hould on, hould on, hould on,' says I. 'Youngfella, what does your mother have with her cup of tay when she manages to turn you off and tuck you in?' He looked around to make sure no-one was listenin' and whispered, 'She loves a digestive or two with her cuppa.' 'Now,' I whispered back, 'would you be so good as to get me a pot of plain tay and one or two of your mother's digestives and leave the flips and flaps and flops for people who live dangerously?' I was exhausted and famished by the time I got what I wanted.

Last Wednesday I found myself in town at grub time and while tryin' to figure out where I'd get the lunch I had a brainwave. Stickie Stakelum's chip wagon: now that's where a fella would get an ordinary, dacent feed. Sure enough, Stickie was parked in his usual spot and had a great welcome for me. 'Ah, Councillor Maurice, you're just in time to sample the most recent additions to my increasingly cosmopolitan menu.' I nearly collapsed in disbelief as he read out his list of pandaleenies, gondaleenies, grabsalas and birettas. 'Jaysus, Stickie,' says I, 'all I want is a burger and chip, not the feckin' Italian soccer team.' I give up.

'WILL YOU STAY ON?'

When I was goin' to the dances twenty years ago, the young wans loved to dance with me. I could jive two women together and could waltz like Fred Astaire. I'd be batin' them back durin' the early sets, but alas and alack, when it came to the slow dances, I was always lackin' a woman. Thinkin' back on it now, I was as well off. My nights spent lookin' at the caper on the dance-floor durin' the slow sets was as good as a course in social studies.

The best way to get a woman for a slow dance was to be on the floor with her for a fast set. As that was comin' to an end you'd ask her if she'd 'stay on' and, if she agreed, the chances are you'd get a shift as well. Let me remind you that in them days, a 'shift' was somethin' couples did with all their clothes on. To put it gastronomically, there might have been a lot of nibblin', but there was no main course. For most people that only happened after the visit to the altar.

To get back to the slow set. As far as I could see there were three types of couples to be found on the floor when the lights dimmed and the tempo dropped. First, there were 'the lovers'. These were couples in the full flush of a strong line for whom the slow dance was an opportunity to cement their relationship. They'd be plastered so tightly to one another you'd need a kango hammer to get them apart. They wouldn't come up for air until the leader of the band announced that the next dance was 'comin' right up'.

The next group I call 'the whisperers'. In this category the male would spend the duration of the slow dance seriously tryin' to 'get off' with his female dancin' partner. The intimacy of the occasion offered him the ideal platform from which to sell his wares. He'd be whisperin' away like a boy, tellin' her that the grand Ford Capri with the go-faster stripes and the furry dice parked across the road was his, and it ready to whisk her off into the night. If he thought he was gettin' somewhere he'd squeeze in a bit closer and sing the praises of the car stereo and how it made Boxcar Willie sound 'feckin' fantastic'. If he thought the whisperin' wasn't goin' too well, he'd go for the nuclear option and offer to let her drive the Capri herself. This offer was made in the mistaken male belief that women will do anythin' to get their hands on a man's machinery.

Many is the eejit who whispered himself into laryngitis durin' slow dances as he boasted about the size of his quota or the latest increment that would catapult him up two points on the scale. He'd let her know in no uncertain terms that if she stuck with him, before she knew it she'd be puttin' her shoes under the bed of a county manager. There's no doubt but the whisperers deserved full marks for persistence, even if they had a bad dose of bullock's notions.

Finally there was 'the waterin' camels'. These fellas were either drunk or had an allergy to soap and water. Only women who knew them well or knew their sisters would dance a slow set with them. These misfortunes would practically fall on their reluctant partners, who, in turn, would spend the duration of the dance tryin' to keep the slobberin' monster at bay. As the poor woman reversed around the hall, the desperate male would be hangin' off her neck with his arse in the air like a camel at a waterin' hole, hence the name. When the dance finished, the relieved female would untackle herself from her camel, who'd inevitably collapse in a heap on the floor only to get up when he found himself in danger of bein' trampled to death by the Siege of Ennis.

Those were the days when men were men and women had a lot to put up with.

WE'RE ALL GOIN' ON A . . .

'Have you been on the holidays?' If I got a pound for every time I'm asked that question I'd be able to buy a feckin' holiday home.

To be honest, I hate the thought of goin' anywhere this year. It reminds me of my recently departed travellin' companion, poor auld Dixie Ryan, and the days and nights we spent on the road. I get very upset. God be good to him.

Enough of that. I've decided to take what I call 'flyin' column' holidays. I'll base myself at home, but if the

opportunity or the fancy for a trip takes me, I'll avail of it.

Such an opportunity presented itself on Monday. Who drove into the yard in a Volkswagen camper van but the bould Breda Quinn, the merry widow of the late Dixie. 'Come on,' says Superquinn, 'we're goin' to Tramore.' 'Where did you get that yoke?' I asked. 'I'm tired of cryin' over Dixie,' she answered. 'I've spent a fortune on bereavement counsellors and now I'm goin' to spend his fortune on myself. Hop in or I'll look for someone else.' 'Are we stayin' over?' I asked. 'Of course we are,' she answered. 'Why do you think I brought the mobile mattress? Grab a toothbrush and a change of drawers.'

I was in a flutter. I had just been ullagonin' over my dear departed friend, Dixie, and here I was takin' off for Tramore in a camper van with his widow! Thankfully, the Mother was gone to the cousins in Kilkenny for a few days so I wouldn't have to explain anythin' to her. As for the rest of the parish, if I was seen takin' off with Superquinn in the camper van I'd be finished.

I felt I had no choice but to go. Anyway, with the sun splittin' the rocks, what would I be doin' hangin' around here? I threw a few things into my Killdicken GAA bag and, with Kenny Rogers blarin' out of the cassette player, meself and Superquinn took off for sun, sea, sand, and whatever you're havin' yourself.

'Twas a great day. As soon as we parked near the beach, Superquinn togged out and took to the water like a submarine. I'm afraid I'm a teetotaller when it comes to full immersion, so I rolled up the trousers and paddled along the shoreline.

When I got back to the camper, the submarine had resurfaced and returned to base. The deckchairs were out, the table was laid and there was a fry hoppin' in the pan. The smell of sausages and rashers in the sea air would rise the hunger of a nation.

After the supper we walked along the seashore before retirin' to a local hostelry for a few drinks. In the course of the second pint, I began to wonder about the sleepin' arrangements. As far as I could see there was one double bed and nothin' else in that camper van. Merciful hour of God, was I about to be led into temptation by the widow of my best friend in a Volkswagen van in Tramore? Were the springs in the mattress up to it?

Were the springs of the Volkswagen up to it? Was I up to it? I thought I'd better do two 'Our Fathers' and three 'Haily Marys' for holy purity. If that didn't work, I'd take me chances.

As we made our way back to the camper, my heart was palpitatin'. Superquinn opened the door and ordered me in before her. Once we were inside she turned and faced me, lifted her arms above her head and said, 'Wait until you see what I have for you, Councillor Hickey.' With that she pulled two levers, up popped the roof of the van and out slid a tiny loft with a single bed. 'That's your scratcher, Councillor,' says she. 'I'm retiring to the presidential quarters. Sweet dreams.'

The springs in the mattress, the springs on the Volkswagen and the state of my immortal soul were saved from eternal alteration.

CAUGHT BY THE PAPARAZZI

There's no doubt but you can do nothin' in this country without bein' seen. Meself and Superquinn were sure we got away with our camper van trip to Tramore. We didn't meet a sinner we knew and returned to Killdicken under the cover of darkness. After she dropped me off, I repaired to the local for a pint and no-one passed a remark, not even me. I'm always the first one to open my big mouth even when it is to my own disadvantage. I have been known to start vicious rumours about myself.

Anyway, I was beginnin' to enjoy the secrecy of my jaunt to the seaside when it all came out. As I walked down the village for my papers on Wednesday mornin' everyone I met was smilin' and noddin' at me. 'Twas as if I had just won the lotto and everyone knew about it but meself. When I got to Gleeson's shop and picked up the local rag, I saw immediately what 'twas all about. Meself and Superquinn were all over the front page of the *Eyeopener*. Under the caption 'Summer Loving', there was a

207

huge photo of the two of us havin' the supper beside the camper van in Tramore. The caption below the photo was worse than the one above: 'Love at last for bachelor Councillor: Killdicken Councillor, Maurice Hickey and friend enjoy a romantic meal outside their motorhome in Tramore.'

When I went to the counter to pay for my paper the new proprietor, young Leemy Gleeson, gave me a big wink as he served me. 'Delighted for you, Maurice. I hope you'll be very happy.' That was the most innocent comment I was to get all day.

I dreaded walkin' back up the village. I felt everyone was lookin' at me – and I was right. Young Niall Cantillon, Pa's son, thundered past on a big monster of a tractor he's drivin' for a local contractor. He nearly blew the ears off me with a blast from the horn as he held up the paper and made a rude gesture with his fist.

From the ridiculous to the sublime. My next encounter was with the women comin' out from mornin' Mass. There was a chorus of, 'Morning Maurice,' followed by gigglin' and titterin' the like you wouldn't hear from a bunch of schoolgirls.

I spent the day locked in at home. The Mother rang from Kilkenny and wondered if there was any news. Of course, I reported all was quiet on the western front. What she didn't know wouldn't trouble her. I planned to stay away from the world till things died down. The slaggin' at the pub could wait for another day. In the meantime I'd watch the telly and go to bed early. However, I was just about to get into the scratcher when the thirst got the better of me and I decided to hit for Walshe's and face the music.

As I walked in the door I could sense they were waitin' for me. 'Twas like a scene from an old western where the gunslinger swaggers into an ambush in the local saloon. The posse was gathered with the sheriff behind the counter ready to fill a drink for the condemned man. They made a bad job of pretendin' they were in the middle of a conversation that I happened to walk in on.

'I wouldn't like them auld camper vans,' says Sheriff Walshe. 'A fella would have no personal space, as Maureen Gaffney might say.' 'You're right,' chimes in Pa Quirke, 'I reckon 'twould be a tight squeeze.' 'Of course,' adds Cantillon, 'it all depends how intimate you want to become with the other occupant.' 'I'll tell ye one thing,' declares Tom Cantwell, 'I'd say they are the ideal job for an adventure holiday. 'Twould be every bit as good as bungee-jumpin'. What do you think, Maurice?' 'Lads,' says I, 'ye haven't lived till ye have been exposed to the delights of the camper van.'

I finished my pint and walked home. The worst was surely over. Or was it?

THEY TOLD ME MA

The camper van saga is set to run and run. The night the Mother came back, I pretended things were still as quiet as they always were. That was a fatal mistake. If there's one thing drives a mother ballistic 'tis hearin' stories about her children from someone else.

As usual, the Mother's first port of call the mornin' after she came home was the post office. She didn't even get to the counter before Nell Regan was in her ear, burstin' for news. She told the Mother how delighted she was with Maurice's 'romantic developments' but 'really expected more from him'. When the Mother enquired as to what romantic developments Nell was on about, the auld biddy produced a copy of the paper with the photo.

I was in Clonmel and by the time I got home the Mother had wound herself into a ball of fire. I opened the back door, announced my arrival and filled the kettle to make tay. I shouted in to know if she wanted a cup, but the response was frosty: 'I don't want any. And, besides, who gave you permission to make tay in my house?'

I put the pot back where I found it and made my way to the sittin' room. 'Who ate your bun?' I enquired bravely. 'No one,' she barked, 'and at the rate you're goin' you'll never eat a bun of mine again.' 'What are you talkin' about?' I asked. 'I'm talkin' about this,' says she, throwin' a copy of the *Eyeopener* on the floor.' Then the lecture started in earnest.

'Since the first day you put one foot in front of the other you've managed to find people who lead you around by the nose. At school you were up to every bit of skulduggery from lettin' the air out of the master's tyres to robbin' orchards. Of course, the smart Alecs like Cantillon, Quirke and Cantwell got away with everythin', but 'twas always our Maurice was caught and 'twas always Mother who had to sort things out. I thought election to public office would cure you of makin' an eejit of yourself. But no, it has given you an even bigger platform to show the world what a complete gom you are.' I couldn't get a word in edgeways.

'When you went off with your best friend's widow did it ever enter your little head that it might be wise to go a small bit farther away? Tramore is not exactly a secluded spot for South Tipp councillors wantin' a fling. You might as well have parked the camper outside the parish hall with the hazard lights on. I don't care whether ye spent the night rattlin' the van off its springs or sayin' the rosary. 'Tis not what you did, 'tis where you did it and the fact that you were caught. That's been your problem all your life. I couldn't care if you'd robbed every orchard in South Tipp or if you'd let the wind out of Master Slattery's car every day of the week. What got to me, and still gets to me about you is that you always manage to get caught. And who is dragged into the mire with you? Your poor Mother. I've had every auld biddy in the parish smirkin', smilin', sympathisin' and whisperin' at me since I came home. All because my brave son thinks with his trousers.

'The next time you want a fling in Ms Quinn's camper van could I suggest that ye fill the yoke with petrol and drive till it runs dry and only then park it? I'm warnin' you, if you drag your Mother into any more muck, you'll find yourself livin' in a camper.'

I was afraid to tell her nothin' happened in the van in Tramore. 'Tis one thing to be caught out doin' somethin', but to be caught out doin' nothin' is a total tragedy.

THE SMELL OF A POUND

With all the talk about college places after the Leavin' results come out, I still think there's no better educator than the university of life. A few pages back I talked about the shortage of water and the sharp increase in bodily smells, especially in church. Canon McGrath is nearly broke from burnin' incense to kill the pong when the parish gathers to pray. Anyway, a young entrepreneur came to the rescue. Willie Quirke, Pa Quirke's eldest youngfella, is at home for the summer havin' completed a master's degree in business studies.

The young man decided to turn the hot summer to his advantage. He was at Mass with his mother and Pa one hot Saturday evenin' and the roof nearly came off the church such was the pong risin' up from the great unwashed. The combination of incense, sweat and socks was too much for his mother and she passed out. Takin' their cue from Mrs Quirke, one woman after another followed suit, and as they collapsed they were carried outside and laid out on the grass. Anyone comin' on the scene would think there had been a drive-by shootin'.

The emergency gave young Quirke a brainwave as to how he might make a few pound from the drought and the smell. I was walkin' home when he pulled up beside me on his bike. 'Hi, Maurice,' he called, 'where is the largest body of water to be found around here?' 'Begod, Willie,' says I, 'I suppose it has to be Lugnagoppal.' 'Wrong,' says he, ''tis Tramore. Watch this space.' With that he took off.

To cut a long story short, he started a swimmin' club and organised a bus trip to Tramore every Saturday afternoon. People who had never as much as put a foot in the water were goin' for full immersion. Young Willie was makin' a killin'. He hired a 55-seater bus from Liam Flynn for €80 and charged the passengers €3.00 a skull. The little hoor was collectin' up to €85 for himself and havin' a swim for nothin'. On the plus side for the community, at least a number of parishioners was gettin' a wash once a week. Even Canon McGrath was goin' along.

Like every good entrepreneur, Willie decided to expand the business. He began to run a second bus, but the expansion stretched his lines of communication somewhat. The two buses were creatin' a bit of confusion when it came to makin' sure everybody had turned up for the journey home.

After a few near misses, things came to a head last Saturday week. The buses had returned from Tramore, the passengers had changed into their Sunday best and were sittin' in the church waitin' for Mass to start. At twenty-five to eight Nell Regan appeared on the altar and declared that the PP was missin'. When passengers from the two buses compared notes, it emerged that the poor Canon had been left behind. What's more, he had changed into his swimsuit on the bus and his clothes had come home without him.

There was panic in the congregation when we realised the Canon was stranded in Tramore in his swimmin' togs. We were on the point of organisin' a posse to rescue our missin' pastor when a mini-bus pulled up carryin' members of the Shronefodda guild of the ICA. They had been on an outin' to Tramore and picked up poor Canon McGrath on their way home. He emerged from the mini-bus wearin' a pair of tracksuit bottoms and a Daniel O'Donnell T-shirt given him by one of the larger members of the guild.

As he made his way up the church he didn't realise that emblazoned on the back of the T-shirt was the slogan, 'Daniel does it 4 me'. There wasn't a straight face in the congregation. Mrs Quirke wiped the smirk off her son's face when she ordered him to compensate the PP by donatin' his profits from that day to the parish buildin' fund. The university of life teaches hard lessons.

A WINDOW ENVELOPE

I gets loads of letters. But I've learned a long time ago to keep one eye on the broad political picture when readin' them.

Drohidnavart
Shronefodda

Dear Councillor Hickey,

I am a pensioner, a bachelor and I live alone. Recently a new house was built next to me by a couple of civil servants 'decentralised' from Dublin. The sale of their house in the capital obviously gave them the wherewithal to build Buckingham Palace in the field beside my humble abode.

Now, I don't mind having near neighbours, but I do object when they have a bird's-eye view of all that is happening in my world.

There's an upstairs window in the gable end of their mansion and I'm sure it was never part of the original plans. Every time I look up at that window there is someone looking out at me. Now, my house is a storey and a half high and I too have an upstairs window in my gable end, but it only reaches the bellybutton of the monstrosity next door. The room inside that window happens to be my bedroom.

One morning, soon after the new neighbours moved in, I went to my window for my morning stretch clad in only in my string vest and long johns. As I finished stretching I opened my eyes to find my neighbour waving down at me from her gable window – a window that should never have been there in the first place. I drew the curtains and went back under the blankets.

I had just recovered from this invasion when, some days later, the man next door flagged me down on the road. He informed me that a number of slates on my roof needed replacing. Obviously his report was based on an examination of my roof carried out from his gable window – a window that should never have been there in the first place.

Insult was added to injury last Friday. Herself met me in the post office and informed the assembled multitudes that the whiteness of the whites on my washing line were an advertisement for Sunlight soap and the wash-board. Her remarks were obviously based on observing the contents of my washing line from the gable window of her house – a window that should never have been there in the first place.

At the rate things are going these neighbours will soon be able to tell me when I need to have the wax taken out of my ears, the hairs in my nostrils cut and my toenails pared.

Councillor, how do I get that window blocked up? Friends have suggested I grow a hedge. This is a non-starter. I'll be a passenger in Tinky Ryan's hearse *before anything that grows naturally will be of sufficient height to restore my privacy.*

I'm at my wits end. I feel naked to the world and if something isn't done soon I will have to engage the services of a bulldozer or invest in a few pounds of semtex.

I hereby formally request your assistance and look forward to your reply.

I remain

Yours sincerely,

Myles P. Slattery

(late of Tipperary S.R. Co Council, Water Department)

To the inexperienced political eye, this is a great letter and a just cause. But let me tell ye, 'tis a political minefield. Myles is the last of them Slatterys. He has cousins in Pennsylvania, but there's no votes for Maurice in that place.

However, if I'm right in my thinkin', the woman in that new house next to him is a Gleeson from Borrisnangoul. There's bucketloads of them there when it comes to the ballot box. The husband is from Dungarvan, but his mother's people are Leahys from Honetyne, and if I get on the wrong side of them I might as well retire.

I think I'll ask Myles to move his bedroom to the other side of the house. I'll try and get a grant to fix the roof and I'll convince him to abandon the washin' line for a tumble dryer. Blockin' that window could mean curtains for my political career.

ONE CAREFUL OWNER

The NCT is due on the Micra and the Mother has decided to change the car. I don't know why. The little wagon she has is a grand yoke that's given no trouble. I keep tellin' her I've travelled the country in a lot worse, but there's no listenin' bein' done since she got this notion into her head. It's the same with clothes. When she decides she needs a new rig-out, it doesn't matter that the wardrobe is full of finery. She still has to go shoppin'.

I'll miss our little Micra. She has landed many a lump of council expenses and carried many a load in her time. When Madge Quigley's Uncle Dan was home from Chicago, she often carried the Mother, Dan, Madge and myself. That's some achievement. Dan must be six foot six and the most of twenty stone weight. Madge is what you'd call a strong woman, and Yours Truly is most certainly built for comfort rather than speed. Gettin' all of us into a two-door Micra was a feat Houdini would be proud of.

Meself and Madge would wedge ourselves into the back while Dan would squeeze into the front once he'd folded himself in two. After much gruntin' and groanin', we'd eventually get the doors closed. With the suspension stretched to the limit and the backside risin' sparks off the road, we'd bounce our way around the country.

Aside from the slightly strained suspension and a scratched bottom, there isn't a thing wrong with that Micra. But I suppose, like everyone else in this country, the Mother has gotten accustomed to the good thing. It isn't too long ago since all that was required in a good car was a steerin' wheel, an engine, wheels and brakes.

I'll never forget the first machine Pa Cantillon owned, a Hillman Avenger. She was a divil to go and a hoor to try and stop. After many a hair-raisin' trip, her final voyage took us to Siamsa Cois Laoi in Cork. There was fierce traffic and 'twas all stop-and-start on the way down. She boiled once or twice, but other than that we got there in one piece. On the way home, didn't the accelerator cable break. The resourceful Cantillon replaced it with a length of baler twine that he attached to the engine and brought in through the driver's window. Quirke, a teetotaller at the time, was in the drivin' seat. He couldn't get a decent pull at the twine so 'twas given to Cantwell in the back. That was a fatal mistake. Cantwell could barely ride a bike and askin' him to co-ordinate the pullin' of the accelerator cable with the pressin' of the clutch was way beyond him.

We were nearly home when he fell sound asleep on the job. As he descended into his slumbers he folded his arms under him and bent over.

This caused the accelerator twine to give the Avenger full throttle and she took off like a rocket as we headed into Clancy's bend on the Bally road. Poor auld Quirke had no option but to go for a controlled explosion. He faced the runaway car towards a heap of county council chippin's piled on the elbow of the bend. She mounted the chippin's, became airborne and landed nose first into a heap of dung in Seanie Dillon's haggard. We got out without a scratch.

Later that day Cantillon was towin' the Avenger to her final restin' place with the aid of his father's tractor when the sergeant flagged him down. 'Air Traffic Control in Shannon was on to me,' says the sergeant. 'They told me you disappeared off the radar somewhere over Dillon's haggard at about five o'clock this mornin'.' 'Is that so?' asked an innocent Cantillon. 'Tis,' replied the sergeant. 'Do you know,' he continued, 'your father warned me you'd meet a bad end in that Avenger. I suppose a heap of cow-shite in Dillon's haggard is as bad an end as you can get. May she rest in peace. Drive on.'

THE BLAME GAME

When the local team isn't doin' well people will often attribute the poor performance to 'trouble in the camp'. Of course, every team kicks off the year with high hopes, but most of them flounder in the early stages. Then the 'trouble in the camp' rumours start. You'll hear that the selectors aren't talkin' to the manager, or the manager isn't talkin' to the Chairman, or the captain was caught in a compromisin' position with the manager's daughter. The shenanigans associated with the local GAA are often more entertainin' than Big Brother.

Killdicken is alive with all this kind of talk at the moment. To put you in the picture, our junior hurlers won their first four matches of the year. 'Twas great, everyone was in mighty form and people that hadn't been at matches in years were turnin' up in their droves. That was until we met our neighbours and fellow parishioners, Glengooley, in the quarter-finals. They bate us by four points.

The disappointment, the shame and the humiliation were made even worse by the fact that they bate us on home ground. They bate us on the pitch that we slaved for years to buy. What's more, when we were scrapin' the price of that piece of ground together we weren't allowed to sell as much as one raffle ticket or put up one poster in Glengooley. And to think they came over here and rubbed our noses in our own dirt.

To add insult to injury, they drove up and down the village fourteen hundred times wavin' their flags and blowin' their horns till we were deaf and blind. I now know how the people of Paris felt when the Germans marched down their Champs-Élysée in 1940.

Anyway, as soon as the post-mortems started, attention focused on 'trouble in the camp'. By all accounts, the chairman and the manager weren't 'pullin' together', and the team was divided. One crowd was sidin' with the manager and the other with the chairman. And then there were rumours that the team was seen in a nightclub in Clonmel the night before the match and they skullin' pints of porter to bate the band.

Of course, the rumour-mongers were joined by the ullagoners and they wailin' like keeners at a wake: 'Sure, how could we win? 'Tis always the same with Killdicken. We only know how to lose. We'll never break the habit.' In the name of God, 'tis valium sangwiches you'd need to stay sane.

Tom Cantwell was the first to get tired of the rumours and the wailin'. Last Wednesday night, at the height of a gossip session about the disaster, he cut loose. 'I'm fed up to my gullet with this talk of trouble in the camp,' says he. 'When will ye get it in to yer heads that we lost that match because the team is useless? It wouldn't matter if the manager and the chairman were in the full flush of a blossomin' homosexual relationship, they still couldn't have made a winnin' team out of that crowd. They could spend the rest of their lives pullin' together and 'twould bring no improvement to the raw material delivered up to them by the mothers and fathers of this parish.'

There was dead silence in the pub as Cantwell continued with his scathin' analysis of the team. 'Lookin' at our back line, you'd imagine you were lookin' at a row of Belgian Blue backsides in the Tullamore show. The only difference is that Belgian Blues carry their hind-quarters better than our backs carry theirs. Now, when you have two ballet dancers at centre field and a forward line that looks as if 'twas drawn from the junior infants class, how do you expect to win? Only that our goalie is twenty-two stone and there isn't a hope you'd fit anythin' else into the goalmouth besides himself, we'd have been baten out the gate. Trouble in the camp, my arse, the trouble is on the field.'

We went back to talkin' about the weather.

OTHER BOOKS FROM
THE O'BRIEN PRESS

The Feckin' Collection

What Are We Feckin' Like by Colin Murphy & Donal O'Dea

For the real lowdown on Irish characters have a dekko at this lot, traditional and contemporary – from the Irish Mammy to Mr Celtic Tiger. You never know you might just recognise yourself!

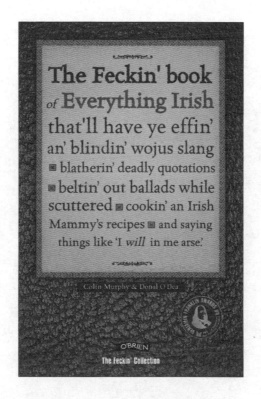

The Feckin' Book of Everything Irish by Colin Murphy & Donal O'Dea

This deadly compendium of all your favourite feckin' books is already an award-winner! It was named Best Humorous Book at The 2007 Benjamin Franklin Awards in New York.

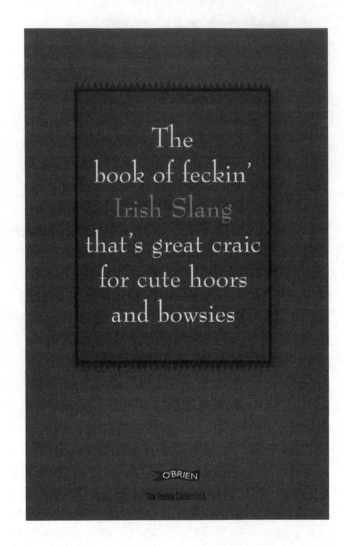

The
book of feckin'
Irish Slang
that's great craic
for cute hoors
and bowsies

O'BRIEN
The Feckin Collection

The book of feckin' Irish Slang that's great craic for cute hoors and bowsies

The 2nd feckin' book of Irish Slang that makes a holy show of the first one

The feckin' book of Irish Sayings for when you go on the batter with a shower of savages

The feckin' book of Irish Sex & Love that's not fit for dacent people's eyes

The book of luvely Irish Recipes yer ma useta make when you were a little gurrier

The book of deadly Irish Quotations some smart fecker in the pub is always blatherin' on about

The feckin' book of Irish Insults for gobdaws as thick as manure and only half as useful

The book of Irish Songs yer oul' fella always sang when he was jarred at a hooley